Lameco Eskrima

Lameco Eskrima

The Legacy of Edgar Sulite

David E. Gould

www.TambuliMedia.com
Spring House, PA USA

Disclaimer

The author and publisher of this book are NOT RESPONSIBLE in any manner whatsoever for any injury that may result from practicing the techniques and/or following the instructions given within. Since the physical activities described herein may be too strenuous in nature for some readers to engage in safely, it is essential that a physician be consulted prior to training.

First Published October 28, 2014 by Tambuli Media
Copyright @ 2014 by David E. Gould

ISBN: 978-1-9431-5503-3
Library of Congress Control Number: 2015935666

All Rights Reserved. No part of this publication may be reproduced or utilized in any form or by any means, electronic or mechanical, including photocopying, recording, or by any information storage and retrieval system, without prior written permission from the Publisher or Author.

Edited by Herb Borkland
www.Herbork.com

Designed by Summer Bonne
bonne.summer@gmail.com

Cover by Rámses Amores Gerardo
diseno.fronterasur@gmail.com

Dedication

We, the members of the "Sulite Orehenal Group" (SOG), would like to dedicate this body of work to the loving memory of our Founder, Punong Guro Edgar G. Sulite (1957-1997) and to Master Cristopher N. Ricketts (1955-2010), both of whom died far too young. May they now and forever rest in peace.

We who were students under Punong Guro Edgar G. Sulite and Master Christopher N. Ricketts were extremely fortunate in our association with these two great masters. We remain thankful and appreciative of everything they shared with us, and for their enduring friendships and outstanding examples, which both established for us by living lives epitomizing what each man represented and demanded of us, their students.

Both of these masters continue to be missed dearly by us, as a group and as individuals. They were incredible teachers, mentors and friends. Without their direct influence, many of us would still be trying to find our ways through life, lost if you will, in search of greatness that we may have never found otherwise, but longed for nonetheless.

We would also like to dedicate this book to the Sulite family and the Ricketts family. They have sacrificed and endured much by having these great men spend so much time away with their students when they might otherwise have spent more "quality time" with their respective families.

May both of these great men rest in peace. Each will be remembered with much fondness, love and appreciation from, not just those of us who trained directly under them and knew them best, but also by the tens-of-thousands around the world who hold them in the highest regard but may have never had the opportunity to meet them or to train with them directly.

Acknowledgments

First and foremost, I would like to thank all of my Lameco Eskrima brothers who make up the "Sulite Orehenal Group" (SOG) for their comradeship throughout our training together during those early days in the "backyard" of Punong Guro Sulite's home in Los Angeles, California. Specifically, I would like to acknowledge Hospecio "Bud" Balani, Jr., Roger Agbulos, Steve Grody, Dino Flores, Arnold A. Noche, and Gary Quan for their respective contributions to this book.

I would like to offer a sincere gesture of appreciation to Master Jun Pueblos and GM Alexander L. Co for their respective contributions to this work. Master Jun Pueblos was one of Punong Guro Sulite's earliest students and training partners as well as one of his sparring partners for many years in the Philippines. He now resides in Glasgow, Scotland. Sifu Alexander L. Co was the one responsible for funding and publishing all three of Edgar's books, in addition to providing Edgar with money to travel and conduct his research.

By collectively adding all of our individual insights and experiences to this book, we hope the reader will get a more complete image of who Punong Guro Edgar G. Sulite was as an instructor, as a mentor, and as a friend. We want to convey him to you as a complete human being, not just his reflection as seen through one source. Punong Guro Sulite used to tell me that, in order to get a more complete image of someone, you need to glimpse that person through more than just one lens. He would say all of us who trained under him carried a different piece of who he was and what his art of Lameco Eskrima was intended to be. He said that we were all like individual pieces of a jigsaw puzzle, and the more of us who were placed together, collectively the more complete the image of himself and his Lameco Eskrima system would become.

Punong Guro Sulite explained that if you see his image through only one perspective you will only see a small part of who he is in his entirety. But if you can see his image through many individual experiences and perspectives collectively, especially through those who know him best, you would get a more complete representation of who he was, what he represented, and what he desired to convey.

The same is true with training in the Lameco Eskrima System. We all carried something different, catered to our own individual inherent strengths and interests. Anybody training under several members of our very select group will experience the Lameco Eskrima system more thoroughly than by training under any one of us and only being able to view who Punong Guro Edgar G. Sulite was from a single perspective.

I would also like to acknowledge all of our recognized official Lameco Eskrima training groups and students positioned in numerous countries around the world. Without their hard work, dedication, and commitment, it would be very difficult to continue spreading the legacy of Punong Guro Edgar G. Sulite, and the Lameco Eskrima system to the next generation of enthusiasts. We are doing our best to ensure that both the man and his art will continue to be acknowledged and appreciated for many generations to come.

I would like to express my most sincere appreciation to Dr. Mark V. Wiley and Tambuli Media for giving me the opportunity to publish this body of work. From the very beginning I expressed to all involved with this long overdue project my intent and greatest desire to preserve the rich lineage and legacy of Punong Guro Edgar G. Sulite and the Lameco Eskrima System over any personal ambitions which I may have for myself.

This project has always been about memorializing Punong Guro Edgar G. Sulite and Master Christopher N. Ricketts for their lifetime of experience, critical contributions and countless sacrifices which resulted in the Lameco Eskrima System that we all know and appreciate today. This was a project of endurement to the nth degree towards cementing the memories of those two great men for countless generations to come and my end goal was to have their names and good reputations eternally kept in the forefront of the Filipino warrior arts community where they rightfully belong.

I have much gratitude for Dr. Mark V. Wiley for all that he has had to endure throughout this project which required dedicating countless hours of editing in an effort to get the best possible product to the reader. He has taken what I wrote and shaped it into an excellent book which now expresses exactly what I was trying to convey to the reader in allowing them to come to know Punong Guro Edgar G. Sulite through my eyes and how I knew him, not only as a teacher but more importantly as a mentor and one of my best friends.

If this book even remotely helps to maintain the good reputation and assists in continuing the rich legacy of Punong Guro Edgar G. Sulite and the Lameco Eskrima System for numerous generations of enthusiasts to come, I will consider it a huge success. I look forward to working more with Dr. Mark V. Wiley and Tambuli Media again in the future.

Mabuhay ang Lameco Eskrima!

Foreword

Edgar Sulite and I went to high school together. In the 1970s, Tuhon Leo T. Gaje, Jr. came from the United States to Ozamis City, Philippines to vacation with his family. It was then that he began training me and my brothers Elben and Lowell in the art of Eskrima. Gaje told us to invite some of our friends into the class, which we did, and this included Edgar Sulite. Our group became organized and then known as Pekiti Tirsia International in Ozamis.

Jun Pueblos and Yuli Romo

One of our other instructors was Marcelino Ancheta. Ancheta then introduced us to Manong Jose Caballero, whom he said was one of the best Eskrima instructors around. Edgar continued to study the Caballero system and I was his sparring partner.

In 1979, the Peketi Tersia group went to attend the first National Eskrima Tournament held at the Cebu Coliseum, in Cebu City. It was on that day that Arnis Philippines Pres. Chief of Staff Gen. Fabian C. Ver officially give the honor to be called "Grand Master" to masters including Tuhon Leo Gaje, and late Tatang Marcelino Ancheta and others. That's our big experience with the group. In the 1980s, Edgar and his family moved to Manila, and after a year Lowell followed him there and I soon followed.

Jun Pueblos and Tony Diego

Tuhon Gaje asked us to teach Arnis at the University of Life. So we meet some exclusive students and two years later Edgar had his own private students. Then we meet Tatang Illustrisimo in Luneta Park, and also Yuli Romo and Tony Diego, who helped us to analyze the

Anthony Lim, Jorge Pineda III, Edgar Sulite, Lou Vallarta-Shih, Jun Pueblos.

Group with Tatang Ilustrisimo

Ilustrisimo system. Edgar then met up with Alex Co, who financed Edgar's first book. Lowell then moved to Los Angeles, CA and many years afterward Edgar followed. I remained in Manila. In Los Angeles, Lowell and Edgar used their backyards as an Arnis training ground. Edgar was soon introduced by my brother to Guro Dan Inosanto and then began to travel across America to teach the Lameco System. And the rest is history.

Edgar Sulite and Jun Pueblos

—Jun Pueblos
Glasgow, Scotland
October 20, 2014

Henry Espera, Mark Wiley, Andy Abrian, Jun Pueblos

Foreword

I first met Edgar Sulite in the early 1980s under very unique circumstances. I was invited by Yuli Romo, an Arnis grandmaster, to attend a tournament sponsored by Master Picate. Yuli told me that the grandmaster considered the "King of Kings" in the field of Arnis, named Antonio "Tatang" Ilustrisimo, shall be present in the tournament. Usually, I don't attend tournaments because I find them boring, as I am already used to their routines. But this time, curiosity got the better of me; I desired to meet the grand master touted to be the king of Arnis. Ironically, as even in kung-fu events, which is my field, I am hardly present; but in this event, with its system then alien to me, I was very visible.

I asked my best buddy, Topher Ricketts, to come along with me. It was when we reached the tournament site that we found out that Yuli will challenge and fight a young master from Cagayan de Oro, one of the provinces of the Mindanao region. Their fight will be the main highlight of the event, using live sticks and without the use of body armor. Unfortunately, their anticipated fight did not push through, as Master Picate failed to come up with the prize money. Considering that the renowned masters were already in the venue, it was decided that there would be a demonstration where each master would be presented. In the event, I was introduced by Yuli to the great "Tatang" Ilustrisimo. I cannot remember the other demonstrators, but what I vividly remembered were the ones presented by Grandmaster "Tatang" Ilustrisimo and Ka Piryong Lanada of the Lanada Style. "Tatang" did the single baston, and Ka Piryong did the double baston. The reason why I singled out these two was simply because they were the ones I knew; "Tatang" having been introduced to me there by Yuli, and Lanada, who had been featured in *Inside Kung-Fu* magazine through the workings of his students in the U.S. So basically, knowledge wise at that time, I could not distinguish the versatility and salient points of their different styles.

After the tournament, Yuli introduced me to Edgar Sulite, whom I noticed to be very well-mannered, respectful and who projected an aura of self-confidence, though still younger than most masters. I had just finished publication of my first book on Ngo Cho Kun, and I was aware that there as a demand for reference materials for the ever-growing market of Arnis practitioners. During those times, the only available book on Arnis was the one published by Remy Presas.

In the course of our conversation, publishing a book on Arnis came up. I thought a book on the art would be a great idea as the art of Arnis, though well-known in the Visayas and Mindanao regions, was then not so well-known in the metropolis of Manila and its neighboring cities. In fact, it was widely believed that Arnis was personified and represented only by the style of Remy Presas, who had established quite a name in this field, by virtue of his book.

I found the young Edgar Sulite very skilled, educated and very passionate about Arnis. I gave my business card to him to pay me a visit, and sure enough, the following week, he appeared at my doorstep, presented me with a manuscript of his work, and was indeed looking for a publisher. This started our business and personal relationship, and together with Topher Ricketts, we three established a lifelong friendship. Edgar would come to my office almost every day to discuss his book and demonstrate his Arnis knowledge to us. I would in turn expose him to the field of kung-fu, sharing my knowledge of Ngo Cho, Hung-gar, Praying Mantis, internal strength training, while Topher would delve into full-contact, pugilistic fighting with boxing basics and scientific training methods. So, in essence, we three became brothers in the martial arts, and at nighttime, would regularly practice at the penthouse of my residence in Makati.

Since the three of us were in constant company, I got to introduce Edgar and Topher to the different kung-fu masters, and Edgar also utilized some internal kung-fu techniques in his Lameco Eskrima, which explains his seemingly internal strength. I also learned Edgar's Arnis style: Lameco. So the three of us each had knowledge in Arnis, Kung-fu, pugilistic fighting with specific strength on our own individual systems.

The publication of Edgar Sulite's book was a great challenge to me. First, we had to change his original manuscript to be able to appeal to the readers. As I was more experienced in the field of book publishing I suggested we incorporate many items to make the book attractive enough to the readers, like putting its history, calisthenics, basics and fundamentals, strides, attack and defense techniques, closed inter-relations between a stick and dagger, plus introduction to some well-known masters. The latter was to expose these masters so their students would like to have their own copies, like a sort of marketing strategy. I published his first book with the title *Secrets of Arnis*.

During those times, I normally traveled back and forth to Hong Kong, to buy stuff for my store, a hobby shop which specialized in model kits and radio control items from Japan and the U.S. Hong Kong, being an Asian free port, was much cheaper to buy goods than to import from their sources. I tried to find a distributor for Edgar Sulite's Arnis book, but unfortunately I was told the market was not yet ripe for that kind of book, and instead was advised to come up with a book on knife techniques, which can be more profitable. I was able to find a worldwide distributor for a book on knife techniques, so after Edgar's first book, we immediately came up with his second book, a book on knife techniques titled *Advanced Balisong*. Both books were distributed and well-received locally, and got positive reviews from practitioners.

Unfortunately, the Hong Kong distributor I got for the knife book encountered domestic problems, and was forced to close his business, so the worldwide distribution of the book was thwarted, and instead we relied on National Bookstore, the Philippine's primary book seller and distributor.

As a martial arts practitioner and publisher, I was greatly intrigued and mystified by the art of Arnis, with this style having no definitive roots. Where did this style originate? From what particular place? Although nobody can specifically say something very definite, I noticed that all styles have three similar movement concepts, although there are certain variations. These three are always present in any Arnis system, so there might be only one origin. These three are the concepts of doce pares, singko teros and siete pares. All Arnis styles rotate on these three concepts, although by now, there might already be numerous deductions and additions, as normally any martial arts system is accorded different adaptations by the master to make it particularly unique and his very own. Arnis styles are commonly defined and named after its master, so we have the Ilustrisimo style, the Lanada style, the Presas style, etc. while some still retain their 'generic' names like Lameco style, Balintawak style, Modern Arnis, etc.

Because of the many questions in my mind regarding Arnis, I told Edgar to go to the different provinces and meet the prominent masters, interview them, get whatever knowledge is available, and delve deeper. With all provinces scattered around, I financed Edgar's odyssey to these local destinations. He compiled all the data, which became the contents for our third book, *Masters of Arnis*. In this book was the very first time these masters were heard about, as most were obscure and secretive.

As Edgar's name rose to prominence since the publication of his first book, he dreamt of hitting it big in the U.S., but the difficulty of getting a U.S. visa even for a short stint seemed impossible. When Topher went to the U.S. to conduct some clinics and seminars, he brought with him copies of Edgar's book *Secrets of Arnis*. At that time (I cannot remember the exact year), Topher conducted a seminar for Richard Bustillo, and gave him a copy of the book. Somehow, Dan Inosanto got a hold of the book, and called the Philippines for Edgar Sulite. Edgar could not believe his ears when he received the call. Dan Inosanto expressed willingness to meet him, which all the more stoked Edgar's desire to try his luck in the U.S., having an extended family which relied on him for support.

After numerous attempts to secure a U.S. visa, Edgar finally got one but with a big letdown: his visa was only a single entry visa, good for 30 days, and in this short time, he cannot come up with the sufficient finances to fund his travels and expenses abroad, so in true blue brotherly passion, I advanced his royalties to pay for his tickets, and advised him to solicit contributions from his students to raise money for his living expenses. He was able to land in the U.S., the fabled land of milk and honey, and in no time, with his skills and dedication, carved a niche for himself in the field of Arnis, and as they say, the rest is history.

With Edgar's knowledge and determination, in no time, he became well-known for his style, and was able to secure his place in the U.S., bringing his whole family from the Philippines to settle in the U.S. With his prominence came the desire to pay back, to help all Arnis masters in the Philippines. He planned to come back every now and then to bring U.S. enthusiasts to study under Filipino masters and meet them personally, and giving income to these native masters, who by then were already old and have passed on their knowledge to their younger generations. But fate intervened and cut short this dream. In one of his homecoming seminars, he suffered an excruciating headache and dizziness during the session, sat down, and collapsed in the arms of Topher Ricketts, while I, at home, was scheduled to see him at the gym in the afternoon.

He died of aneurysm in his late thirties, so young and accomplished. Perhaps the books we published, all three of them (*Secrets of Arnis, Advanced Balisong, Masters of Arnis*), all happened for a reason: they would serve as his legacy, a reminder to all Arnis practitioners of his unequaled passion for the arts. Constant reminders that although he is already gone, his legacy will forever live on in his books. Fate willed us to meet each other, so we could work as a team to publish his works. We were brothers in the martial arts, and it gave me great joy to know that some of his students pay homage to him by continuing his legacy, the Edgar Sulite Lameco style of Eskrima (the Visayan preferred term for Arnis). As the founder/forerunner of the Lameco style, Edgar Sulite's name and memory shall forever be remembered for all lifetimes. Here is one person who has shown unequaled, exemplary passion and dedication to his craft. Not that he and our brother Topher have both passed on, I am saddened that my brothers and our penthouse training will have to wait for our eventual reunion.

Sifu Alexander L. Co
June 27, 2014
Beng Kiam Makati Branch

TABLE OF CONTENTS

Dedication v
Acknowledgments vii
Foreword, Jun Pueblos ix
Foreword, Sifu Alexander L. Co xi

CHAPTER 1: TACLOBAN CITY, LEYTE AND VISAYAS, PHILIPPINES 1
    From the Very Beginning.. 1
    Helacrio L. Sulite, Sr. and the Sulite-Rapelon System 2

CHAPTER 2: TRAINING WITH MASTERS OF OZAMIS CITY, MINDANAO 7
    GM Jose Diaz Caballero and De Campo 1-2-3 Orehenal 7
    Tuhon Leo T. Gaje, Jr. and Pekiti-Tirsia Kali 17
    GM Jesus Abella & GM Pablicito "Pabling" Cabahug and "Modernos Largos"........... 22
    GM Ireneo "Eric" Olavides and "De Campo 1-2-3 Orehenal" 28

CHAPTER 3: THE FOUNDING OF LAMECO ESKRIMA 31
    Edgar G. Sulite: The Young Master 31
    The Founding of the Lameco Eskrima System: September 25, 1981 33

CHAPTER 4: CRITICAL INTRODUCTIONS AND THE EARLY PERIOD OF LAMECO ESKRIMA IN MANILA, PHILIPPINES 39
    Roland Dantes and His First Meeting with Edgar G. Sulite 39
    Master Christopher Ricketts: His First Meeting with Edgar G. Sulite 42
    Master Tony Diego: A critical Sparring Session which Influenced Lameco Eskrima 46
    GM Antonio "Tatang" Ilustrisimo and "Kalis Ilustrisimo" 49

CHAPTER 5: THE FIRST EXPOSURE OF LAMECO ESKRIMA TO AN INTERNATIONAL AUDIENCE 55
    Edgar G. Sulite's First Two Books: "Secrets of Arnis" and "Advanced Balisong" 55
    The "Masters of Arnis" Tour of Australia 57
    Fighting Challenges in the Philippines 58

CHAPTER 6: LOS ANGELES, CALIFORNIA: A NEW OPPORTUNITY TO EXPAND LAMECO ESKRIMA 61
    Indian Creek, Tennessee Pekiti-Tirsia Camp (1989) 61
    Relocating to Los Angeles, California from the Philippines (1989) 63
    Guro Dan Inosanto and How He Came to Train in the Lameco Eskrima System 67
    Sifu Larry Hartsell and the Lameco Eskrima System 69

CHAPTER 7: THE LATE PERIOD OF LAMECO ESKRIMA AND EDGAR SULITE'S LAST DAYS 75
    Edgar G. Sulite: Focus on Training (1993) 75
    Punong Guro Edgar G. Sulite's Concerns with Flying in an Aircraft 77
    Germany Seminar Flight and Conversation 79
    Punong Guro Edgar G. Sulite's Medical Condition and Demise 84

CHAPTER 8: EDGAR G. SULITE'S INVITATION-ONLY "BACKYARD" LAMECO ESKRIMA GROUP 89
    "Sulite Orehenal Group": Edgar G. Sulite's Private "Backyard" Group 89
    The "Sulite Orehenal Group" in the Aftermath of Punong Guro Sulite's Death 100

CHAPTER 9: SELECT MEMBERS OF THE "SULITE OREHENAL GROUP" IN THEIR OWN WORDS 107
    Hospecio "Bud" Balani Jr. — Lameco "SOG" Member (11LA) 107
    Roger Agbulos — Lameco Eskrima "SOG" Member (23LA) 109
    Steve Grody — Lameco Eskrima "SOG" Member (24LA) 111
    David E. Gould — Lameco Eskrima "SOG" Member (43LA) 115
    Dino Flores — Lameco Eskrima "SOG" Member (60LA) 150
    Arnold A. Noche — Lameco Eskrima "SOG" Member (62LA) 157
    Gary Quan — Lameco Eskrima "SOG" Member (77LA) 164
    Pantaleon R. Revilles Jr. — Lameco Eskrima "SOG" Member (79LA) 166

CHAPTER 10: THE LAMECO ESKRIMA SYSTEM IN APPLICATION 171
    Hospecio "Bud" Balani Jr. Photo Sequence 171
    Steve Grody Photo Sequence 174
    David E. Gould Photo Sequence 181
    Dino Flores Photo Sequence 254
    Gary Quan Photo Sequence 264

Afterword 269
About the Author 271

CHAPTER 1

Tacloban City, Leyte and Visayas, Philippines

From the Very Beginning

Edgar G. Sulite was born to Helacrio L. Sulite and Cristita G. Sulite on September 25, 1957 in Tacloban City. Tacloban is a rugged barrio on the isle of Leyte in the Visayan region of the Philippines, where it was commonplace to see skirmishes and deadly brawls play out with machetes or knives. Here, in this less than ideal part of the world, is where Edgar grew up fast, learning and enduring life's most important lessons as he began his initial training in the Filipino warrior arts.

When Edgar spoke later of his training during those early days of his development, he emphasized the reality of training in Eskrima for survival more than for sport. He would often speak of the many dangers involved in growing up in the Philippines and the necessity of being able to defend oneself and one's family from troublemakers whom lurked

Edgar G. Sulite circa 1995

in every shadow. He would often say there are no guarantees in combat, only opportunities, and either you will take advantage of those opportunities as they reveal themselves to you in real-time, or you will not, and possibly be left for dead as a direct result of a failure to act. Edgar lived a hard life in the Philippines, and he wanted to convey to students, not just the Filipino warrior arts, about which he was extremely passionate, but also the culture which brought forth this rich heritage of indigenous Philippine combatives.

Circa 1974, before his 17th birthday, Edgar and his family moved from Tacloban City to Ozamis City, Mindanao, Southern Philippines. It was there that he really began to develop and grow in the indigenous warrior arts, which would eventually help establish him as one of the most well-known and influential ambassadors of Eskrima the world over.

On April 10, 1997, Punong Guro Edgar G. Sulite, at the early age of thirty-nine, died from a stroke which he had suffered weeks before while training in the Philippines. His demise was primarily due to complications of an enlarged heart exacerbated by a lifetime of high blood pressure.

The impact that he had on the Filipino warrior arts community as a whole, in such a short lifespan, was profound to say the least and, in that realm of existence, Edgar G. Sulite was a deeply respected warrior who stood firmly on the shoulders of giants. His loss is felt deeply by many around the world but by none more-so than his personal "backyard" students and members, known affectionately as the "Sulite Orehenal Group," of which I am honored to be one of his handpicked students and member of that prestigious group, in addition to being a long time private student and appointed Standard Bearer of the Lameco Eskrima system.

Helacrio L. Sulite, Sr. and the Sulite-Rapelon System

Edgar Sulite recalled that the very first time he was made aware of his ancestral warrior arts was around 1962. At the age of five he and his father were visiting Edgar's Grandfather, Mateo Sulite, at his home in Tacloban City. It was here that Edgar recalled hearing the clacking of sticks and went to investigate the noise. He saw his father and his grandfather apparently fighting with sticks, not understanding at such an early age that they were just training. Edgar said that this scared him because he thought that they were angry with each other, and he did not want to see either one get hurt. As the sticks would violently meet each other, they made a very loud noise which made Edgar feel uneasy, as he had never witnessed such a thing before. He was struggling to understand what his father and grandfather were fighting about. They calmed Edgar down by explaining that they were not fighting but rather only training to fight. This first image of them training together never left him and was burned profoundly into the deepest recesses of his young mind.

Edgar G. Sulite and Helacrio L. Sulite Sr.

Edgar recalled that it was about seven months later when he received his very first lesson in Eskrima from his father, Helacrio L. Sulite Sr. Edgar's earliest memories regarding training were not fond ones but instead filled with much pain and dislike for his ancestral arts. With a wince on his face Edgar, often talked about his initial early "bad" impressions of Eskrima. At this time Edgar was only six years old, and his first lessons were given at his father's convenience, done as a kind of experiment. When his father came home from work, and after eating and relaxing for a bit, Edgar dreaded hearing the call to him and his three brothers for Eskrima lessons. The lessons would be long, torturous, and painful. His father was very "strict" and "rigid" in his teachings, and often the manner of teaching would be "heavily laced with discipline," Edgar recalled.

Edgar told how his father taught him and his brothers using a bamboo stick he had himself cut from his backyard. He ordered them to parry and counter his strikes as he randomly struck at each one of them individually. Most of the time, his father struck at them along awkward and unexpected angles designed to confuse and deceive them, slipping his attacks just past their best attempts at a defense. Edgar recounted how he and his brothers "suffered" greatly during these early training sessions, receiving their fair share of bruises and sometimes even boils which formed on their hands and on the top of their heads from their father's heavy strikes. Edgar was hit in the mouth, on occasions, with the rough tip of freshly cut bamboo, making his mouth bleed. This was one of his father's favorite targets while utilizing a thrusting attack or counter attack towards the face of his opponent.

Regardless of what Edgar was told to do during those early training sessions, he recalled his father would counter immediately, hitting him in numerous places on his body, most often on top of his head, on his hands, arms, and shins. Many lessons were held outside in the dark of evening, with the only light coming from either the stars or the moon. He often spoke of his father placing him on three tortoise shells as a way to train his footwork while also forcing him to defend against random attacks from his father, who would hit him with the freshly cut bamboo sticks when Edgar would fail to block or deflect appropriately. As a direct result of those early experiences, Edgar said that, as a small child, he did not care much for his ancestral warrior arts since all they meant to him were the pain and discomfort associated with those early lessons. He had no choice early-on but to train in his family's Rapelon Eskrima system, but his heart was not yet in the training. Simply put, he could not go against the wishes of his father.

Edgar did develop an interest in one form of fighting, but it was not Filipino in origin. Western boxing and Japanese Karate are what captured his earliest interest. His father was a reputable ten-round boxer, which initiated an interest in that discipline, and so Edgar asked his father if he could train him to box, which he did. Edgar also developed a keen interest in Karate after reading a book written by Mas Oyama (circa 1967) titled *Vital Karate*. This lead Edgar to taking a local Karate class offered close by his school. He was also influenced by his eldest brother, Helacrio Sulite Jr., under whom he received much of his Karate training. After seriously training in both disciplines for a while, and doing a comparison analysis, Edgar eventually began to see more clearly the advantages which his ancestral Filipino arts may have possessed and could offer him as a young warrior in training. It was around the age of 12 (circa 1969) that Edgar developed his genuine interest in learning Eskrima. From this point forward it was no longer a forced activity, but rather a passion and way of life for him.

The Sulite family style was called Sulite-Rapelon, which was first created a couple of generations ago by Edgar's grand uncle, Luis Sulite, the brother of his grandfather, Mateo Sulite. Edgar's father, Helacrio L. Sulite Sr., began his training primarily under the tutelage of his father, Mateo Sulite, during the 1930s, but also received training from his uncle, Luis Sulite. As Edgar began to immerse himself in his Eskrima lessons under his father's watchful eyes, he developed more of an interest in Eskrima, which eventually opened up doors for him to more formal training under some of the most prominent masters of the Ozamis City region of Mindanao, which went well beyond the scope and size of his family system and of his father's tutelage.

Edgar was fortunate that many of the local masters from the region would often drop by his family home and train with his father and eldest brother, who, around their community, were both known to be effective fighters. Because of his local fame, from time to time various masters would show up to "test" the elder brother, Helacrio Sulite Jr. This became an opportunity for the young and hungry Edgar to associate with these masters and provided him an "in" should he wish to pursue training with them at a future time. And Edgar did eventually go on to train under some of these local masters, and the result of that involvement would be pivotal in his development of the Lameco Eskrima system, which he would develop decades later.

Aside from everything, Edgar was always highly impressed by his father's prowess in Eskrima. He did, however, have one concern, which was how his father appeared to others while doing it. Edgar would often say, with a smile on his face, that his father was quite fond of the "unorthodox" approach in fighting, and a lot of the techniques looked "made up." That did not diminish the fact that these techniques were effective in combat! Unorthodox looking or not, they still hurt when they struck their mark, and numerous bumps and bruises left on Edgar's hands, arms, shins, and head were the proof. Edgar would say that his father's signature strike, which he would call *pintok*, would unexpectedly come hard and fast directly from overhead, as if he were attempting a hook shot in basketball. It would hit Edgar square on the top of his head every time because it was so awkward and unusual that it was hard to recognize and defend against. Helacrio was also very good at disarming his opponents so quickly, they would not notice what was happening until their weapon was gone from their grasp.

The Sulite-Rapelon system was named after a specific training device which Edgar's grandfather Mateo, and his granduncle Luis often used. The *rapelon* (meaning, "propeller") was a stick perfectly balanced and tied in the center by a string and then hung at different levels from a tree limb. It primarily developed alertness, hand, eye, and body coordination, deflections, blocking, and the ability to pass the weapon, as well as footwork and proper body mechanics. Hitting one end of the *rapelon* forced the other end to swing around, and the harder they struck the one end, the faster and more erratic the other end would swing back around at them.

The longer and heavier the hanging stick, the slower it would move about when hit. The shorter and lighter the stick, the quicker and more erratic its response, greatly increasing the level of difficulty in executing defenses against it. In the beginning levels of the Sulite-Rapelon system, the student used a heavier and longer stick, and as the student improved his ability to locate the stick as it moved around faster and faster, the shorter and lighter the hanging stick would become. At the level that Luis, Mateo, Helacrio Sr., and Edgar were training, they would hang a much lighter and shorter stick with both ends sharply pointed, forcing them to use *praksyon* techniques to be able to intercept the *rapelon* as it would spin almost out of control at lightning speed. *Praksyon* are off-timing movements and techniques found in advanced Eskrima training.

Years later as Punong Guro Edgar Sulite was training me with this device, he told me that I would be well advised to wear head gear in the beginning, until I had adjusted to the much quicker spin of the stick coming toward me as compared with a person's strike. That was sound advice, as the harder I hit the *rapelon*, the quicker it would spin around, often striking me in the head, well before I was able to locate the threat and adequately respond to it.

Another primary characteristic associated with the Sulite-Rapelon style is the movement concept known as *praksyon*. Meaning "fraction," this is the method of countering an opponent and intercepting him before he can execute his initial line of attack, and thereby reducing the threat early before collateral damage could be done to self. According to Edgar's grandfather Mateo, *praksyon* is a very efficient and highly effective concept considered by many to be one of the most advanced levels of the indigenous Filipino warrior arts. It forces you to strike first and strike last, even when your opponent initiates the attack. Edgar used this concept to his advantage often in later years after he had founded the Lameco Eskrima system. The concept allowed him to end a fight before it could begin. He would later see *praksyon* also used years later by Antonio "Tatang" Ilustrisimo, under whom Edgar studied Kalis Ilustrisimo in Manila from 1982-1989. This is interesting because Edgar's father Helacrio had trained under Melicio Ilustrisimo, the uncle and a teacher of Tatang. Maybe there is a connection there, or, I suppose, it might just be happenstance.

One thing that Edgar specifically recalled was, as a teenager, being made to feel slightly embarrassed by his father's inability to twirl sticks well as he warmed up. He would regale us with stories of his father performing public demonstrations, and, as his father's accomplishments and status as a well-respected *eskrimador* were being introduced to the spectators, Helacrio began to warm up by twirling his *garotes* (sticks). Edgar would say, with a huge smile on his face, and just a hint of stifled laughter, that it looked as if he were a beginner because of the rough un-coordinated appearance of the two sticks "jutting" out from all positions in a jerky awkward manner when his father twirled them around. After the warm up was over Edgar felt relieved because he knew that his father would then impress the crowd with his combative effect and movement.

Edgar loved his father beyond what words could express, and, over the years, he did come to understand why the early training was so demanding. However, from the perspective of a young child, regardless of effective combative movement, pain was pain, and it took the fun out of the experience. As a young adult, however, Edgar came to understand perfectly why he was challenged so soon in his training. Fighting is not an enjoyable thing to experience; nor was it ever intended to be. So, why should we train to contend with it as if it were? Besides, this laid a realistic functional foundation under what would come – Edgar would simply call it "fighting form" – when he began his first formal training in De Campo Uno-Dos-Tres Orehenal, under the expert eyes of Jose D. Caballero, the longtime undefeated *juego todo* ("anything goes") champion fighter from the region in which Edgar spent his teen years. Later on, Manong Caballero began building on the foundation that Edgar's father had created. Edgar said that, at the very least, his father bequeathed to him and his three brothers a rich legacy and heritage in indigenous martial arts. That was his father's gift to his four sons and Edgar was proud to receive such a gift.

The Sulite-Rapelon system is one of the five major influences on Lameco Eskrima – and with good reason. Many have found how effective developing broken rhythm in a combative context can be. Most "polished" practitioners have a difficult time adjusting and countering against an ugly, awkward attack coming from unexpected angles with broken timing. Since the passing of Helacrio L. Sulite Sr. the system is now headed by Helacrio "Jun" Sulite Jr., who is well-known in his community for his fighting ability. Some of the more notable qualities and characteristics of the system are *pangilog* (disarms), *praksyon* (fractioning), *pintok* (wrist snap) – overhead wrist snap strikes to the top of the head, or a quick snap to the shin bone – and, of course, the namesake of the system: the propeller-like *rapelon*.

Chapter 2

Training with Masters of Ozamis City, Mindanao

GM Jose Diaz Caballero and De Campo 1-2-3 Orehenal

Punong Guro Sulite told me many times that even though he began his training under his father and his eldest brother (in his father's absence), his first real "formal" training in Eskrima came from Jose D. Caballero in the De Campo 1-2-3 Orehenal system. Mang Caballero and his system were absolutely essential to the future creation, founding, and eventual worldwide popularity of Lameco Eskrima.

The views of Jose Caballero regarding fighting were simply this: you are only as effective in fighting as you are in training. You will fight the way you train; hence, one of his favorite sayings: "Suffer during training, not during a fight." Simply put, if you fight with weakness and compromise, it is because you have trained with weakness and compromise, and so, to alleviate this, you must remove both elements, and allow yourself to train as you would expect to fight. Permit your training to brush up against reality. Mang Caballero never allowed his students to rest on their haunches while training in De Campo 1-2-3 Orehenal. He would push them until their hands bled from striking so much with their *garotes*. He expected students to improve after their first tries, one hard strike behind another, all done with full intention for two or three hours straight, without being given a chance to rest.

De Campo 1-2-3 Orehenal is truly combat effective, having been created to win fights and nothing more. It is definitely one of the most effective systems in which I have had the privilege to train, as its foundation is anchored in reality and governed by combative truth. Cause and effect seem to dictate response and counter response as opposed to some orchestra of speculation which may or may not ever come to pass. You are truly effective only when you are in the moment, as it were, on any given day. Punong Guro Sulite used to say: "An ounce of reality is worth a pound of speculation." In other words, combative truth speaks loudest when based on actual experience and rings more valid than arts whose techniques are based on mere speculation.

GM Jose D. Caballero

GM Jose D. Caballero and Edgar G. Sulite posing in front of the De Campo 1-2-3 Orehenal Banner which Edgar had made and presented to his teacher. The garote which Jose D. Caballero is holding in this photo is now in the authors private collection.

Nong Otek, as Manong Caballero was known to his family and closest friends, formed De Campo 1-2-3 Orehenal in 1925. It is based on his observations of local masters in Barrio Ibo, Toledo City, Cebu, as they would "play" with one another with sticks, knives, and swords during local fiestas, duels, and challenge matches. Since Mang Caballero didn't have formal instruction, he would go to tournaments, watch street fights evolve, and observe challenges played out, sometimes to the death, during his childhood and adolescence. The techniques of De Campo are based on the actions and reactions which Caballero saw in these fights, and he would teach himself to duplicate their movements. Even as a young man, he noticed the smallest curiosities while these masters fought, and he made mental note as they were revealed to him.

One of the things that he noticed right away, Edgar told us, was that, when the matches would start, both fighters typically walked around each other, watching the other's movements, analyzing and waiting for the other to strike first. Sometimes there would be no action at all for the first minute or so of the fight, and Nong Otek saw a lot of advantage in acting to the contrary. So, he established a series of three-second rules for initiating a fight. He usually waited for his opponent to strike first, as he was a counter fighter by nature. However, at the start of the fight, he counted to three, and if his opponent was not ready and had not thrown his first strike within three seconds, then Nong Otek launched his own attack with lightning speed and with strong purpose, catching his opponent by surprise and either break his head or his hand: the two primary targets in De Campo. As his opponent reacted to the damage inflicted, Nong Otek would back just outside of his reach, to see if the opponent could continue or not, but always at the ready to counter attack should the fight continue. In most cases, the fight would be over in mere seconds as few of his opponents could recover and continue fighting, thereby accepting defeat.

Nong Otek would constantly get into trouble as a young boy because he never made it to school on time. As he walked to school, he would see a stick laying on the ground, cut a piece of rattan out of a stalk, or else break a tree branch hanging down low. He just could not resist the temptation to practice Eskrima, resulting in his losing track of time and making him late for school, if he made it there at all. The young Jose Caballero used to get much grief from his father since he wanted only the best for his son and thought education was a necessity that would give him a chance to lift himself out of poverty one day and have a better life than that of his father. However, young Jose had other interests and fighting was at the top of the list. In 1925, when he was eighteen years old, Caballero formally formed, founded, and named his own system, "De Campo 1-2-3 Orehenal Combat Arnis," and started fighting in tournaments and playing with local masters at fiestas. Based on his successes or failures in these matches, he would update and expand his system appropriately.

Nong Otek always sought to strike two primary targets: the head and the hands. These essential targets were both simple and effective because one or the other would always be made available to him during a match. Nong Otek felt there was an additional advantage to striking to the hands in training sessions: it really developed a high sense of awareness and accuracy, which involved location and relocation principles while busy perceiving a moving threat. He often said the hands were faster, three times smaller, and had four times the mobility of the head; so, if you could locate and strike the hands at will in real-time speed, then you would have no problem striking the head, with all of its restricting limitations of movement. He would go on to explain that if you had problems locating and hitting the hands in a fight, you should instead target the elbows, saying: "If you find the weapon hand hard to hit, target the elbows since they travel within a much narrower radius." In this way, he looked at things others made difficult and make them simple and achievable.

I have to admit that it is the secondary targets of Manong Caballero which peak my interest the most. They are, in my opinion, nothing short of absolutely brilliant! There were times when Caballero could not hit the head or hands, and so he would, out of necessity, choose to strike at less than ideal targets in order to manufacture opportunity where none readily existed. In utilizing these more painful secondary targets, a distraction was created and, once a reaction was committed to by his opponent, he could then easily break the head of his opponent with finality and claim victory.

In utilizing these secondary targets, the intent was to strike to "maim" or "injure" the opponent. In doing this, Manong Caballero would use the first inch or so of the tip of his *garote* to inflict painful yet "less-than-lethal" wounds. By using the first inch or so of the *garote*, the very edge of the tip, he could choose to create a distraction by breaking the smaller bones of the opponent's hand, the fingers, thumb, wrist, tip of the elbow, or knock out the knee cap, break and knock the bridge of the nose loose from the face, tear off a piece of an ear, tear off a lip, or tear chunks of tissue from either the forearm or biceps. I think any of these secondary targets more than qualify as a major distraction! Imagine seeing a piece of your biceps dangling from the tip of your opponent's *garote* as he stands before you awaiting an opportunity to break your head and bring you to the ground in agonizing pain, while securing your defeat and his victory.

If a more serious outcome were sought with intent to produce "lethal" results, Nong Otek would utilize the upper six inches of the *garrote*, targeting the opponent's temples to – as Manong Caballero would say – "Strike through the eyes." By striking this far up the *garote*, even striking the hand or wrist can have a devastating effect, more than enough to distract and create an opportunity to strike and break the opponent's skull. Regardless of whether one chooses to use the tip or the upper six inches of the *garote* to strike the intended target, precision and intent are required. "Every strike that you throw has to be able to break the head of your opponent, or you should not throw a strike at all," Caballero warned, "as a strike thrown in weakness and without intention can only invite defeat from a skilled and determined enemy."

I think it also important to note that, when Manong Caballero fought, he did not look directly at the weapon hand or the head of his opponent. Instead, he used his peripheral vision and would pick a spot located just above the shoulder of the weapon-holding hand, almost as if he were looking off into the distance. By doing this, he would say that he could notice even the slightest movement of his opponent's weapon. He would explain that peripheral vision creates an appearance that the opponent's strikes are slower than they really are, allowing you to perceive the threat much more quickly because you are reacting to general movement as opposed to specific movement. By using his peripheral vision, Nong Otek could follow the weapon hand of his opponent wherever it went, and be able to hit it at will with power and focus.

Jose Caballero believed that when an opportunity revealed itself in a fight, it was split equally between you and your opponent. As such, the first one of you to recognize it and take advantage of it will gain the advantage. He used to warn his students that there were no guarantees in combat, only opportunities. Either you take advantage of those fleeting opportunities at the very moment they are presented, or you hesitate, and the same opportunity can be seized by your opponent to break your head. In other words, your failure to act in the moment can cost you the match or your life. Caballero also warned his students not to wait for the opportunity they desired but instead to take the first opportunity that presented itself, and work off of that advantage to end the fight. In any fight, very few opportunities will present themselves in any form, and if you allow even one to pass without seizing it, another may not come along at all; so take any and all opportunities and use them to your advantage. If you do not, your opponent will.

Caballero's De Campo 1-2-3 Orehenal system focused on only two weapon categories: *solo garote* (single stick) and *doble garote* (double sticks). It is said that he fought challenges against opponents brandishing knives, bolos, and swords, and still he maimed, defeated, and sometimes killed them by using only medium weight rattan sticks. Caballero was the undefeated *juego todo* ("anything goes") champion of his region, which gained him much notoriety and respect from his fellow *eskrimadors*. He would often go to tournaments during local fiestas and place his name on the list of fighters, only to find many who had previously enlisted to fight, rushing to withdraw their names for fear of fighting him. Caballero would then withdraw his own name and watch the other fighters run back to the table to get back on the list. Nong Otek was fond of doing this, for no other reason than just to gauge the response. He enjoyed the profound respect of his peers as well as from all of the battle-hardened *eskrimadors* in his region. In fact, sometimes, when he would walk down the road, people crossed to the other side to greet him out of respect, leaving Caballero to ask: "When are we going to play?" To which they would respond: "Joe, mine is only for playing. Yours is for killing. So, you and I will not be playing

Certificate of Authenticity for several weapons in the authors private collection which belonged too and were hand carved by GM Jose D. Caballero over 70 years ago. The certificate is signed by: Mrs. Amparo Lebumfacil Caballero, the widow of Manong Caballero, his Daughter, Edilberta Caballero Liawao and Manong Eric Olavides.

anytime soon." To which Nong Otek replied: "If yours is not for killing then why waste your time training?"

De Campo 1-2-3 Orehenal is classified as a "largo-medio" (long to medium) range fighting system with close range implications. It has only seven strikes, three double stick patterns, no blocks, no hand contact between players, no disarms, no *punyos* (butt strikes), only three types of footwork, 10 striking groups, a plethora of group mixing, three finishing strikes, alertness training, and specialization of grouping/striking, and thousands of hours of sparring against single and multi-person scenarios. It is simply a system of a continuous series of hard destructive strikes, counter strikes, and strike combinations designed to work well against chaos and uncertainty, which are all too commonly found in a street fight as it dynamically evolves from second to second. Even though the system was designed to be most effective in the "medio-largo" range, it is also quite effective in the close range as well. Caballero said that he would shorten the path of his strike to accommodate the strengths of his system at that distance by drawing the *punyo* closer to his body while striking, thereby decreasing the radius of his strikes but not sacrificing his power or lightning-quick hand speed.

Caballero was a counter fighter by nature. When attacked, he would retreat to just within an inch of *largo* range while striking to break the hand of his opponent. Once the tip of his opponent's weapon barely passed his nose, Caballero would immediately charge forward to strike his opponent's head. Anticipating a counter attack, Caballero would then retreat back into *largo* range, just outside of his opponent's reach; again waiting to attack whatever angle his opponent might counter with. Manong Caballero would say that the perfect fighting range was found "when you could feel the fibers of your opponent's stick brush up against your nose. At this range you cannot possibly get any closer to your opponent without being more in harm's way and you cannot possibly get any further away from your opponent without being found in deficit." The master would gauge the proper fighting distance based on these criteria and, on average, his fights were said to have lasted only three to five seconds each, before his opponent would be on the ground bleeding from the head, unable to continue.

Jose Caballero made his living for several decades traveling from island to island in the Philippines, challenging various masters to a fight for money, bringing along his father-in-law to act as his referee. He would go to an island and challenge the best fighter there, make side bets with the residents of the village, then fight and defeat his opponent. He then returned home to Barrio Ibo, Toledo City, Cebu, and lived off the profits made from the fight. When he ran low of money, once again he would be off to another island for another fight. Caballero

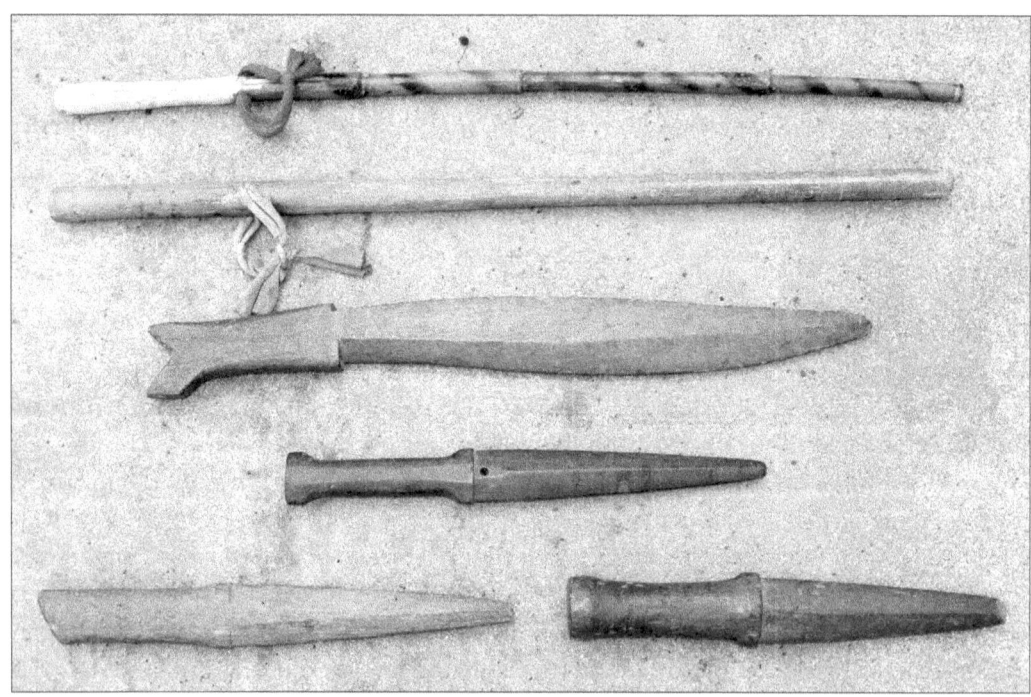

These were all hand carved by GM Jose D. Caballero circa 1940s and were all used often by him during his personal training. The second stick from the top was used by GM Caballero in the books : "Secrets of Arnis" and "Masters of Arnis, Kali and Eskrima" both authored by Edgar G. Sulite. The stick on top was used by both Manong Ireneo "Eric" Olavides and Edgar G. Sulite to spar against Manong Caballero during their private lessons with him at his home in Ozamis City, Mindanao, Philippines in De Campo 1-2-3 Orehenal. The bolo and training knives were used by Manong Caballero in training. One of his students would feed him while holding these and he would work his counters with either solo garote or doble garote against a knife wielding or bolo wielding attacker.

did this until he got too old to fight for a living and was forced into teaching. That was when, after hearing of Caballero's reputation, a young and impressionable Edgar Sulite sought him out as a teacher.

From the onset it was quite difficult for Edgar to gain the confidence of the "old man," as Edgar would fondly refer to him. In fact, it would take one full year of "courting" him with much patience and determination, in addition to providing him with poultry and dairy products when Edgar had collected enough money to purchase such things. All of this was done in an honest attempt to convince the master of his sincere desire to be accepted as an earnest student seeking only combative knowledge and not presenting himself as a "spy" out to steal his secrets, as was the belief of old warriors back in the day.

In order to gain the confidence of Caballero, Edgar would go by his house almost every day and inquire if he could train with the "old man," yet day after day he would be denied and told to go away. When Edgar could get a small amount of money together he would buy small gifts of chicken, eggs, or milk and place these items on the doorstep of Caballero's house, as a good will gesture. He hoped these would gain him a small measure of influence with the very sought out and highly respected Eskrima master. Edgar's persistence and dedication were unwavering, and soon Caballero came to recognize this. After almost a year of this "courting" the "old man" gave in and accepted Edgar as a student of De Campo 1-2-3 Orehenal, several months before Edgar's 18th birthday in 1975, and an odyssey began.

The problem from the beginning was that Jose Caballero felt that, if you had trained in any other system, the only goal you could possibly achieve by training under him was to "steal his secrets" and teach them to your group or clan. It was feared that one day those "secrets" might be used in combat against him or his best students. This was a common way of thinking among the "old warriors" of that time, and for good reason; at one point in time it was true. Indeed, many systems were violated in this manner during the turn of the 20th century when Caballero was raised, and the mistrust of anyone not of one's family or clan was quite common. Since Edgar was neither of the Caballero family nor of his clan, naturally, he was met initially with suspicion and was much scrutinized. However, Jose Caballero, by then feeble and old and not able to fight challenges for a living any longer, had little choice but to offer himself as a teacher to try and make a little money to help pay his bills and provide sustenance for his family.

Edgar told me several times that when he was learning De Campo 1-2-3 Orehenal from Manong Caballero, it was the training itself he initially hated most because it was so demanding and challenging to him physically. But in only a short time he came to appreciate fully the combative value being laid at his feet by training in this system under such a great and experienced warrior. Because there are no blocks or disarms in De Campo 1-2-3 Orehenal, and there are only two types of strikes (one to kill and one to maim), it was sometimes very difficult to train because you would repeat the same grouping and finishing strikes again and again, thousands of times per training session. That said, the results were highly effective, and that fact could not be argued.

The author posing with two of the hand carved garotes which belonged to GM Jose D. Caballero and are now in the authors private collection

Because training and sparring sessions were conducted without protective equipment, Edgar got hit thousands of times on the hands, wrists, and forearms, making each strike painful beyond belief. This is what forced him to further develop his hand evasions revealed in Caballero's well thought-out progression of *kaabtik*, or "alertness" training. In *largo* range, even though the body and head are kept just out of the opponent's reach, the hands, wrists, and forearms can still be struck. In order to stay close enough to one's opponent to take advantage of opportunities as they revealed themselves during the fight, one had to master hand evasions for those times when one's opponent tried to target those extremities of the body.

At the earliest stages of their student-teacher relationship, Edgar felt that Caballero was being stingy with his teachings as he kept forcing Edgar to repeat the same thing every time. What he eventually came to understand was that Caballero was trying to get him to master the basics against all situations and probable scenarios, and to learn all that each had to offer in street combat. To learn them so well, that he not only learned the strength of the technique, concept, or principle, but also gleaned the inherent weakness which was the opposite side of the strength itself. Only when he fully understood the weakness of what he did could he then assess fair value to the strength. Only then could he come to depend on it, as sometimes the weakest part of a technique proves to be greater than the strength, and, therefore, becomes ill-advised to use under certain conditions or circumstances. De Campo 1-2-3 Orehenal became the confidence system of Edgar Sulite in regard to impact weapons, and every time he was forced to defend life and limb, fight a challenge, or spar, he reverted back to the lessons learned and combative abilities instilled during his time under the tutelage of Jose Caballero. In the words of Jose D. Caballero: "You train to live, not die."

De Campo 1-2-3 Orehenal utilizes one hard strike thrown after another. You strike until your hand bleeds, and then you strike some more. Caballero's requirement was that you strike as hard and as fast as you could for 15 minutes without slowing or stopping. Then you did two minutes of hard aggressive footwork followed by 15 more minutes of striking without resting, continuously, for three hours a day. He would have you break small coconuts, hit tires, and the daily sparring was rough – no head gear or padding. The rules of training were such that, if the head were open, you were required to take the shot. The only way that you could truly protect your head and weapon hand was to constantly keep both just outside of your opponent's reach, all while staying highly aware of your opponent's every move and maintaining the ability to act

A closer look at two of the hand carved garotes which belonged to and were used by GM Jose D. Caballero.

on any additional opportunities as they reveal themselves to you in real-time, until the fight has been won. Another of GM Caballeros favorite sayings regarding this concept was: "Strike first and strike last, even when your opponent initiates the attack." Even though his opponent might try to throw the initial strike, GM Caballero beat him to it and then strike last, as well, ending the fight to his advantage.

It got so bad at times during his training sessions that often Edgar, being absolutely exhausted, would pretend that he had to relieve himself just to be able to get away from the "old man's" critical eyes for only a few minutes, so he could catch his breath enough to continue training. Edgar recalled GM Caballero thinking he had a faulty bladder because he needed to "relieve" himself so many times in a three-hour session. Edgar would excuse himself, head for the bushes, and, bent over, resting on his knees and catching his breath, he would think to himself: "Surely, this old man will be the death of me!" Trying to steal one more minute to recoup from his exhaustion, then came the words he hated to hear the most from the "old man": "Gar! Back!"

Edgar went to the home of GM Caballero for training whether or not he had the money to do so, because he really wanted to train, and he hoped the "old man" might make an exception due to Edgar's poverty. As he arrived at the house, GM Caballero would approach him and ask if he had any money. Edgar replied with a "yes" or "no," depending on his circumstances. If the answer was "no," GM Caballero went into his home and got his receipt book showing the receipt for the student who had just trained before Edgar, that day, and say: "You see? 'So and so' was just here, and he paid this much." Then he told Edgar that, without money, he would not be able to train today. Edgar always hung his head in disappointment, as he truly desired to train.

I remember a situation where Edgar told me that he did not have any money to pay and Manong Caballero refused to teach him for the day. He was told that, since he was there already, he should go into the back yard and train by himself, swinging his garote. GM Caballero went and sat on the porch with his back turned to Edgar and looked off into the distance. If Edgar began to relax in the execution of his strikes, the "old man" shouted, "More sound!" Although still sitting with his back turned, he was actively teaching Edgar, if only by audible sound. Edgar would then start striking his garote with gusto at the prospect of GM Caballero offering something more for his efforts. Manong Caballero used to demand that each strike which you threw in training had to have enough power to break the head of your opponent, or, he said, you should not throw the strike at all. If he did not hear the wind swishing across the tip of the garote as each strike cut the air with full intention, he would quickly say: "No sound!", "Wrong sound!", or "More sound!" He taught Edgar that, when his stick was silent, his capacity to fight was diminished.

It was hard training, but Punong Guro Edgar G. Sulite realized how blessed he was for being given the chance to train and learn from GM Caballero, and he valued their friendship and all that GM Caballero shared with him. It is funny because later Edgar told me he first thought GM Caballero to be his stingiest teacher because he taught so few techniques and made him repeat tens of thousands of times what he did teach him. Where some of Edgar's other Instructors overwhelmed him with techniques, sometimes showing him hundreds of different techniques per training session, even though Edgar said he walked away from those training sessions remembering only about 10 techniques if he were lucky and forgetting the rest. Yet, he remembered 100% of what he was required to do in each session with GM Caballero. Hence, one of Punong Guro Edgar G. Sulite's favorite sayings: "Repetition is the mother of all skills." This reference was made specifically regarding how GM Caballero taught his students, and what was required of each of those who trained under him in De Campo 1-2-3 Orehenal.

When Edgar looked back on his previous training, he realized most of the things he had received from some of his other Masters, he did not truly master because he spent so little time evaluating each technique, concept, or principle to the point where he fully understood them. Whereas, GM Caballero forced him to truly master each strike, counter strike, and counter-to-counter strike as well as forcing him to verify each one every time they faced one another in hard sparring. By forcing Edgar to repeat those same strikes and combinations of strikes against an unexpected random attack or counter attack in real-time by literally hundreds of thousands of repetitions and countless hours of sparring, Edgar had no choice but to master the combative equation itself, the "art of fighting," if you will. He came to realize that GM Caballero was not the stingiest of his Teachers but rather the most generous because he cared enough to force Edgar, not to become a master of meaningless techniques and countless series of redundant drills, but rather to master combative movement and the fight itself.

De Campo Uno-Dos-Tres Orehenal is one of the five major influences of the Lameco Eskrima System, and, since the passing of GM Jose Diaz Caballero in 1987, the system has passed on to his number-one protégé; Master Ireneo L. Olavides, who resides, and can be contacted, in Cagayan do Oro, Mindanao, Philippines. For anyone who truly wants to connect with the true combative essence of Lameco Eskrima, it is essential to investigate further into De Campo 1-2-3 Orehenal. A few years ago, Mang Eric Olavides transferred full authority back to the Caballero family when he announced GM Manuel "Mawe" Caballero as the head of the system; and both Mang "Mawe" and his son can be reached in Toledo, Cebu, Philippines for training and further information regarding the system.

Tuhon Leo T. Gaje, Jr. and Pekiti-Tirsia Kali

Edgar G. Sulite first met Tuhon Leo Tortal Gaje, Jr. of Pekiti-Tirsia Kali fame through two of Gaje's nephews, Lowell and Jun Pueblos. Both of these men were good friends, training partners, and early sparring partners of Edgar. Leo Gaje is a living legend, having been one of the first Filipinos to introduce their ancestral warrior arts to the world, first in New York circa 1970 and eventually in Europe and beyond in the decades to follow.

Tuhon Leo Tortal Gaje Jr. taken in March 1996 at Mambukal, Negros, Visayas, Philippines during a trip where the author was training with him in the Kali Pekiti-Tirsia System.

According to Leo Gaje, he was first taught Pekiti-Tirsia by his Grandfather, Conrado Tortal, who is credited with formally founding the system in 1898. However, Tortal family history recorded the system being taught by the family as many as four generations before, but not in the same form as the now-recognized system with its rich curriculum and identifiable moves, known today as Pekiti-Tirsia Kali. Tuhon Gaje was well-known in the Philippines at the time Edgar met and trained with him. In fact, Gaje had political clout at the highest levels of the Philippine Government, all the way to President Marcos, General Estrada, and General Ver, all of whom he would eventually introduce to Edgar. This was fortunate because, years later, he would be in need of employment when he relocated to the Metro Manila around 1981.

Edgar would recall Gaje's ability to speak with such eloquence that he could convince a man to do anything with nothing more than his words. Edgar once said of Gaje, "As well as having *anting-anting* for fighting, he must also have had a buried amulet for the art of speaking, because he could speak as if he had a silver tongue." I found this to be true in my own training under Tuhon Gaje; he can be quite convincing, and he is indeed a very eloquent speaker. Even so, he speaks loudest and with greatest clarity when he moves, since he allows his movement and abilities bespeak his combative capability and effect. Tuhon Gaje was one of Edgar's favorite and most respected teachers.

Tuhon Leo Tortal Gaje Jr. and the Author taken in March 1996 at Mambukal Resort, Visayas, Philippines during a training session in Kali Pekiti-Tirsia.

Edgar would say that the most important lesson which he received from Tuhon Leo T. Gaje Jr. was to always go straight to the top. Never waste your time with anyone who answers to someone else, but rather go to the very person who has complete authority, and then everyone below him will bend to you and your demands. This is true in all aspects of life and business in general, as well. This philosophy did Tuhon Gaje well in his years of doing business since, eventually, he met with Heads of States and other people of power in order to perpetuate his trade. Edgar learned much of business through his association with Tuhon Gaje and, through their interactions, he witnessed the advantages and disadvantages which politics bring to any situation, and the added risks associated with that activity.

Tuhon Leo Tortal Gaje Jr. and his Nephew, Master Jun Pueblos who in addition to being a practitioner of Kali Pekiti-Tirsia was also the training partner, sparring partner and long time student of Edgar G. Sulite in the Lameco Eskrima System.

Out of all of the Masters under whom Edgar trained in the Philippines, he said, more-so than any other, it was probably Tuhon Gaje who had prepared and placed him on the long road to success. He was the first to bring Edgar to Manila and put him up in a nice hotel when he relocated there in 1981 from Ozamis City, Mindanao, Philippines. Tuhon Gaje created the opportunity for Edgar to get a job in personal protection for both General Estrada and General Ver, who, as Secretary of State and Secretary of Defense in the Philippine Government at that time, were both only answerable to President Marcos. It was also Tuhon Leo T. Gaje Jr. who created the environment for Edgar to meet and subsequently become the Eskrima teacher of Roland Dantes, a huge action star in Filipino Cinema. This opened up many essential doors for Edgar to pass through on the way to propagating the Lameco Eskrima System as we know it today. That pivotal meeting set the stage for Edgar to eventually meet GM Antonio "Tatang" Ilustrisimo and the rest of the Bakbakan group, who later played a critical role in the exposure of Lameco Eskrima, both in book form and through opportunities for Edgar to share his teachings internationally, for the first time, and so to establish long-lasting friendships and bonds with people he met as a direct result.

Tuhon Gaje was indeed a very important component in Edgar's future, and regardless of how the waters of history may become muddy on this particular subject, when the waters eventually become clear, people will see the influence that Tuhon Gaje really had on Edgar and the Lameco Eskrima System since it was the logistics pertaining to the Pekiti-Tirsia Kali system which became the model for how Edgar formulated and organized his own system of Lameco Eskrima's infrastructure and propagation. Tuhon Leo T. Gaje Jr. never saw himself simply as an Instructor of the Filipino Warrior Arts who limited himself to the Philippines, exclusively. Rather, he felt himself to be an Ambassador of the Filipino warrior arts and culture, and so he took both to the world and did not wait for the world to come to either him or the Philippines. This, then, was the seed also planted in the mind of Edgar G. Sulite when he was training under Tuhon Leo T. Gaje Jr., as it gave him a world view of what Lameco Eskrima could become and a determination not to wait on others to act on his behalf but rather to go out and act on behalf of himself; and that is exactly what Edgar went on to do in propagating the Lameco Eskrima System throughout the world.

Tuhon Leo Tortal Gaje Jr. in Visayas, Philippines (1996) training with the author along with one of his students, Mr. Brian Lane who also was a student of PG Edgar G. Sulite in Lameco Eskrima.

Edgar said of Tuhon Leo T. Gaje Jr. that he was probably the most versatile of all of the Masters under whom he had trained, that he was one of the few who possessed all three qualities required of a great Master: 1) he knows his discipline inside and out, not just the strengths

Tuhon Leo T. Gaje Jr. teaching at the Mambukal Resort Pekiti-Tirsia Kali Training Camp in Visayas, Philippines in March 1996.

Tom Sotis (AMOK! Founder), David E. Gould and Tuhon Leo T. Gaje Jr while the three were traning together in Bacolod City, Visayas, Philippines.

but also any weakness' which also exist in the system; 2) he has the ability to teach his progression with pristine clarity in a manner by which a student could learn his system thoroughly, and; 3) he has the ability to fight with effect and to apply all that has been learned in a realistic environment. Tuhon Gaje was the "whole package," Edgar would say.

Training in Pekiti-Tirsia Kali was not easy for Edgar as Tuhon Gaje was a very demanding instructor. He would have Edgar get up really early in the morning, long before the sun came up, and drill him in hard aggressive footwork and strikes for hours before entering into the core of their lesson for the day. Edgar used to say that Tuhon Gaje made him get up so early, he had turned the roosters against him because he woke them up long before even they wanted to get up and announce to the world the morning sun. Edgar recalled, at one point, he would try and get up before Tuhon Gaje (a rare thing indeed!), then quickly go out and begin his footwork, so he could tell Tuhon Gaje he had already completed it, so they could skip it and move right into the lesson. Tuhon Gaje would not have this and always made Edgar repeat the footwork again under his observation, which was a grueling task in and of itself. Since hours of exhausting footwork are one of the essential elements of Pekiti-Tirsia Kali, you were required to do it, and a lot of it, under the tutelage of Tuhon Gaje.

Tuhon Leo T. Gaje Jr. teaching Espada-y-Daga during a training session with the author in Bacolod City, Visayas, Philippines.

Edgar remained a dedicated and loyal student of Tuhon Leo T. Gaje Jr. and, at one point, was rewarded by becoming the head representative for the Pekiti-Tirsia Kali Organization in the Philippines, answering only to Tuhon Leo T. Gaje, Jr. and Tuhon Jerson "Nene" Tortal, and to no one else below them, making Edgar G. Sulite the third highest-ranking person in Pekiti-Tirsia Kali during that period. At this time, people were even calling Edgar "Little Gaje" because the two men were inseparable, spending so much time together, and had become such good friends. In those days, whenever you saw Tuhon Gaje, Edgar was never far behind.

In addition, it was Tuhon Gaje who first introduced Edgar to Guro Dan Inosanto, in the United States of America, during the Indian Creek, Tennessee Camp in 1989. This was a pivotal meeting which began a mutually beneficial relationship lasting until Punong Guro Edgar G. Sulite passed away on April 10, 1997. Tuhon Leo T. Gaje Jr. was also the one that recommended that Guro Dan Inosanto accept Edgar as his instructor and begin training in the Lameco Eskrima System under him, and the rest, as they say, is history.

The author and one of his students in Lameco Eskrima, Mr. Brian Lane training during the Mambukal Resort Pekiti-Tirsia Kali Training Camp in Visayas, Philippines in March 1996 under the tutelage of Tuhon Leo T. Gaje Jr. and Tuhon Jerson "Nene" Tortal.

Pekiti-Tirsia Kali is one of the five major influences of the Lameco Eskrima System, which is still headed by Tuhon Leo T. Gaje Jr., who, to this day, actively propagates the system worldwide, based out of his hometown of Bacolod City, Negros, Philippines. Anyone wishing to further explore into the origins of Lameco Eskrima, or simply interested in expanding his or her knowledge of the Filipino Ancestral Warrior Arts would do well to contact him for training.

Tuhon Leo Tortal Gaje Jr. and the Author taken in March 1996 at Mambukal Resort, Visayas, Philippines during training in the Pekiti-Tirsia Kali System.

GM Jesus Abella & GM Pablicito "Pabling" Cabahug and "Modernos Largos"

Both GM Jesus Abella and GM Pablicito "Pabling" Cabahug had vast experience regarding the indigenous warrior arts of the Philippines because both fought against the invading Japanese Army as "voluntarios" during WWII. As well, both had endured and survived several attacks made on their lives while separately doing business throughout the very dangerous regions of Mindanao, sometimes being forced to fight against "basag uleros" and "tulisans," who were men of bad reputation always looking for trouble and often finding it at the expense of those who were not able to defend themselves. When both GM Jesus Abella and GM Pablicito "Pabling" Cabahug dealt with these types of men, they always found a way to tip the balance to their advantage and survived these attempts to take their lives and treasures. Both Grandmasters became fast friends and were also sparring partners who combined their individual experiences together to cofound the "Modernos Largos" System of Eskrima.

GM Pablicito "Pabling" Cabahug and Edgar G. Sulite training in Ozamis City, Mindanao, Philippines.

While Edgar G. Sulite was training under both Manong Jose D. Caballero in De Campo 1-2-3 Orehenal and Tuhon Leo Tortal Gaje Jr. in Pekiti-Tirsia Kali in Ozamis City, Mindanao, Philippines circa 1975, he first met GM Pablicito "Pabling" Cabahug. They met innocently enough. Every morning, Edgar went out in his front yard and, as part of his daily routine, hit the tires with his garote. After a while, he noticed, while he trained, an "old man" routinely walked by and would stop to watch for a while as Edgar swung his garote. Then the "old man" would turn and walk away without ever saying a word. Every day this would take place, and it began to intrigue Edgar enough to find out more about who this "old man" was and what his interest in Edgar's training could possibly be.

The more often this happened, the more Edgar would hit the tires with intention, trying to impress this "old man." Finally, one day Edgar spoke to him: "Grandmaster, who are you, and why is it that you pass by here every day, stop and watch me swing my garote but never say anything?" The "old man" then introduced himself as Cabahug, a veteran Eskrimador, and said he was simply curious about Edgar's training. Edgar, having heard of this old man in his local province, asked for an opinion of his skills? GM Cabahug told Edgar his movement was very good, which provoked Edgar into asking if the "old man" could give him any pointers. GM Cabahug responded, "No, you move good already," and, with that, he just turned and walked down the road, as had long been his custom.

This encounter made Edgar very apprehensive, so every day from that point forward he would look for the "old man" to come back down the road and, as soon as he saw him off in the distance, turning the curve in the road, Edgar would really start pounding the tires with all his might, hoping the "old man" would be in a more talkative mood, that day, and offer some pointers regarding his training. Finally, after months of this, GM Cabahug did begin speaking with Edgar more and more, and, finally, he invited Edgar to meet with GM Jesus Abella, his sparring partner and the co-founder of "Modernos Largos." The three of them were to form a long-lasting student and teacher relationship, as well as an enduring friendship. Edgar went on to train for years with the two old Grandmasters of Ozamis City, and, when they died, they left Edgar G. Sulite as the sole heir to their system of "Modernos Largos."

The system of "Modernos Largos" was named, not for the long range implication which the name implies, but rather for "largo," the act of following the strikes through to the ground, which both GM Cabahug and GM Abella referred to as "luhod-luhod": following each strike to the ground with their body weight, on impact, while striking through their selected target. This was distinctive of both GM Abella and GM Cabahug. One of the signature principles regarding their system was never to use "wetik" strikes, which were strikes thrown with a "wrist snap," as both Grand Masters felt those specific strikes had little effect due to a lack of power. Instead, they hit with their garotes as if they were striking with blades, relying on proper weight distribution and body mechanics to make their strikes effective as they followed each strike through the intended target and down, taking their bodies low to the ground so as to glean as much impact power as possible. GM Cabahug told Edgar that every strike was thrown as if made by a bolo (machete), as though they were guiding the edge of a blade through each body part struck during the execution.

Most people think, because of the name "Modernos Largos," that, it was a long range system. When asked about this by Edgar, GM Cabahug explained that, even though long range was heavily addressed in their system because they primarily trained and fought using 36-inch sticks, they also sometimes did use shorter sticks and were very comfortable in close range. GM Cabahug pointed out that, in close range, even with the longer sticks, he would recalibrate the strike by pulling the punyo closer to his body and shortening the path of the strike to accommodate closer targets. If his opponent did impede, block, or intercept his strikes in close range, then GM Cabahug would deviate his strike by simply retracting or withdrawing his stick a little bit and then let his strikes follow through or rebound from the point of contact as it continued past the obstruction encountered. PG Sulite later referred to that concept as "drifting," "de kadena," and "patalon" – three separate concepts which allowed him to deviate his

GM Pablicito "Pabling" Cabahug and Edgar G. Sulite

strike just enough to not allow his opponent to block or intercept his strike, which would open up immediate counter opportunities to him along his opponent's violated center line, exposed to him as a direct result of those actions.

When people saw Edgar move, especially his finishing strikes which took him low to the ground, this was the direct influence of "Modernos Largos" and is one of the signature principles of both GM Jesus Abella and GM "Pabling" Cabahug. Another of the principles Edgar shared with us in the Lameco Eskrima System which was directly influenced by GM "Pabling" Cabahug and the "Modernos Largos" System. GM Cabahug referred to it as "weapon transfers." He was able to fight equally well with either hand. GM Cabahug was known for this ability to transfer his weapon from one hand to the other in mid-stream, while striking seamlessly, without calling attention to it. He was so good, you could not keep up with which hand wielded the garote. This was one of the most valuable lessons Edgar learned from GM Cabahug, that we should not identify ourselves as being predominantly right handed or left handed but rather make both equally capable, since the closest hand to the most immediate threat inherited the task of intercepting that threat, regardless of whether it was located on the left or the right sides of the body.

Because of this mindset, Edgar trained me to be ambidextrous while still retaining the ability for both hands to work together when the situation demanded it. Edgar often told me: "Dabe, why should you have problems with the left hand? If you can do it with the right hand, then you can do it with the left hand equally well, as the same mind operates both sides." He made a valid point, and, in time, finally bringing to fruition what he had expected of me, I became as proficient with the left as I was with the right. In like manner, I demand the same thing of my students.

GM Jesus Abella was also quite experienced and well-versed in the indigenous Warrior Arts of the Philippines. He began training in his ancestral arts at a young age and, by sixteen, had gained a reputation for being a very effective fighter in Arnis in his native region of Mindanao, Philippines. However, he was better known there for fighting with the bolo, dagger, and the garote. Edgar said he could wield any of the three weapons with "breath taking propensity," having fought as a "voluntario" during WWII against the invading Japanese Army in the Malangas, Zamboanga del Sur region of the Southern Philippines. This experience gave him, Edgar said, a "wealth of knowledge in the art of killing men." After the War, GM Jesus Abella had reportedly survived several attempts to murder him made in various parts of his native Mindanao by "robbers" who were looking for an easy

GM Pablicito "Pabling" Cabahug and Edgar G. Sulite

target. He was able to thwart each attack on his life as they played out.

Because of his vast experience, GM Jesus Abella had reached a very basic understanding of the best way to train and develop for real combat. He felt that the best way to gauge one's true effectiveness as a fighter was simply to fight more, since this alone ensured learning the more important lessons about fighting while being taught and guided by the very experience itself. Only actual experience could adjust your expectations and shape your understanding of what was most required of you to do well in an environment shrouded by sheer uncertainty. GM Jesus Abella often reminded Edgar G. Sulite: "Fighting is the real gauge of how much you have developed in your training, as well as revealing to you how much more you have to learn in your pursuit of becoming a better fighter."

GM Pablicito "Pabling" Cabahug and Edgar G. Sulite

He would go on to tell Edgar that: "A fight improves your skill because, while you fight, your movements are spontaneous and un-programmed, and this forces you to react to what your opponent actually does, making you rely on your own reflexes as the fight naturally evolves and not to anticipate what your opponent is supposed to do." Edgar took this mindset to heart as one of his core beliefs when teaching the Lameco Eskrima System to his students in the future. Because of this insight, Edgar began to see the importance of inserting adversity into his training model, and to always strive to engage against uncertainty, dealing not so much with what was expected in training or in fighting but, more readily, with what was not expected, as this alone will heighten one's awareness of the unexpected attack in regards to the combative equation and all things found there-in.

When GM Jesus Abella and GM Pablicito "Pabling" Cabahug developed the "Modernos Largos" System, they pieced it together based on their collective and individual knowledge, a lot of which was derived from their experiences during WWII fighting in the jungles of the Philippines against the Japanese, as well as from their experiences soon after the War had ended. The two Grand Masters from Ozamis City were looking to build a good reputation for their system, so they went in search of the best way to accomplish this goal. GM Jesus Abella was well aware of and revered the skill of GM Jose D. Caballero of De Campo 1-2-3 Orehenal fame, who was the long time undefeated "Juego todo" fighter of the region where young Edgar G. Sulite was training at the time. GM Abella felt the need to challenge GM Caballero to prove to himself that "Modernos Largos" was in the same league as the art of Nong Otek. So, now that he had found the platform by which he could immediately elevate his system of Modernos Largos, all that was left to do was something no one else had been able to do for several

GM Pablicito "Pabling" Cabahug and Edgar G. Sulite

decades, and that was to beat an undefeated "Juego-todo" champion widely recognized as one of the best fighters of all time in that region. Even at ripe old age, GM Jose D. Caballero was deemed a dangerous threat to even the most-talented younger eskrimadors coming to challenge him.

During this time GM Jesus Abella was aware that Edgar was training under Nong Otek in De Campo 1-2-3 Orehenal and asked him what he thought his chances were of him beating GM Caballero in a fight. He also asked Edgar about some of GM Calleros secrets. Edgar did not want to say anything, as he respected GM Abella, and did not want to see him get hurt, and he was most definitely not going to share the secrets of GM Caballero out of fear of the "old man" finding out and dropping him as a student. So, Edgar kept his tongue silent but knew deep in his heart that GM Caballero could easily defeat GM Abella in a duel, a certainty based entirely on the way each moved, and that GM Abella would do well to end the confrontation with his life in tact should they engage each other in battle. Regardless of everything, GM Jesus Abella became convinced he could beat the "old warrior" and, with that conviction, he sent word to GM Caballero, challenging him to fight a duel; and GM Caballero sent word back that he would fight with GM Abella, but, first, he would have to prove himself worthy by defeating GM Caballeros protégé, Eric Ireneo Olavides, first, to earn the right to challenge GM Caballero himself. This was the custom at the time regarding issuing challenges in that region of the Philippines. So, the date was set, and GM Abella showed up at the home of GM Caballero at the announced time.

There he found Eric Olavides warming up for the match. After a small measure of time had passed, the two met in the center of the yard, and the match began. GM Abella twirled his garote as he scanned for opportunities. While Mang Eric Olavides just watched, trying to time his own opportunities, GM Abella struck first, and Mang Eric countered right away, hitting GM Abella in the wrist, forcing him to drop his garote to the ground. This resulted in GM Abella not being able to continue due to a severely injured wrist, and the fight was called declaring Mang Eric Olavides the victor. GM Jesus Abella paid his respects to GM Caballero, telling him that, when he recovered, he would like to reissue the challenge. GM Caballero told him, "Fine with me." Both Punong Guro Sulite and Mang Eric Olavides agreed it was not really much of a fight since it was over so quickly. GM Abella shared their reservations about the match when asked at a later date by Punong Guro Sulite.

After thoroughly analyzing his defeat, GM Jesus Abella decided to go back to the country side for a number of years, to reconfigure "Modernos Largos," and, upon his return to Ozamis City years later, he had come to respect the abilities of GM Caballero and De Campo 1-2-3

Orehenal and never reissued his challenge to Nong Otek, who was in his eighties by then. When Edgar spoke to him, GM Abella honestly stated that Mang Eric Olavides was just too fast and powerful, so much so that he could not see his strike coming, only felt its immediate pain. That really made him respect the ability of Mang Eric Olavides, immensely, as well as the teachings of GM Jose D. Caballero and the De Campo 1-2-3 Orehenal System. GM Abella went on to tell Edgar that incident made him question everything about his own system and had forced many changes for the best in regarding the "Modernos Largos" system.

One of the signature pieces of both GM Jesus Abella and GM Pablicito "Pabling" Cabahug was what they referred to as their "Hurricane" footwork. They would mostly use it either fighting in water or on sand. They kicked their feet back and up from the ground, attacking their opponent's position while simultaneously kicking up dust or water into the air, while also using the tips of their custom long garotes to direct water or sand into the eyes of their opponent as a form of distraction. Edgar said that both GM Abella and GM Cabahug were masters of this technique and would use it to good effect when training, sparring, or fighting.

Both GM Jesus Abella and GM "Pabling" Cabahug were strong believers and advocates of "anting-anting" as well as "orasyon," the spiritual side of the Filipino Warrior Arts. They believed in both the invincible factors and the healing side of "orasyon." They were also practitioners of the healing arts of Eskrima known as "Hilot Palina," which both Grand Masters claimed to use to cure things not even a Medical Doctor was able to cure. Both would conduct daily ceremonies, invoking the power of "anting-anting" by chanting prayers, anointing themselves with oil and burying amulets holding certain properties which offered their protection to both Grand Masters against any dark spirit which may bring harm to them.

Edgar recalled one time that GM Jesus Abella wanted to rub his head with oil and say an "orasyon" over him, to protect him before their lesson together. Edgar, not really convinced of "anting-anting," did not know what to think of the ceremony, but, in an effort to accommodate the Grand Master's wishes, he complied. Edgar was told after the "orasyon" that he could now allow someone to strike him with full power in the head and the strike could not hurt him because he was protected by the ointment and the "orasyon" spoken over him. To demonstrate this, GM Jesus Abella – also under the protection of the "orasyon" since he had included himself while speaking the prayer over Edgar – was willing to demonstrate his point, personally.

GM Jesus Abella asked Edgar to hit him as hard as he could in the head with his garote. Edgar, not believing in "anting-anting," told him no because he did not want to hurt him. GM Abella explained Edgar would not hurt him because he was protected by the "orasyon" spoken over him during the ceremony. Edgar still felt that he would surely kill GM Abella if he were to hit him with full power in the head and again respectfully declined. GM Abella insisted, and so Edgar hit him in the head, albeit controlling his strike, just to be sure, but even so hitting with enough force to draw blood from the side of the Grand Master's head. Edgar felt terrible, and he asked GM Abella, who stood there with a noticeable trickle of blood rolling down his face, what had gone wrong? And GM Abella pointed out Edgar was using a wooden stick, which is why he was able to draw blood. Apparently, the "orasyon" was only good at protecting him from anything made of metal, like a sword or machete, but not from something out of the earth like a stick cut from a tree or a plant. GM Abella told him "orasyon" only offered protection from something not natural, like metal blades or bullets. Edgar, being somewhat confused and dismayed, found an excuse to leave before GM Abella could insist Edgar hit him in the head with something made of metal, to better illustrate his point.

Edgar really liked both GM Abella and GM Cabahug a great deal and respected their system of "Modernos Largos" immensely. However, after training under GM Jose D. Caballero for years, he knew that De Campo 1-2-3 Orehenal was for fighting, and he had not witnessed anything in the area that could compete with it, which is why it would later become the nucleus of the Lameco Eskrima System and become the adopted confidence system of PG Sulite when it came to fighting with impact weapons.

GM Jesus Abella co-founded "Modernos Largos" with GM Pablicito "Pabling" Cabahug in Ozamis City, Mindanao, Philippines, and it was one of the five major influences in the creation and founding of the Lameco Eskrima System. Edgar G. Sulite was first introduced to GM Jesus Abella circa 1975 by GM Cabahug and became a student of the two Grandmasters from Ozamis City, training in their system of "Modernos Largos."

The account of GM Jesus Abella and GM Eric Olavides fighting was told to me by Edgar G. Sulite at his home in Palmdale, California in September of 1995 inside his garage after one of our private training sessions together.

GM Ireneo "Eric" Olavides and "De Campo 1-2-3 Orehenal"

Manong Ireneo "Eric" Olavides of De Campo 1-2-3 Orehenal was always one of the masters whom Edgar looked up to the most. Edgar told me numerous times that, if he could move like only one of the Masters under whom he had trained, his hands-down choice would be Mang Eric Olavides. During my personal training with him, Punong Guro Sulite used numerous analytical comparisons to get across how Mang Eric Olavides moved or would execute a certain technique, concept, or

Mang Eric Olavides and Master Jun Pueblos

principle. He always had great things to say about Mang Eric Olavides, and rightly so; all of the comments were well deserved according to what I have been able to find out about Mang Eric's combative knowledge and abilities. To say that Mang Eric Olavides was impressive would be an understatement. I do not think that I have ever seen anyone as fast and seamless in putting combinations together with a stick in his hand more-so than Mang Eric Olavides. Incredible is the only word that comes to my mind in describing him.

Mang Eric Olavides had been training with GM Jose D. Caballero for six years before Edgar was finally able to convince the "old warrior" to accept him as a student, and Edgar looked up to him immediately because Mang Eric was beyond impressive when he moved. His strikes were then and are now lightning-quick, and his power and accuracy are unmatched. Edgar always held him up as the example, and when he would move against GM Caballero in training, it was Mang Eric's example he was trying to follow and project in his own movements.

Even with the great respect in which Edgar held Mang Eric Olavides, there was a little competiveness between the two from time to time, as sometimes Mang Eric would tell Edgar that the "old man" was not teaching him everything, that he was holding back secrets from him regarding the De Campo 1-2-3 Orehenal System, and this gave Edgar much anxiety early on and compelled Edgar to investigate further, to see if there were any truth to it.

Mang Eric Olavides and Edgar G. Sulite training in Ozamis City, Mindanao, Philippines.

Edgar would say that he had to know for sure if the "old man" was holding anything back from him. So, there were times when he would go early to GM Caballero's home and hide in the bushes, hoping to notice a difference in the "old man's" warm-up done before Edgar was supposed to arrive for his training. Edgar said he saw nothing out of the ordinary on the few occasions that he did this but one day was deeply embarrassed when he tripped and fell out of the bushes and rolled downhill into GM Caballero's view. GM Caballero asked him what he was doing. Edgar told him that he had arrived early and did not want to disturb the Grand Master while he was warming up. GM Caballero suspecting Edgar was spying on him told him to never to do such a thing again, and Edgar honored GM Caballero's warning from that day on.

Yet Mang Eric went on telling Edgar that the "old man" was not showing him everything, and again Edgar would wonder if it were true. So, one day Edgar confronted Mang Eric about this and told him that he had to know. He told Mang Eric that the only way that they could be sure who was telling the truth was for him and Mang Eric to fight, and see if he was getting all of the "old man's" secrets or not. Mang Eric Olavides told Edgar that, if they fought, he would surely break Edgar's head. Edgar replied it was worth it to find out for sure and then warned Mang Eric that he might get his own head broken. Mang Eric just laughed.

This conversation continued for a few minutes, and, finally, Edgar took off his sandals and folded one to cover his hand and the other over his wrist and a portion of his forearm, then he securely tied both sandals down so they would stay in place around his hand, wrist, and forearm, for protection when they fought. Edgar said that since they were both De Campo and were both trained to hit to the hands with much speed, power, and accuracy, the sandals would allow them to fight for a little longer, so that Edgar could be convinced if what Mang Eric had been telling him was true or not. Mang Eric repeated again that, if they fought, he would break

Mang Eric Olavides and some of the "Sulite Orehenal Group" taken in Los Angeles, California.

Mang Eric Olavides and some of the "Sulite Orehenal Group" eating after some training in Los Angeles, California.

Edgar's head, and the conversation was dropped right there. And this incident was what gave Edgar the idea later on to invent the Lameco hand protector and forearm guard which proved to be a novel idea and helped allow Lameco Eskrima to flourish and become one of the most effective and sought-after Filipino warrior arts around the world.

Edgar would tell me that, from time to time, Mang Eric would still tease him that the "old man" was not showing him everything, but by now Edgar was convinced that he was. Edgar told me numerous times of how quick and powerful Mang Eric's strikes were. So I asked Edgar if he really thought he could keep up with Mang Eric in a fight, and he told me probably not, because Mang Eric's hand speed was just too fast. He said that, in reality, had the two fought that day, he would have needed to place two pair of sandals on his hand, wrist, and forearm because just one pair would have offered little protection against the speed and power of Mang Eric Olavides. Over the years, Edgar and Mang Eric stayed close, and Edgar always held him in the highest regard and valued everything he would share with Edgar regarding De Campo 1-2-3 Orehenal.

Mang Ireneo "Eric" Olavides was the protégé and best student of GM Jose D. Caballero's "De Campo 1-2-3 Orehenal" System and is currently located in his hometown of Cagayan De Oro, Mindanao, Philippines. He has formed his own system named "De Campo 1-2-3 JDC-IO" which he teaches to students globally. For anyone who wishes to train under him, he can be contacted through his representatives around the world. Anyone who wishes to learn more about the origins of the Lameco Eskrima System owes it to them self to look him up and pursue training with him. Punong Guro Edgar G. Sulite had nothing but the utmost respect for Mang Eric Olavides as both a man and as an Eskrimador. You will not regret contacting him for training.

This account was told to me several different times by Edgar G. Sulite between 1992-1997 at both of his homes first in Los Angeles, California and later in Palmdale, California.

CHAPTER 3

THE FOUNDING OF LAMECO ESKRIMA

Edgar G. Sulite: The Young Master

Around 1980 Edgar was given consideration for the rank of Master in the Filipino Warrior Arts by several of the Masters and Grand Masters under whom he had trained for many years in the Ozamis City area of Mindanao, Philippines. Namely: GM Jose D. Caballero, Tuhon Leo T. Gaje, Jr, GM Pabling Cabahug, and GM Marcilino Ancheta who were all present among other notable Masters representing the region of Mindanao in Ozamis City on that fateful day.

Edgar G. Sulite circa 1987 in Manila, Philippines

Edgar told me that he was notified by Tuhon Leo T. Gaje, Jr. that he was being considered for the rank and title and to show up on the day, time, and location of the testing. When he did so, he was tested in the respective systems by each of the Masters under whom Edgar had trained. All of them drilled him heavily regarding aspects of their respective systems of expertise, and the ordeal took several long hours before it was complete.

Edgar requested that he be allowed to spar with each of his Masters and Grand Masters during the testing just so that he could confirm that he was ready for such a high position, title, and rank of Master, proving both to himself as well as to his Masters and Grand Masters he was ready for such a promotion.

One by one, Edgar said, he sparred that day with GM Jose D. Caballero, Tuhon Leo T. Gaje, Jr., Master Pabling Cabahug, and GM Marcilino Ancheta. He remarked that, at the end of the day, after all was said and done, he was happy with his performance and felt worthy of their recognition. When all of the proceedings were complete and the sparring had been finished for the day, all of the Masters and Grand Masters welcomed him into that prestigious elevation of rank and title, and it made him very happy.

Punong Guro Edgar G. Sulite was one of the youngest people ever to have earned the rank and title of a bonafide Master in the Philippines as he was only 22 years of age when this took place. Edgar expressed high emotions regarding the ranks of Master and Grand Master and felt that it was not something one was able to award oneself, rather, it had to be awarded and acknowledged by someone else for it to have significance.

Group photo of Edgar G. Sulite circa 1980 in Ozamis City, Mindanao, Philippines; right to left: Dr. Caballero, GM Marcilino Ancheta, Master Jun Pueblos (shaking hands with Dr. Caballero), GM Jose D. Caballero, Edgar G. Sulite (sitting) and Tuhon Leo T. Gaje Jr.

The following is something Punong Guro Edgar G. Sulite gave to me in 1994 regarding the definition of what makes a Master and Grand Master:

"To be recognized as a Grandmaster or Master of the warrior arts in the Philippines, you must have made your reputation and show mental maturity and physical age. Grandmasters question the rankings of other Grandmasters.

"Grandmasters and Masters are criticized and questioned regarding their skills and abilities. Among the many pertinent questions they ask are: Who bestowed their title? Do they have enough skills for the titles they carry? How many years have they been practicing the art? How old are they? How many followers and students do they have?

"In other Martial Arts, the attainment of a certain level automatically designates the title of Master or Grandmaster. In the Philippines, there are certain norms to be satisfied before one can be called and can be accepted as a Master or Grandmaster.

"A Master of the Warrior Arts must be a Master of himself. He must be in control. His daily life epitomizes a man in control of his life, his destiny. A Master of the art must know his art, its origins, its history, its philosophy. He must know the techniques, the interplay of techniques, and the reversals of techniques.

"A Master must know the basics, the intermediate forms of techniques, and the advanced levels of the art. Mastery of the art does not only mean so many years in the art, but the amount of experience using the art, one's personal evolution with-in the art, and personal dedication and contribution to the art.

"A Master of the art must know how to teach and impart knowledge of the art. He must be able to communicate, elaborate, and present the art in such a way that each student learns on a personal basis. Each instruction is adapted to the learning process and ability of the student. A Master must be a real "Maestro," a real teacher.

"A Master of the art must be of good character. He should epitomize the qualities of a leader, the majesty of a noble, and the courage and strength of a warrior.

"A Master of the art is called and acknowledged a Master by other masters, never by himself."

Edgar's above-written words ring with much truth and, looking back, this was the epitome of who Edgar was as a teacher, a fighter, a mentor, and a friend: humble, sincere, dedicated, and very serious regarding his training and fighting prowess.

The Founding of the Lameco Eskrima System: September 25, 1981

Soon after arriving to Manila, Luzon, Philippines on his 24th birthday, a young Edgar G. Sulite formally founded his own personal style which he named the Lameco Eskrima System. Several of his Masters had expected him to carry on their specific systems, but he felt, if he chose any one system over the others, he would not be able to fairly represent just the one system without disrespecting the others, since he would also be teaching by drawing from the lessons of all his Masters but doing so in the name of the one system which he would claim to represent.

Early Group photo including Edgar G. Sulite and some of the founding influences credited with the creation of the Lameco Eskrima System. Back row left to right: unknown, Tuhon Leo T. Gaje Jr., GM Jose D. Caballero, Dr. Caballero (no relation). Middle row left to right: unknown, unknown, Lowell Pueblos, unknown, GM Marcilino Ancheta, unknown, Helacrio "Jun" Sulite Jr., Edgar G. Sulite, Mawe Caballero. Front row sitting: Jun Pueblos.

Instead of disrespecting the Masters from whom he received his knowledge, he decided to form his own system, inclusive of all the Masters' collective knowledge, and give them each credit for their knowledge and, thus, for the founding of the system. He came up with an acronym, "LA-ME-CO," which represented all three major ranges in fighting, by combining the first two letters of the long range (largo), medium range (medio), and the close range (corto). "Lameco Eskrima" seemed to be the perfect compromise as he would be representing all of his Masters knowledge equally and be able to give them all credit.

One of the first Lameco Eskrima Logos created by Edgar G. Sulite when the system was first formed in 1981.

Below is a list of the Five Major Influences, Six Minor Influences, and Two of the un-credited Influences which were responsible for the creation of the Lameco Eskrima System.

The Major Influences were Masters and Systems which Edgar G. Sulite formally trained under extensively for years and was certified to teach.
The Minor Systems were from Masters with whom Edgar G. Sulite trained to some degree and with whom he collaborated but never received ranking in their respective Systems.

Five Major Influences on the Lameco Eskrima System:
1. De Campo 1-2-3 Orehenal (GM Jose D. Caballero)
2. Kalis Ilustrisimo (GM Antonio "Tatang" Ilustrisimo)
3. Pekiti-Tirsia Kali (Tuhon Leo Tortal Gaje Jr.)
4. Modernos Largos (GM Jesus Abella & GM Pablicito "Pabling" Cabahug)
5. Sulite-Rapelon (GM Helacrio L. Sulite Sr.)

Six Minor Influences on the Lameco Eskrima System:
1. Doce Pares (GM Diony Cañete)
2. Balintawak (GM Johnny Chiuten)
3. Lapunti Arnis De Abanico (GM Felimon E. Caburnay)
4. Siete Teros Serado - Serado no Puede Entrar (GM Marcilino Ancheta)
5. Abanico De Sungkiti (GM Billy Baaclo)
6. Tres Personas Eskrima De Combate (GM Maj. Timoteo E. Maranga)

Uncredited Influences on the Lameco Eskrima System:
1. Moro-Moro System (Master Alejandro Abrian)
2. Simaron Style (GM Abdul Hai Qahar Madueño)

When Punong Guro Edgar G. Sulite first formed and founded the Lameco Eskrima System on September 25, 1981 in Manila, the nucleus was then anchored securely in the De Campo 1-2-3 Orehenal Combat Arnis System under the teachings of GM Jose Diaz Caballero. Then, various techniques, combative principles, combative concepts, and methodology were added to that nucleus drawn from the other four major influences: Sulite-Rapelon, Pekiti-Tirsia Kali, Modernos Largos, and later Kalis Ilustrisimo, in addition to the six minor influences of the system.

As Punong Guro Edgar G. Sulite grew and became more proficient in Kalis Ilustrisimo, he began to see the combative value of the system and the teachings of GM Antonio "Tatang" Ilustrisimo, and then began incorporating more of this methodology into the curriculum and basic foundation of the Lameco Eskrima System, especially regarding the edged and thrusting weapons curriculum: specifically, blade and dagger. When the Lameco Eskrima System had reached its height of development and evolution in the early to mid-1990s, the confidence system of Punong Guro Edgar G. Sulite was the De Campo 1-2-3 Orehenal system in regards to the single and double garote; and his confidence system regarding the blade and knife was Kalis Ilustrisimo. So, depending on which weapon or weapon combination Punong Guro Sulite would fight or spar with, his choice would determine which of his confidence systems he would draw from, so that he could end the fights quickly, with intensity, precise execution, and finish with a very dominating performance that would secure him the victory.

When you break the Lameco Eskrima System down, you can clearly see the core systems and their influence from the time of development in 1981, through its evolution, until it hit its peak of performance in the early to mid-1990s. In the very beginning, circa 1981, you could really see the influence being drawn from De Campo 1-2-3 Orehenal, then, in the mid-1980s, Pekiti-Tirsia Kali was definitely the clear influence of choice, and you could see this when Edgar would move, specifically around 1984–1986. From the mid- to late 1980s, the Kalis Ilustrisimo system, as it was influencing the evolution of the Lameco Eskrima System, was obviously reflected in Punong Guro Sulite's movements. There are some of us who were either private students of Punong Guro Edgar G. Sulite or part of his private "backyard" group, or sometimes both, such as is my case, who will move differently than our other brothers because we have specialized in specific influences of the founding systems and Masters, and we tend to operate specifically within those systems and styles, and this is evidenced by the way we move as individuals—even though we all learned the same curriculum in the Lameco Eskrima System, and we had the same instructor and influences, that being Punong Guro Edgar G. Sulite.

My specialty then and still today is the De Campo 1-2-3 Orehenal system, which inspired me the most. Second came Kalis Ilustrisimo, and then Pekiti-Tirsia Kali, as I was also a student of Tuhon Leo T. Gaje Jr. before beginning my training in the Lameco Eskrima System under Punong Guro Edgar G. Sulite in October 1992. Others, such as my brothers Hans Tan, Hospecio "Bud" Balani Jr., Arnold A. Noche, and Dino Flores, preferred to train in aspects of the Kalis Ilustrisimo system, and that was evidenced by their individual movements, even though they learned the complete curriculum of Lameco Eskrima under Punong Guro Edgar G. Sulite as did the rest of us. Both Guro Jun Pueblos and Guro Lowell Pueblos prefer to express themselves through the Pekiti-Tirsia Kali system as they had trained in that discipline directly under their uncle, Tuhon Leo T. Gaje Jr., for years, and, thusly, moved accordingly but also were instructed in the rest of the Lameco Eskrima curriculum, too.

> **Oath of Allegiance**
>
> I, (member's name), do solemnly pledge my allegiance to the ideals and covenant of Lameco Eskrima International.
>
> I promise to uphold the covenant of the brotherhood, to support, propagate and assist in the continuing development of the Warrior Arts of the Philippines. I will willingly and unselfishly teach, support and assist in the advancement and growth of my brothers in Lameco Eskrima. I will accord allegiance, respect and obedience to the esteemed Punong Guro, Instructors and Seniors of Lameco Eskrima.
>
> As God is my witness, I swear to keep this oath, on my honor as a Maharlika and a Mandirigma, a Noble Warrior sworn to the glory of God, the service of my country and the brotherhood, ideals and covenant of Lameco Eskrima International.
>
> So help me God.

The oathe of Allegiance that we all had to swear too in order to be accepted as members in good standing into the Lameco Eskrima International Association.

That was the unique thing about Punong Guro Edgar G. Sulite. He had the ability to look within each of us and see our individual strengths, weaknesses, and varied interests. His job as our instructor was to enhance our individual strengths and diminish any perceived weaknesses as much as was possible, and he would modify or adjust those changes which needed to be made in each of us, or get rid of some things within our individual movement altogether, if these would lead to compromise and become a weakness. It was always about your fighting ability, or "the way that you moved," as he would often say, which mattered most with Edgar. He often warned us that, when we do nothing more than collect techniques, drills, and disarms, all for the sake of collecting these things, that in the end all we would become would be Masters of mere techniques, numerous redundant drills, and disarms, and not the combative equation itself in its most basic configuration, which was of most value. He felt that we were to Master "the fight," and all the things which would accompany "the fight" in its rawest form, including uncertainty and the unexpected element of combat. The way in which we would respond to these things, while being forced to defend life and limb in the streets, would dictate if we were to survive the combative equation, or perish.

Punong Guro Sulite used to say that he did not want a thousand students moving in his "exact image" as if they were clones of himself, rather he wanted a thousand different warriors who moved with individual strengths but were influenced by his guidance and instruction. He would tell us all the time that what worked for him may not work for us and vice-versa, that what he may personally dislike might be the very thing one of us was looking for. So, he would offer the whole curriculum to us, and, as individuals, we would pick and choose those things that worked best for us in fighting and disregard or enhance the rest. He felt the "combative equation" was our greatest teacher as it alone could tell us what would work and what would not work in the fight itself. So, fighting and sparring became our barometer of sorts for reality in verifying the things that we trained in during our classes. If something would not work, we would try to modify it until it did work, or else dismiss it altogether, and replace it with something that would work. He told us that fighting either confirms or refutes that which we learn and practice in our training environment, always holding our individual performance and realistic expectations to numerous combative truths. One of his mantras regarding the Lameco Eskrima System was "Truth to self, truth in training, and truth in combat." These three things would guide you well in your search for excellence in combative movement.

The Lameco Eskrima Members Training Passbook which was given to every member with which we were required to log all of our training as well as rank and grades as we were promoted with-in the system.

As Lameco Eskrima grew in popularity around the world, Edgar would constantly improve upon its overall combative effect. He would determine what needed to be added, taken away, or improved-upon based on our "Sunday gatherings," where we would come together as brothers in the "backyard" group and fight all day long. If he noticed a weakness, he would try and shore up that weakness, drawing from the countless lessons which he had received from his Masters and their specific disciplines in the Philippines. Towards the end of his life, he was adding into the system more and more material influenced by De Campo 1-2-3 Orehenal regarding single stick and double stick, as well as material from Kalis Ilustrisimo regarding the blade and knife.

I can only imagine what the system would have looked like today, some years after Punong Guro Edgar G. Sulite was taken from us in 1997, if he had somehow lived. No doubt in my mind that the system would be considerably different, being improved upon greatly under his direct influence in shoring up a lot of things he may have felt could have been done with more success, as well as adding to areas which needed to be strengthened to some degree, including a ground game regarding empty hand, blade, and stick. One thing that I know for sure is, whatever the probable outcome or changes might have been, I would still be right there by his side, assisting him in every way I could – a sentiment, I am sure, all of my Lameco Eskrima brothers from the "backyard" would share equally.

Early photo of Edgar G. Sulite and Jun Pueblos during a Lameco Eskrima demonstration in Manila circa 1984.

CHAPTER 4

CRITICAL INTRODUCTIONS AND THE EARLY PERIOD OF LAMECO ESKRIMA IN MANILA, PHILIPPINES

Roland Dantes and His First Meeting with Edgar G. Sulite

When Edgar G. Sulite first met Master Roland Dantes, the two were initially introduced to one another by Tuhon Leo T. Gaje Jr., Edgar's teacher in Kali Pekiti-Tirsia. Roland Dantes was a famous world-level competitive body-builder and movie action star in the Philippines. Outside of his notorious body-building career, he was best known for the movies "Arnis: Sticks of Death" and "The Pacific Connection," and watching how he moved in those movies is how Edgar had perceived him to be during their first introduction to each other. Edgar was convinced that Master Roland Dantes could perform all of his movements in real life with precise execution, just as they had appeared in his movies, both of which impressed Edgar immensely.

Master Christopher Ricketts and Master Roland Dantes.

Edgar was from the hinterlands in the Philippines, and, while living his whole life in the provinces, he had seen very few movies before and some of the very first only after he had moved to Manila, which was when and where he saw two of the movies starring Roland Dantes. So, he looked forward to talking with Master Roland Dantes in great detail about some of the Filipino warrior arts he had witnessed him performing on the big screen. Roland, being pressed for time, told Edgar he would like to talk further with him but had to leave and meet someone, but, if Edgar wanted to learn more, he should come by his Gym, and he would discuss the topic at length with Edgar.

So, Edgar met with Master Roland Dantes at his Gym at a later date. Edgar told me the conversation between them initially was a little confusing to him as Roland was under the impression that Edgar was there to learn about body-building, and Edgar thought they were meeting to discuss the Filipino warrior arts in-depth. Edgar remembers asking Roland what he should start with to achieve the same success as Roland had enjoyed regarding his training. Roland directed him to the weight bench and had him start with isolated curls for his biceps. Edgar, not fully understanding what this had to do with Eskrima, tried it for a few minutes and

Master Christopher Ricketts and Master Roland Dantes training.

asked Roland how this was supposed to help his Eskrima. After they both realized they were talking about different things, Roland asked Edgar why he had come by the Gym if not to lift weights and learn more about how to develop his body. Edgar replied that he was there to learn more about what he had seen Roland doing in the movies. So, they began to talk about the Filipino Warrior Arts and the Movie Industry, and Edgar quickly realized the majority of what he had seen in the movies was scripted and choreographed for optimum effect.

Roland asked Edgar what his background was in the Filipino warrior arts, and Edgar, only having been in Manila for a very short time, told him he was from the hinterlands of the Philippines and, besides training with Tuhon Leo T. Gaje, Jr. in Pekiti-Tirsia Kali, he had trained under some local Masters in Ozamis City, Mindanao, Philippines, mentioning by name GM Jose D. Caballero, GM "Pabling" Cabahug, GM Helacrio L. Sulite Sr., and GM Jesus Abella as his formal teachers there. Roland, who grew up in the Mindanao region, had heard of some of these Masters but had never met any of them. He then asked if Edgar could give him a personal demonstration of his Eskrima skills, and Edgar obliged. As they were speaking, two of Roland's students came into the room where he and Edgar were having their conversation.

Edgar asked if he could warm up before he demonstrated his style, and Roland told him to go ahead. Edgar began warming up with single garrote, drawing from the grouping and group mixing with finishing strikes from

Group photo including Master Roland Dantes; left to right: Tony Diego, Edgar G. Sulite, Roland Dantes, GM Antonio "Tatang" Ilustrisimo, Christopher Ricketts and Alex L. Co.

De Campo 1-2-3 Orehenal, and saw the mesmerized look on Roland's face as he was only a few seconds into his warm up. Roland was surprised and commented on the speed and power of Edgar's strikes as well as his fluid and smooth combinations, which were seamless and continuous. Edgar performed a very powerful demonstration which really captured the interest of Roland as well as his two students who were standing next to him. Edgar proposed to Roland that they should spar, so that he could experience his skill first hand. Roland agreed and told Edgar that he would love to see more of his style. Edgar said to Roland, as he was looking at his two students standing next to him, "Since there are three of you, I will use doble baston."

Master Roland Dantes and Lameco "SOG" Member Arnold A. Noche.

So Roland and his two students, using single garote, squared off against Edgar using double garote. Right away Edgar started striking furiously with strong purpose, quickly hitting the hands of Roland's two students, forcing them to drop their garotes, and he then immediately countered three uncontested strikes in front of the face of Roland Dantes as he stopped the last strike in mid-air with the tip of his garote suspended

Master Roland Dantes and Master Jun Pueblos

only an inch in front of Roland's face, waiting for him to move. Roland was speechless, and to say that he was impressed would be an understatement. Edgar had told him he was hoping to find a place to train and teach some classes in his newly formed Lameco Eskrima System, which was still very much in its infancy. Roland, who seemed fascinated by what he had just experienced, told Edgar that, if he wanted to use his Gym in which to train, that would be fine, and he even offered to try and find Edgar a few students to start a Lameco Eskrima class there. Roland also became a student of Punong Guro Sulite in the Lameco Eskrima System and trained with him for years as the two men grew to become great friends over their time together.

This was an important meeting for Edgar because soon it would be this very contact which brought Master Christopher Ricketts to Edgar, which in turn directly led to Edgar meeting for the first time Master Tony Diego, Master Yuli Romo, and GM Antonio "Tatang" Ilustrisimo. Roland Dantes has since passed away, but he was a staunch supporter and long time student and friend of Lameco Eskrima, and one of the biggest fans of PG Edgar G. Sulite.

This story was first told to me by Edgar G. Sulite after a private lesson at his home in Los Angeles, California in the Lameco Eskrima "backyard" circa 1993.

Master Christopher Ricketts: His First Meeting with Edgar G. Sulite

Master Christopher Ricketts first became acquainted with Punong Guro Edgar G. Sulite at Master Roland Dantes Gym in Manila, Philippines not long after Edgar had relocated there from Ozamis City, Mindanao, Philippines and had formed his system of Lameco Eskrima. The two met innocently enough one day when Master Topher walked into Master Roland Dantes Gym looking for someone to fight in an up-coming tournament Master Topher was assisting a friend of his in organizing. He needed to find fighters for the event and thought that a good place to look would be at his friend Master Roland Dantes Gym, where he might be able to persuade a couple of his students in Modern Arnis to fight on short notice.

Master Christopher N. Ricketts

Master Christopher Ricketts had been a longtime friend of Roland Dantes going back to his early days of training when he was quite young. Master Topher walked into the gym and saw Edgar sitting by himself stretching and loosening up, and Topher went over to talk with him, thinking he was one of Master Roland Dantes' students and hoping he could talk him into fighting at the tournament. At this time, Punong Guro Edgar G. Sulite had been training Master Roland Dantes in the Lameco Eskrima System for only a few months, and he had not really gotten his name around the Manila area to a point where people would recognize it when they heard it spoken in public.

Master Topher Ricketts introduced himself to Punong Guro Edgar G. Sulite, saying he was a longtime friend of Master Roland Dantes and that he came into the gym to find fighters for his fast-approaching tournament, and then asked Edgar if he trained Eskrima. Edgar said yes he did. Topher wanted to know if he would be interested in fighting at his tournament, and Edgar told him he would only be interested if he would get paid to fight. Topher told Edgar that there was prize money for the fighters, and Edgar would be paid something for the fight. He further told Edgar to ask around the gym, to see if any more of Master Roland Dantes' guys would be interested since they were short of fighters for the event. Edgar told him he would ask around but, before Master Topher could leave, Edgar asked him again if he would be paid for the fight, Master Topher again reassured him that he would be paid something for fighting. With that, Edgar agreed to fight, and Topher gave him the address of the tournament and the time and date when he needed to be there. They shook hands, and Topher left.

The day of the Tournament came, and Edgar showed up ready to fight. Edgar began to warm-up, the same as he had done when he had first met Roland Dantes at his gym, and gave him a demonstration of his style for the first time. He began striking his garote, utilizing the

Edgar G. Sulite and Master Christopher N. Ricketts training at the Lameco Eskrima Headquarters in Los Angeles, California, aka the "Backyard" circa 1992.

grouping and group mixing with finishing strikes from De Campo 1-2-3 Orehenal. Everyone's eyes were fixed upon him as he was putting on a very aggressive and powerful demonstration just in his warm-ups. Edgar not knowing any of these people, and, with the event being held in public, he thought he would have to knock out the guy he was fighting, so that there would be no disagreement as to who won the fight. It might have been just a tournament to everyone else, but, to Edgar, it was a real fight, and he was going to make sure that he won and got paid.

The person that Edgar was scheduled to "fight" against was none other than Master Epifanio "Yuli" Romo of Kalis Ilustrisimo fame, and he was watching Edgar's movements very closely. Edgar began to strike heavily during his warm ups and had a very serious yet disturbing look on his face while he showed off incredible hand speed and power while moving his stick in fluid yet precise motions. It became evident to all who witnessed his warming up that there was something different about this Eskrimador. It looked like he was there to kill someone and not to just participate in a local tournament.

Master Topher went over to Master "Yuli" Romo and they discussed the turnout for the tournament. Master Topher had just spoken with his friend, the promoter of the event, and was told that there were not going to be

Master Christopher N. Ricketts training.

Master Jun Pueblos training with Master Epifanio "Yuli" Romo.

any fights because of a poor turn-out. There were far fewer paying spectators than anticipated, and even fewer fighters, so he was told that the fights would be cancelled since what little money that they had taken in at the door for the event would not cover all of the cash prizes. As Master Yuli and Master Topher were talking, they both were watching Edgar warming up as he prepared for his fight. Master Yuli commented that the guy he was supposed to fight looked angry and asked who this guy was. Master Topher told Master "Yuli" Edgar was one of Roland Dantes' students in Modern Arnis, and that he had met him a few days before at Master Roland Dantes' gym. But, watching Edgar, they both noticed he did not move like any of the other students of Master Roland Dantes, not like them in the way Edgar was moving and striking with so many lightning-quick strikes and seamless hard aggressive combinations striking in such a fluid yet destructive manner. One thing became quite clear: this was not Modern Arnis as they had ever witnessed it demonstrated before.

Master Topher went to Edgar and told him he would not be fighting after all because of low turnout, but instead wanted for Edgar to do a demonstration of his style. Edgar told Topher right away that he came to fight and was promised money. Master Topher agreed to pay Edgar something for a demonstration of his style, but there would not be a fight. Edgar agreed but only if he got paid. Topher again reassured him and then asked Edgar point blank if he were a student of Master Roland Dantes. Edgar said no, that in fact he was the teacher of Roland Dantes in the Lameco Eskrima System. Topher then asked who his Instructors were. Edgar responded that he was from the Hinterlands of the Philippines and had trained under GM Jose D. Caballero, Tuhon Leo T. Gaje Jr., GM Jesus Abella, and GM "Pabling" Cabahug as well as under his father, GM Helacrio L. Sulite Sr. They briefly discussed a little of his back ground before the time came to introduce Edgar's demonstration.

Master Christopher N. Ricketts posing with his student Guro Viko Aquino Perrine.

Once Edgar was ready, he exploded with precise execution, violently countering the random feed of his training partner, Lowell Pueblos, with great focus, accuracy, speed, and so much power he literally drove his training partner to the wall time after time while bombarding him with lightning-fast, powerful strikes, one after another. Edgar impressed all in attendance with his demonstration. Edgar said that as he was performing, no one was talking, and the only thing he could hear in the whole place was the wind swishing from the tip of his garote every time he struck. No other sounds were being made other than from him and the squeaking of his shoes from the hard contact with the floor beneath him as he would aggressively move forward. He said that he looked into the eyes of some of those in attendance after he had performed his demonstration and saw that a lot of them were beyond impressed with his movement. People began to applaud loudly and started to talk amongst themselves.

Master Christopher N. Ricketts training with his student Guro Viko Aquino Perrine.

Master Christopher Ricketts was extremely impressed as well and went over to Edgar after the demonstration to speak with him. The more they talked about Edgar's previous experience and his personal views regarding the Filipino Warrior Arts, the more he was impressed. After which, Edgar was, for the first time, introduced to Master Tony Diego and GM Antonio "Tatang" Ilustrisimo, both of whom were guests of honor

Master Christopher N. Ricketts training with his student Guro Viko Aquino Perrine.

at the event. This led to another meeting later on between Edgar, Master Tony Diego, and GM "Tatang" Ilustrisimo which would lead to Edgar training under "Tatang" Ilustrisimo in Kalis Ilustrisimo. Master Epifanio "Yuli" Romo was also impressed, so he approached Edgar and began a conversation. When he found out Edgar had received his training in Mindanao, this news excited Master "Yuli" Romo because he, too, was from that region of the Philippines, and a great friendship sprang up between the two.

The one thing of greatest importance that Master Christopher Ricketts saw in Edgar was his willingness to fight and to give everything he had when he fought. This was a trait Master Topher also had in common with Edgar. Both felt the true path to better fighting was fighting itself as only through the medium of actual fighting could you truly learn more. Both the Lameco Eskrima System and Bakbakan International relied heavily on the lessons learned through countless hours of sparring or fighting. This is one of the reasons why the two men became such close friends for life and understood each other so well: they were both cut from the same fabric, so to speak. They would spar literally thousands of times together over many years as training partners. I would have to say that some of the most significant contributions made towards the evolution of the Lameco Eskrima System came from the numerous sparring sessions between Edgar and Topher when the System was still in its infancy.

Punong Guro Edgar G. Sulite and Master "Yuli" Romo became fast friends and developed a lasting relationship until the day Edgar passed away. Edgar used to tell me that "Yuli" was the one who was always trying to find a way to make the others laugh, and that he was truly comical when he wanted to be. But, Edgar also said, when Maser "Yuli" got serious, he could more than handle himself in a fight. Edgar had many fond memories of Master "Yuli" and would often tell stories about their experiences together, always with a smile on his face while trying to restrain a slight hint of laughter. They were great friends, and both respected the other a great deal.

I later asked Master Topher Ricketts about their first meeting, and he told me he had gone to Roland Dantes' gym looking for Edgar because he had heard he was training Master Roland Dantes in Lameco Eskrima there. Master Topher also mentioned that Alex L. Co. had asked Master Topher to check out Edgar, to see if he was legit as Edgar had recently approached Alex L. Co about possibly publishing his first book, "The Secrets of Arnis," which he would go on to write in 1984 and release in 1985 along with the other two books Edgar wrote thereafter. So, that is why Master Topher invited Edgar to fight at the tournament – to see him move and report back to Alex L. Co. When he reported back to Alex L. Co, Master Topher told him Edgar was beyond legit and was a true Master in the Filipino Warrior Arts.

This story was first told to me by PG Edgar G. Sulite circa 1994 in the Lameco Eskrima "backyard" in Los Angeles, California.

Master Tony Diego: A critical Sparring Session which Influenced Lameco Eskrima

After initially being introduced to GM Antonio "Tatang" Ilustrisimo, Master Epifanio "Yuli" Romo, and Master Tony Diego at the Rizal Coliseum in Manila during an event where Edgar gave a demonstration of the Lameco Eskrima System, PG Edgar G. Sulite was invited to come witness "Tatang" Ilustrisimo first-hand. Edgar accepted the invitation, and a meeting was arranged.

When Edgar arrived and first saw the Ilustrisimo system in action, he said it was already familiar to him because a lot of its sword and knife movements GM Jose D. Caballero duplicated with a garote in his system of De Campo 1-2-3 Orehenal. The difference being

GM Antonio "Tatang" Ilustrisimo demonstrating a technique on Master Tony Diego with Tuhon Leo T. Gaje Jr. looking on.

that GM Caballero would use full strokes, as his need to create momentum to generate power required him to use a big circle; whereas, GM "Tatang" Ilustrisimo, striking with a "pinute" (sword), only needed a small circle to be effective in using the principle of "walang bunot," which always left the tip of his blade in front of him, never allowing the tip of the "pinute" to travel behind his body at any time but instead always facing forward toward his opponent to facilitate the process of "finding the opening," as he was fond of saying.

Master Tony Diego demonstrating a technique for Tuhon Leo T. Gaje Jr. with GM Antonio "Tatang" Ilustrisimo looking on.

There were numerous similarities between the two systems yet those similarities were governed by two totally different perspectives. Edgar asked Tony if he would care to spar, and Tony agreed. They chose to spar with single garotes and faced off with one another. Edgar threw lightning-quick and very aggressive strikes and combinations but was forced to recover his centerline quickly as Tony's counters were so fast, and, since he was using the small circle to counter Edgar, it was very critical that Edgar move immediately to recover center once violated.

When Edgar hit Master Tony on his wrist and hands, they began to swell because of their power, and when Master Tony hit Edgar with his small circle strikes, it was not with a lot of power but his speed was forcing Edgar to move more quickly. After the sparring, Edgar said, "I won." Master Tony, baffled, said: "No, I won." Edgar replied to Tony: "Look at how swollen your hand and wrist are from my strikes. Mine only have white lines where you hit me, with no swelling. If it were a real fight, and my strikes were full force, I would have broken your hand and wrist, and you would not be able to continue." Tony answered: "I was using a sword, and if this were a real fight, I would have cut your hand from your wrist, and you would not be able to continue–not to mention me hitting you twice as much as you hit me."

Edgar thought about this, and he came to realize that Tony was right. Yes, Edgar hit Tony and did more damage to Tony's hand and wrist than Tony did to him, but Tony did hit Edgar twice as much by striking with the small circle. So, he came to realize that, if the fight were between two sticks, he would have beaten Tony because his strikes would do more damage to Tony than Tony's strikes would have done to him. But, if Tony were using a sword, Edgar would have been beaten since Tony would have certainly cut his hands from his body and then taken his head, being the much quicker of the two and violating less of the center line as he moved.

So Edgar came to the conclusion that when he would fight with a sword or knife, he would use the Ilustrisimo system to govern his movements, and when he used a garote, he would use De Campo 1-2-3 Orehenal as his confidence system.

This was a very critical time in the development of the Lameco Eskrima System, which had only been in existence for a little more than a year on the occasion of their sparring together for the first time. Kalis Ilustrisimo was the missing piece to the puzzle, and, without this meeting

Master Tony Diego demonstrating a sequence of techniques with PG Edgar G. Sulite.

and sparring session between PG Edgar G. Sulite and Master Tony Diego, Edgar would most likely have never realized what was missing, and the Lameco Eskrima we enjoy today would have a much different appearance and effect to it than we are accustomed to.

This story was told to me by Punong Guro Edgar G. Sulite in 1995 in Edgar's garage during one of my private sessions with him soon after he moved from Los Angeles, California to Palmdale, California.

GM Antonio "Tatang" Ilustrisimo and "Kalis Ilustrisimo"

GM Antonio "Tatang" Ilustrisimo learned his family system from both his father, Isidro Ilustrisimo, and his Uncle Melicio Ilustrisimo. Who, in turn, had learned from their father, Regino Ilustrisimo, who learned from his father, Juan De Dios Ilustrisimo, who learned from his father, Pablo Ilustrisimo. It is reputed that GM Antonio "Tatang" Ilustrisimo has fought in more "death matches" than perhaps any other FMA Master in recorded history and has had his share of real-life violent encounters over his very long life span. Regardless of whether you choose to believe this or not, one thing speaks with pristine clarity, and that is the fighting ability of GM Antonio "Tatang" Ilustrisimo. When you stood in front of him in training or fighting, his combative capability was the one thing that cannot be refuted, and anyone who has stood before him with a weapon in their hand profoundly understands the truth of this. The man was simply one of the best reactionary fighters in existence and his abilities showed this time and again.

GM Antonio "Tatang" Ilustrisimo

It is reputed that GM Antonio "Tatang" Ilustrisimo killed his first man in self-defense at the age of 15 circa 1919 while living in Jolo, Mindanao, Philippines. During World War II, he was a guerrilla fighter (voluntario) who fought in the Sierra Madre Mountains of Luzon and used his blade fighting techniques (sword) in many close-quarter encounters with Japanese soldiers in the jungles of the Philippines. There, he gained a vast knowledge regarding the taking of lives, vital lessons which he would much improve upon during the remainder of his long life.

As a young man, GM Antonio "Tatang" Ilustrisimo had his share of run-ins with the law, and he was reputed to have been arrested more than 20 times for violence in the mean streets of Manila. He spent a lot of time in the Tondo region of Manila, where he lived and labored as a dock worker along the harbor; and this is where GM Antonio "Tatang" Ilustrisimo really acquired and earned his hard reputation as a fighter, being an enforcer for one of the more feared organized gangs there, in addition to his working on the docks at the same time. "Tondo" was a very hard "barrio" in the metro Manila area, and it attracted a very rough crowd. Many men of ill-repute flooded the area engaging in numerous illegal activities, and "Tatang" Ilustrisimo often came into contact with this caliber of unscrupulous men, and, many times, violence would ensue.

Siok, Tuhon Leo T Gaje Jr., GM Antonio "Tatang" Illustrisimo and Jun Pueblos.

As GM "Tatang" Ilustrisimo aged, he was neither able to work on the docks any longer nor was he able to perform his duties as an enforcer for the gang bosses there, so he was forced to find another means of income. Thus, in 1976, Antonio "Tatang" Ilustrisimo accepted his first students, Antonio "Tony" Diego and Epifanio "Yuli" Romo. These two dedicated themselves to his teachings for the remainder of his life. After GM Antonio "Tatang" Ilustrisimo passed away in 1997, Master Tony Diego was elected head of Kalis Ilustrisimo. Some of the more notable students associated with the rich legacy of GM Antonio "Tatang" Ilustrisimo include Romy Macapagal, Christopher N. Ricketts, Edgar G. Sulite, Roberto Morales, Pedring Romo, Norman Suanico, Reynaldo S. Galang, and Mark V. Wiley. But it was only five of these students who are specifically credited with formulating and organizing the fighting style of GM "Tatang" Ilustrisimo into a formal system with a written curriculum. These five individuals became known as "The Five Pillars of Kalis Ilustrisimo."

Group photo of GM Antonio "Tatang" Ilustrisimo and the Bakbakan Group in Manila Philippines. In the front row are "Tatang" Ilustrisimo sitting at center with his two most senior students at his side, Master Tony Diego and Master Epifanio "Yuli" Romo. In the back row among others are Master Christopher Ricketts, Master Rey Galang and Master Jun Pueblos.

The Five Pillars were Master Tony Diego, Master Epifanio "Yuli" Romo, Master Christopher N. Ricketts, Punong Guro Edgar G. Sulite, and Master Reynaldo S. Galang. Among their peers, these five spent the most time training with GM "Tatang" Ilustrisimo, dedicating countless hours to observing how "Tatang" moved against various attacks, and then recording their findings on paper, giving names to all of the techniques, concepts, and principles. GM "Tatang" Ilustrisimo had very few names for the techniques and counters with which he responded to random attacks. Rather, he would simply move against each threat, always making the most appropriate reaction according to what each strike from his opponent demanded of him, but void of any specific name or term. The few names and terms for these things which he knew, he gladly gave to his students during their training together, but the vast majority of the techniques and counters were actually named and organized into an official written curriculum by the Five Pillars. The only way possible for them to extract this information was for one of them to constantly feed GM "Tatang" Ilustrisimo random unexpected attacks and counter attacks while the other four watched his reaction and then recorded how he responded. This was a daunting approach to learning, but, over time, it was well worth the enormous effort since the rewards for their years of sacrifice amounted to a well spring of knowledge concerning one of the very best reactionary fighters that the Philippines had ever produced.

The way that "Tatang" Ilustrisimo would teach his system was for students to feed him an attack to which he responded with the most efficient counter response likely to "find the opening," as "Tatang" was fond of saying. You could feed him the same strike five times in a row and would get five different responses. He would say that, even though you threw the same angle of strike five times in a row, each strike showed different weaknesses and opportunities, and he would react to the first opportunity which revealed itself to him at random in real-time speed, and then counter that weakness. One strike might be early, or another late, or the one after that thrown telegraphing intent, and he would just react to the most immediate threat, depending on how the strike was thrown in general and not on the specific angle of strike represented in the numbering system of basic strikes. GM "Tatang" Ilustrisimo reacted to "movement" not "numbers," as Punong Guro Sulite would often tell me. "Tatang" was a true fighter who reacted in direct response to how his opponent would attack him, as opposed to giving a planned reaction merely because that might be the expectation of others.

GM "Tatang" Ilustrisimo could be very smooth in his response, or very jerky and awkward, as he would intentionally respond with a broken rhythm in an effort to make it more difficult for his opponent to counter his attacks or counter attacks. He worked on the basis of efficiency, always following the most direct route to his intended target so as to end the fight quickly. Punong Guro Edgar G. Sulite once told me that Kalis Ilustrisimo was like water in a bucket. He explained it to me this way: "You have to be like water finding a hole in the bucket, not wasting time and space in swirling around in an effort to splash out over the top, but going straight to the hole and out of the bucket through that hole as the most direct route to its final destination, that being the ground." Edgar G. Sulite told me that this was the approach of GM Antonio "Tatang" Ilustrisimo when fighting with the blade. He always allowed the tip or edge of his blade to "find the opening" as soon as it was detected where ever that opening was made available by his opponent. Since it was a blade-oriented style, thrusts were heavily relied on, and. when necessary, they were used in concert with fine strategic slashes and cuts to various parts of the body meant to aid in quickly finding an opening, with an intent to thrust deeply into the body, to end the fight as soon as was possible.

GM "Tatang" Ilustrisimo was amazing with a blade, and his simple and straight-forward approach was highly effective. Anytime the blade of his opponent made even the slightest contact with his

GM Antonio "Tatang" Ilustrisimo demonstrating techniques from Kalis Ilustrisimo with his student Edgar G. Sulite.

own blade, "Tatang" Ilustrisimo would then quickly slide his blade down his opponent's blade, cutting off fingers in the process, and then driving the tip of the blade forward into the body of his opponent, either disemboweling him or severing his head, hand, or a limb. He did not believe in going force to force with his opponent but rather in disrupting his opponent's force and using it against him. "Tatang" would always tell his students to never use 100% of their strength against only one opponent but, rather, no more than one-third of their total strength for each opponent. He did this by deflecting or intercepting his opponent's strikes on his position, instead of blocking, and, since he would displace his opponent's weapon, he could force his opponent to violate his centerline, and "Tatang" Ilustrisimo would cut deep to center before his opponent could recover from that center line violation.

GM "Tatang" Ilustrisimo also thought it was very important to teach proper range, and what he called "fighting form," which was the proper body mechanics utilized on impact which would increase the power of his strikes when the tip or edge of his blade came into contact with his opponent. A lot of this was in the hips, and he demanded that his students stand in a natural stance, keeping their body weight up and centered over their feet instead of distributed over their knees, which would slow them from being multi-directional when they were required to move. He taught students to walk forward, suddenly tell them to stop, then to look down, and that would be their fighting stance. He felt your fighting stance should be your natural stance as you move when you walk or stand up straight with your feet pointing forward until you were forced to move. The more natural you allowed yourself to become while fighting, the better the results gained would be. When you could not move with your feet, "Tatang" demanded you use "de lastiko," which is a body evasion that allows you to lean back just enough out of reach of your opponent for just long enough for you to rebound quickly, as you would then have an opportunity to take advantage of weaknesses left behind in the aftermath of your opponent's missed strike on target.

When fighting, establishing the proper fighting range is of utmost importance to the combative equation. GM Antonio "Tatang" Ilustrisimo distanced himself in a natural stance just outside of his opponent's reach, prepared to launch an attack or counter attack toward any opening accessible to him at any point during the fight. He would call this "una pulgada," meaning "an inch," so as to move wherever the situation dictated ,with sufficient movement in a fight being measured in "inches" and not in "feet" or "meters." If you maintain the proper fighting distance, you should only be required to "inch" forward to take advantage of opportunities and move only "inches" backward to remove yourself from harm's way by placing yourself just outside of your opponent's reach again. GM "Tatang" Ilustrisimo would say that if you were moving in terms of "feet" and "meters," then you were not properly maintaining the correct fighting distance, to begin with.

Another reaction that GM "Tatang" Ilustrisimo was fond of using when he found himself too close to his opponent in close range was what he referred to as "praksyon" (fractioning). He would apply this conditioned response against very sudden attacks or counter attacks, usually when he would find himself too close to his opponent as he was attacked. By using this

GM Antonio "Tatang" Ilustrisimo demonstrating techniques from Kalis Ilustrisimo with his student Edgar G. Sulite.

response, he could counter the pending attack as he saw it initiated and be able to intercept and stop it before it had a chance to evolve and become a danger. This was one of the responses taught to him by his Uncle Melicio Ilustrisimo, who used it as one of his favorite reactions to an unexpected attack. "Tatang" Ilustrisimo was very fond of "praksyon," and he would often use it, especially in resisting and countering his opponent's counter responses. Since he could feel their energy shifting, he would immediately obstruct their pathway to hit him with "praksyon," and then "find the opening" and make them pay dearly for any and all of their mistakes.

GM Antonio "Tatang" Ilustrisimo demonstrating techniqes from Kalis Ilustrisimo with Master "Yuli" Romo, Tuhon Leo T. Gaje Jr., Master Jun Pueblos and Master Tony Diego looking on among others in 1992.

When it came to edged weapons, Kalis Ilustrisimo was Punong Guro Edgar G. Sulite's confidence system. For those who want to understand more about the origins of the Lameco Eskrima System and to better understand blade-oriented combat, you have to experience Kalis Ilustrisimo for yourselves. Although Master Tony Diego passed away during the production of this book, he has many students teaching in Manila, and there are several students of "Tatang" still teaching around the world. You will not be disappointed with the results gained by training with him or his people.

GM Antonio "Tatang" Ilustrisimo was one of Five Major Influences which led to the founding of the Lameco Eskrima System, under whom Punong Guro Edgar G. Sulite trained in Kalis Ilustrisimo predominantly from 1982 - 1989 in Manila, Luzon, Philippines. Kalis Ilustrisimo is a blade-based Filipino Warrior Art reputed to have been founded more than seven generations before in Cebu, Philippines. The style is said to have been in the Ilustrisimo family for several hundred years, according to family folklore, experiencing its meager beginnings on the Island of Cebu during the pre-Hispanic period and based on traditional Filipino Sword Styles of that time mixed with sword styles influenced and evolved by Spanish fencing in the post-Hispanic era of the Philippines.

Chapter 5

The First Exposure of Lameco Eskrima to an International Audience

Edgar G. Sulite's First Two Books: "Secrets of Arnis" and "Advanced Balisong"

Punong Guro Edgar G. Sulite really made his claim to fame as an author of his first book; "The Secrets of Arnis", which was released in 1985 through Socorro Publications. The book was bitter sweet to Edgar though. On one side of the equation he gained international fame and notoriety as a recognized author of a best-selling book on the Filipino warrior arts and this book specifically show cased his own style which he founded himself in 1981 being the Lameco Eskrima System which was an extra bonus for Edgar.

However, there was a misunderstanding between him and someone whom he held in the highest regard and that was GM Jose Diaz Caballero, his teacher in the De Campo 1-2-3 Orehenal system. When Edgar went back to Ozamis City, Mindanao, Philippines in 1984 when he was writing this book he had made mention to GM Caballero that he was writing the book and asked him if he could interview him for the book and take some photos of GM Caballero performing some of the De Campo 1-2-3 Orehenal system to be used for the book. GM Caballero agreed and had his interview recorded by Edgar and they took a lot of photos of GM Caballero demonstrating key components of his system.

An autographed first edition copy of "The Secrets of Arnis" which was gifted to the Author by PG Edgar G. Sulite in 1993.

An autographed copy of "Advanced Balisong" which the Author received from PG Edgar G. Sulite in 1993.

An autographed copy of "Masters of Arnis, Kali and Eskrima" which the Author received from PG Edgar G. Sulite in 1995.

A photo of the Author with Guro Wolfgang Mueller taken when the two were training together in Frankfurt, Germany in 1999.

As Edgar continued to write and compile the book eventually he sent it to the publisher for final editing. When he did he let GM Caballero know that it was due to be released later in 1985 and that he would give GM Caballero a little money in appreciation for his participation in the book. So when the book was released he made a special trip back to Ozamis City to bestow the gift of money to GM Caballero for his participation in the book. But when he gave the money to GM Caballero he was expecting more money than what he received.

GM Caballero was under the impression that the book was only going to be solely about him and the De Campo 1-2-3 Orehenal System and he was wanting at least half of what Edgar was going to profit for the book. Edgar tried to tell him that his contribution to the book was only but a portion as quite a few other Masters were interviewed and photographed for the book as well. That the book was entitled *The Secrets of Arnis* because it was written to include several different Masters contributions to show case Edgar's Lameco Eskrima System.

Edgar showed GM Caballero and gifted him a copy of the book and as GM Caballero thumbed through its contents he could see that there were other systems represented other than his. Out of 241 pages only 14 pages were committed to tell the story of GM Caballero and the De Campo 1-2-3 Orehenal System. Actually the majority of the book was based on Pekiti-Tirsia Kali and the views of Tuhon Leo T. Gaje, Jr. Edgar felt bad for the misunderstanding and gave GM Caballero a little more money for the confusion but he said that he could feel the distance that was placed between them after that. Which is sad because GM Caballero would pass away a little more than a year from then due to complications of old age in 1987.

GM Caballero would not live to see Edgars next two books be released; *Advanced Balisong*, which was released only months after GM Caballero passed away in 1987 and *Masters of Arnis*, which was released in 1994 all three of Edgars books being published by his good friend, Alex L. Co through his publishing company, Socorro Publications. The book was later expanded to include masters whom Edgar met in the USA and retitled *The Masters of Arnis, Kali and Eskrima* for the U.S. market in 1997, and republished by Bakbakan International.

The Secrets of Arnis did amazing things for Edgar's reputation and he saw many people coming to the Philippines wanting to train with him in the Lameco Eskrima System due to them purchasing and reading that book. One of which was Guro Wolfgang Mueller who flew to the Philippines from Frankfurt, Germany in 1987 not knowing anyone there but wanting to train in the Filipino Warrior Arts. He went to a local book store in Manila and saw the book and purchased it. He went back to his hotel and fully read it without putting it down.

Within a few days he reached out to Punong Guro Sulite establishing contact with him from information which was provided through the book. Wolfgang spoke briefly with Punong

Guro Sulite over the phone and made arrangements to train. This started a great student / teacher relationship between Punong Guro Sulite and Wolfgang Mueller that would last for two months straight as the two would train privately five times a week for several hours a day. After Wolfgang went back to Frankfurt, Germany it was only a small amount of time until he opened the Frankfurt Lameco Arnis Club in 1988.

Edgar told me that this happened quite often to him getting contacted by people from different parts of the world based on them reading that book in specific to which he credited with a lot of his success regarding the Lameco Eskrima System in gaining an international audience for him and his international association.

The "Masters of Arnis" Tour of Australia

The thing that really put Edgar on the road to international notoriety was the "Masters of Arnis" tour of Australia in 1986 which was initially suggested and planned out by Master Reynaldo S. Galang. Up until that time Edgar only had students flying to him from abroad to train with him in the Philippines. This would be the first time that he traveled out of the Philippines to train others in the Lameco Eskrima System and Kalis Ilustrisimo in other countries, thereby truly placing the notoriety and reputation of the system on an international level.

A reunion photo of the 10th year anniversary of the "Masters of Arnis Tour" taken in Manila, Philippines in 1996. Left to right: Master Tony Diego, Edgar G. Sulite, Christopher N. Ricketts, Reynaldo S. Galang and Alex L. Co.

Punong Guro Edgar G. Sulite, Master Tony Diego, Master Christopher N. Ricketts and Master Reynaldo S. Galang all decided to go to Australia and show case their respective skills and abilities. The tour took them to several Kendo and Aikido schools in Australia where they gave numerous demonstrations and offered instruction in the Lameco Eskrima System, Bakbakan International and Kalis Ilustrisimo respectively.

Edgar would say that when he was giving a demonstration with the balisong knife that he would stab into the chest of his training partner really hard with a live blade, only he would turn the blade up at the last second hitting with the handle as opposed to the blade, but to the spectator it looked as if Edgar was really stabbing his training partner. He would say that he would see those who were watching the demonstration wincing and diverting their eyes when he did this as they thought that he was actually stabbing with a live blade. Edgar would always laugh when he would tell me the stories of that trip as he was truly amused regarding the reactions of those spectators watching in disbelief as he would quickly turn the blade up on impact while striking with the handle of his balisong.

This tour really brought a lot of attention to Lameco Eskrima, Bakbakan International and Kalis Ilustrisimo and because of it a lot of students would come from Australia to learn more of each of these systems from these men soon after they returned to the Philippines from that trip. It was good for everyone, but especially for Edgar as this was the trip that made him start thinking that he could possibly move away from the Philippines and become a true International Instructor regarding Lameco Eskrima having students and representatives positioned in numerous countries all over the world, which appealed to him greatly. Seeds initially planted in his mind some years before by Tuhon Leo T. Gaje Jr. now starting to sprout into concrete manifestations. Which would soon firmly take root and see Edgar realize those dreams just 3 years later from that point in his life in 1989 when he would relocate from the Philippines to Los Angeles, California and vastly expand the Lameco Eskrima System to numerous countries around the world.

Fame had found Punong Guro Edgar G. Sulite but not without a cost. As he became more and more known and his reputation became greater he would be approached by more and more people who wanted to take his reputation from him and use that for themselves.

Fighting Challenges in the Philippines

Punong Guro Edgar G. Sulite gave me several varying accounts of him having to fight numerous challenges back in Manila after he became famous for writing his first two books, the *Secrets of Arnis* and *Advanced Balisong*, as well as becoming instructor to famed action star of the Filipino cinema, Master Roland Dantes.

Edgar said that things got so bad in 1989, before he relocated to Los Angeles, that he had to get someone to teach his classes at his club because he was being challenged so much that he did not have time to teach. People would walk in off of the streets and issue a challenge, and he would have to fight them, or they could brag that he had refused to fight them, making him lose face and, with it, his good reputation and students.

Punong Guro Edgar G. Sulite circa 1986

The way that it worked then was the same as in the old days in the Philippines, where, if someone came into your school or club and could beat you soundly in a fight, then they would tear down your banner on the way out the door and take your students with them. Edgar said he had to hurt some of these men very badly because they refused to quit, since beating a man with his worldwide reputation would automatically elevate them to a good position in the Filipino

Warrior Arts community as a whole. So, Edgar would say, they had nothing to lose, only something to gain, and were, therefore, very determined and would not give up easily. He had to knock them out or, worse yet, hurt them to the point where they could not continue, just to be able to declare the fight over.

One incident that really made Edgar feel terrible was when an Aussie flew all the way from Australia to train with Edgar after reading the *Secrets of Arnis*. A taxi driver took him to Edgar's Lameco Eskrima Club in Manila. The Aussie walked in off the street and asked if Edgar was there. Edgar was told that someone was asking for him, and he suspected the worse—that it was just another guy coming to challenge him to a fight—so he goes out and grabs his garote and told the guy to grab his garote. The guy did not question the command.

Both men squared off, and Edgar, wanting to end this quickly, struck at the guy with lightning- quick speed, hitting the guy hard in the hand and forcing the Aussie to drop his stick right away. The Aussie fell to the ground, holding his hand, trying to figure out what was happening. Edgar was hovering over him, ready to break his head if he tried to get up and resume the fight. As he winced in obvious pain, the Aussie asked Edgar why he had hit him so hard. He thought his hand might be broken. Edgar looked down into his eyes and saw something different about this man; he recognized that he was not trying to hurt Edgar at all. It was an obvious misunderstanding. Seeing Edgar's

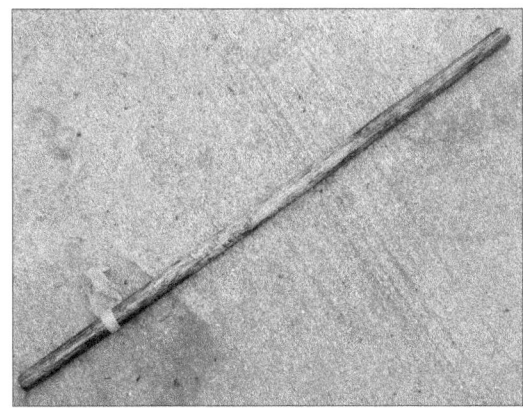

The Bahi garote which belonged to Edgar G. Sulite with which he fought his challenges in Manila, Philippines which was autographed and gifted to the Author by Edgar G. Sulite in 1996 and remains in his private collection to this day.

A look at the signature of PG Edgar G. Sulite on his personal Bahi garote with which he fought his challenges in Manila which he gifted to the Author in 1996.

eagerness to grab a stick, abrupt as it may have been, the Aussie thought Edgar was going to demonstrate a Lameco Eskrima System technique, not that the two were going to fight.

The Author posing with the bahi garote with which PG Edgar G. Sulite fought his challenges in Manila.

Edgar said that he immediately recognized the error of his actions and took the Aussie personally to the hospital. He felt bad that this had happened and told himself that he would never again jump to conclusions so quickly. The Aussie did understand and, with his left hand, he managed to train with Edgar for two weeks free of charge; Edgar felt that this was the least that he could do after breaking his hand.

In July 1996 Punong Guro Edgar G. Sulite told me this story regarding the Aussie and, on that day, PG Sulite presented me with the very same stick with which he had fought his challenges in the Philippines from 1985–1989. It was a small but solid bahi stick which felt very comfortable in the hand, and upon it he wrote: "To Dave, Keep Up the Flow!!! Punong Guro," then he signed it "E.G. Sulite" It is one of my most prized possessions, and I will cherish it for as long as I live.

CHAPTER 6:

LOS ANGELES, CALIFORNIA: A NEW OPPORTUNITY TO EXPAND LAMECO ESKRIMA

Indian Creek, Tennessee Pekiti-Tirsia Camp (1989)

This was the meeting which was responsible for Edgar G. Sulite deciding to become the Lameco Eskrima Instructor to Guro Dan Inosanto. It was Edgar's first time to visit the United States of America, and it was his first meeting face-to-face with Guro Dan Inosanto, and it also marked the first time they trained privately together, after the camp was over, in addition to the first time they sparred together, which took place during the camp. The three instructors for the training camp were Tuhon Leo T. Gaje Jr., Punong Guro Edgar G. Sulite, and Guro Dan Inosanto, with each of the three teaching his own portion of the camp.

During this training camp, Edgar made quite an impression on many in attendance but especially on Guro Dan Inosanto. For many years, Guro Dan Inosanto had been aware of who Punong Guro Edgar G. Sulite was through Tuhon Leo T. Gaje Jr. as both were long time students of his Pekiti-Tirsia Kali System. In addition, Guro Dan Inosanto bought the first two books Edgar wrote – *The Secrets of Arnis* (1985) and *Advanced Balisong* (1987) – and, on July 29, 1987, endorsed Edgar's third book, *The Masters of Arnis* which took some years to complete. So Guro Dan Inosanto knew who Edgar was and was well aware of the reputation which preceded him.

Punong Guro Edgar G. Sulite circa 1989. This is how he would have appeared when he relocated from Manila, Philippines first to the Indian Creek, Tennessee Pekiti-Tirsia Camp and then to Los Angeles, California.

The Indian Creek, Tennessee Pekiti-Tirsia Kali Camp was held on the weekend of August 12-14, 1989. Edgar was brought there on a work visa to help Tuhon Leo T. Gaje Jr. and Guro Dan Inosanto teach the event. After the training camp was finished, Edgar returned to the Philippines for a short time and then relocated to the United States a few months later, moving for good to Los Angeles, California and not returning home again until seven years later, in 1996. Tuhon Leo T. Gaje Jr., Punong Guro Edgar G. Sulite, and Guro Dan Inosanto presented material to the participants of the training camp and each would assist the other with demonstrations and also walk the room to make sure all of the participants understood what each of the three instructor's demonstrations were trying to convey to them. Towards the end of the first day, the camp got really interesting when Tuhon Gaje suggested that Guro Dan Inosanto and Edgar give a sparring demonstration. They both agreed but obviously had very different views pertaining to the word "sparring" and the definition of "demonstration."

Guro Dan Inosanto saw it as just that—a demonstration: a friendly sparring session between the two—but Edgar saw it as "sparring," which to him conveyed a totally different definition: more like "fighting." Edgar told me that, when they began to spar, he would see an opening and counter hard to the wrist or the hand of Guro Dan, who would try and move his hand but was not having much success at evading Edgar's extremely fast and powerful strikes. Even using padded sticks and hand protection his strikes were very heavy and painful. Tuhon Gaje called Edgar over during the sparring and asked what he was doing, and Edgar replied, "Sparring." Tuhon Gaje then told him to take it easy, and then reminded him that it was just a demonstration and a friendly sparring and not a fight, and Edgar replied that he was taking it easy.

To Edgar, "sparring" was the same as "fighting," and it was commonly viewed as such by him and his instructors back in the Philippines. In the "backyard," Punong Guro Sulite often warned us of sparring in public locations where the sparring might be video-taped. He told us, anytime we sparred in public, to always treat it as if it were a fight because someone could take the video footage and "prove" to others they had beaten you, by editing the footage, when, in actuality, they were only using certain small clips of the video to falsely portray something that did not happen. When you might be video-taped sparring in public, he said, try really hard to win impressively, so the video could never be misused against you at a later date. So, understanding this, Edgar was not trying to be difficult with Guro Dan Inosanto; he was simply doing what he was told to do by his Masters when being viewed in a public venue and being videotaped, which was happening in this case.

During the training camp something unexpected occurred involving a former student of Tuhon Gaje who had broken from the Pekiti-Tirsia Kali group to train in another style. This person was living very dangerously, considering the kind of comments he was directing toward both Tuhon Leo T. Gaje Jr. and Punong Guro Edgar G. Sulite, since both men surely would have just killed him had this offense taken place in the Philippines instead of Tennessee.

This person was going on and on about how effective this other style was and how no system could compete with it, including those of Tuhon Gaje and PG Sulite. Edgar took this very personally and confronted the individual by telling him that, if they were in the Philippines, he would be dead already and his body thrown in a garbage can, which started an already dangerous situation spiraling toward an even more dangerous conclusion. Edgar only had a dull metal training sword on his person with which he was assisting Tuhon Gaje during the camp. But someone who was also in attendance and standing close to Edgar had a real "pinute" (sword) on his side with a very sharp blade. Edgar had enough of this person talking nonsense and threw his training sword to the ground, grabbed the real sword off the hip of the person close to him, and went after the person who was disrespecting him and Tuhon Gaje.

Once people saw that Edgar was going for this person with very deadly intentions with a live sword, they immediately started scrambling for safety. Edgar said that, even though he was purely focused on killing this person he could hear something very familiar in the background. It was the voice of Tuhon Leo T. Gaje Jr. shouting to Edgar: "No, do not kill him!" Then Edgar felt someone holding him back, and it was Tuhon Gaje telling him in his ear that this was not the Philippines and, if he killed someone here in the United States, he would go to prison for life and never see his family again. Hearing this and listening carefully to what Tuhon Gaje was telling him, Edgar came to his senses. The other person had already gotten the message loud and clear and left, albeit threatening to return the next day. Edgar told him he was fortunate to be alive and, if he came back the next day, he would not be so fortunate.

The next day of the three day training camp came and went, as did the one after that, and the person who was so much the focus of Edgar's rage at the end of the first day did not return to make another appearance. Apparently he showed a little wisdom; and the rest of the training camp went well, more than exceeding everyone's expectations. Soon after this camp, Tuhon Leo T. Gaje Jr. relocated back to his native Bacolod City, Philippines and would remain there for quite some time, not returning to the United States again until after 2005.

This account was told to me by Punong Guro Edgar G. Sulite at his home in Los Angeles, California after one of my private training sessions with him in 1994.

Relocating to Los Angeles, California from the Philippines (1989)

A couple of months after the Indian Creek, Tennessee training camp, which was held from August 12-14, 1989, Punong Guro Edgar G. Sulite conducted his first official Lameco Eskrima Seminar in the United States, hosted by Roberto Torres (New York); and his second seminar was with Ron Balicki soon afterward, hosted at a little school where Ron Balicki was teaching called the "American Martial Arts Academy" in Berwin, Illinois. It is a little suburb just outside of Chicago, Illinois.

Punong Guro Edgar G. Sulite with Lameco "SOG" Member Ron Balicki during Edgar's second seminar in the United States in Berwin, Illinois circa 1989.

Punong Guro Edgar G. Sulite was doing what he could do in those early days in Los Angeles to make ends meet financially. He worked part-time at a few small jobs, to help with money and expenses. One of those places was Universal Studios in Los Angeles, California where he worked as a busboy, clearing tables in one of the restaurants in the Adventure Park. Slowly people began to develop an interest in Punong Guro Edgar G. Sulite and the Lameco Eskrima System both locally and from within the United States, and he soon became more sought out as an instructor.

Punong Guro Edgar G. Sulite with Lameco "SOG" Member Ron Balicki among others eating after Edgar's second seminar in the United States in Berwin, Illinois circa 1989.

Punong Guro Edgar G. Sulite and Guro Lowell Pueblos training Lameco Eskrima circa 1990 at the Lameco Headquarters ("Backyard") in Los Angeles, California. This is where Lowell Pueblos was living and where Edgar stayed when he first relocated to Los Angeles in 1989.

Punong Guro Edgar G. Sulite and Master Topher Ricketts training Lameco Eskrima circa 1991 at the Lameco Headquarters ("Backyard") in Los Angeles, California.

When Edgar first relocated to Los Angeles, California in 1989, he was living with his student and friend Guro Lowell Pueblos until he could get on his feet and get his own place. The house where they were living was small, so Edgar sometimes slept in his car out in the front yard of Lowell Pueblos' house, thinking about his family back in the Philippines, whom he missed dearly. Edgar would tell me that there were many seemingly endless nights when he felt estranged in this new land with its very different culture from what he was accustomed to. He looked up among the countless stars and thought of his wife Felisa and his three children, Don-don, Em-em and Glady Lea, and wonder what they were doing at that time and if they could possibly miss him as much as he missed them. It was very hard on him being without his family, and that was the thing which drove him in those early years: the desire to make enough money to be able to bring his wife and kids to Los Angeles, where they could all live together as a family again.

Slowly Edgar built up his student base and reached out to those who would train under his tutelage and, increasingly due to the assistance of Tuhon Leo T. Gaje Jr. and Guro Dan Inosanto, he began to be hosted for more and more seminars, which eventually allowed him to quit his part-time jobs and focus on teaching Lameco Eskrima for his living full time. My Lameco Eskrima brother Ron Balicki told me that, when Edgar conducted seminars with him in Berwin, Illinois, (just outside Chicago) in those early days, sometimes Edgar asked Ron if he could possibly stay with him for a few weeks before heading back to Los Angeles. Ron would oblige him, and the two would spend the time training in the Lameco Eskrima System.

Punong Guro Edgar G. Sulite's first official new student in Los Angeles, California in 1989 was our "backyard" brother Eric Koh, who was invited by Edgar to train with him at Guro Lowell Pueblos' home. The second student of Edgar's in Los Angeles was Guro Dan Inosanto. Edgar would train him either at the home of Guro Dan, or at the Inosanto Academy, whichever was more convenient on that particular day. Edgar said that early on the training in Lameco Eskrima was very demanding for Guro Dan Inosanto, mostly because Edgar demanded a lot of sparring, and Edgar always gave a good accounting of himself whenever he sparred with any of his students, in order to keep their awareness heightened and ready to react to unexpected attacks. Once I asked Punong Guro Sulite why he demanded so much sparring with Guro Dan Inosanto in those early days. He

Punong Guro Edgar G. Sulite in the "Backyard" circa 1994.

said their mutual teacher, Tuhon Leo T. Gaje Jr., had told Edgar that Guro Dan really needed to spar a lot since, with his worldwide reputation as the best-known student of Bruce Lee, people would try to use his reputation for their gain by trying to best him in public. So, Tuhon Gaje told Edgar that he must spar with Guro Dan at the end of every class, to make sure Guro Dan would be well prepared to deal with these types of trouble makers.

Edgar said that his job as an instructor was to always position himself just above the reach of his student's capability. Not so far above them in skill and ability that it would intimidate or overwhelm them and prevent his students from making a valiant effort to train with strong purpose, but rather he wanted to keep the students challenged enough to keep giving one hundred percent in everything required of them. As the students increased in both skill and ability, then Edgar would ratchet himself up to the next level, again positioning himself just above their skill and ability to keep them motivated. He often said his sole purpose in teaching was to unbalance the combative equation, and the students' job was to rebalance

Punong Guro Edgar G. Sulite and the Sulite Orehenal Group in the "Backyard" circa 1994.

Punong Guro Edgar G. Sulite refereeing a sparring match between Dino Flores and Mang Leo Revilles Jr. in the "Backyard" circa 1994 with Steve Tarani watching on.

it as soon as was feasible and maintain that balance as they intercepted every attempt to unbalance it again. As our teacher, his job was to pass along all of his strengths and none of his weaknesses, which was exactly what he did. Edgar was an outstanding teacher, my only regret is that more people were not able to train under him and find that out for themselves.

By 1991 Edgar had been successful in getting his wife Felisa to Los Angeles but was still having difficulty going through the immigration system to bring his three children to America, where they could all live as a family once again. By 1993, they had given birth to Edgar Andrew Sulite, and, by 1995, next came Leslie Grace Sulite, and, finally, in 1996, Edgar was successful in bringing over his other three children, Don-don, Em-em, and Glady Lea, and he along with Felisa finally had their entire family living under the same roof for the first time since he had left the Philippines seven years before, in 1989. Edgar fulfilled two of his dreams during this time: moving away from the city, he bought a brand-new house in Palmdale, California (1995) in the high desert of Los Angeles County; and he finally reunited his family (1996). I remember how Edgar and Felisa were so excited, it was difficult not to celebrate these two great accomplishments with them. They were all so happy, then, and we were all happy for them.

Punong Guro Edgar G. Sulite with a select few of the hand picked members of his invitation only Lameco Eskrima "Backyard" Group circa 1995 in Los Angeles, California. This Group would later become known as the "Sulite Orehenal Group".

Edgar believed in affirmation, and he credited getting both a new home and his children here from the Philippines as successes for positive thinking. He would write down all the things he deeply desired in life and send prayers and positive energy towards realizing those desires. I remember he had taped a piece of paper to his bathroom wall and wrote several things which he wanted most in life. At the top of that list was written: buying his new home and receiving his kids from the Philippines. Those were the two most important things to him in life during that period, and he felt that, through affirmation, both were made possible.

It was not easy for Punong Guro Edgar G. Sulite to pull up his roots in the Philippines and relocate so far away, to a totally different life in a new country with a very different culture and so far away from all that he had grown to love, but Edgar made the best of it, and, through much determination and persistence, he had begun to make it work for him. He could finally see his hard labor bearing fruit, bringing successes he could only have dreamt of so many years ago in the Philippines. He was happy, and his future was bright, and we all much desired to see him succeed in every aspect of his life.

Guro Dan Inosanto and How He Came to Train in the Lameco Eskrima System

This is the story of how Punong Guro Edgar G. Sulite became the Instructor of Guro Dan Inosanto in the Lameco Eskrima System. As Guro Dan Inosanto stated in his "Free Voice" interview conducted in the spring of 1997 at the Inosanto Academy in Los Angeles, California, he and Punong Guro Sulite were first introduced by their shared teacher Tuhon Leo T. Gaje Jr. at the Pekiti-Tirsia Kali Camp held at Indian Creek, Tennessee on August 12-14, 1989. After sparring against and training his first private lesson with Punong Guro Sulite there, Guro Dan Inosanto was very impressed with the Lameco Eskrima System and Punong Guro Sulite. So much so that he inquired more about him from Tuhon Leo T. Gaje Jr.

Punong Guro Edgar G. Sulite and Guro Dan Inosanto during a private Lameco Eskrima lesson at the Inosanto Academy in Los Angeles, California circa 1990.

When Edgar relocated to Los Angeles from the Philippines a couple of months later, he received a phone call from Tuhon Leo T. Gaje Jr., during which he told Edgar Guro Dan Inosanto was impressed with him and that Edgar would be training with Guro Dan in Los Angeles from now on. Edgar agreed and, with this in mind, he called Guro Dan and set up the first class at the Inosanto Academy. Tuhon Leo T. Gaje Jr. had also called Guro Dan Inosanto a couple of days before he had called Edgar and told Guro Dan that he would be training under

The Author with Guro Dan Inosanto at the Inosanto Academy in Los Angeles, California circa 1996.

Edgar G. Sulite at the Inosanto Academy in Los Angeles, California circa 1995 posing in front of Bruce Lee's Mook Jong from 1968.

Edgar G. Sulite and the Author at the Inosanto Academy in Los Angeles, California circa 1995 after a training sesion in Lameco Eskrima.

Punong Guro Sulite in the Lameco Eskrima System. Guro Dan was glad to receive such good news as he truly wanted to train under Edgar.

Edgar met with Guro Dan Inosanto on the date and time agreed upon, and, when the two saw each other again for the first time since the Tennessee Camp, they exchanged pleasantries and went inside. Edgar began twirling his sticks to warm up before the class, as did Guro Dan. Edgar looked at Guro Dan, waiting for the class to begin, and Guro Dan looked at Edgar, waiting for the same thing. After a few awkward moments, both were becoming anxious to begin the training. Finally Dan asked Edgar: "What will we be training in today?" Edgar replied: "It does not matter. You tell me, Dan. I am good with whatever you suggest." Dan then said: "Well, you are the teacher, so you make the suggestion." Edgar was surprised because he was under the impression he was Dan Inosanto's student, which was fine with him, and not the other way around. He had misunderstood what Tuhon Gaje had told him during their phone conversation. Once the confusion was cleared up, he looked at Dan and said "Okay, Dan, we will begin with our footwork and then the abesedario." And with those words, their personal odyssey together began.

Guro Dan Inosanto recognized right away the immense value of both the Lameco Eskrima System and training with Punong Guro Edgar G. Sulite. Guro Dan Inosanto was quoted as saying about Lameco Eskrima: "In my opinion, Punong Guro Sulite's system of Lameco Eskrima has one of the most practical and highly developed progressions of teaching and training." He also stated: "Lameco Eskrima takes a student from A-to-Z in such an organized and enjoyable progression that both training and learning is fun and practical. The Lameco Eskrima methods and progressions enable a student to learn both quickly and efficiently what will work and what is applicable in a multitude of combative situations." Finally, Guro Dan Inosanto said: "Punong Guro Sulite always gave credit to the Grandmasters of the Philippines who had trained him and always gave proper respect and acknowledgement to the techniques, drills, methods, and material that was developed by those men, which he used to form the core of the Lameco Eskrima System. What was unique about Punong Guro Sulite was the manner in which he was able to combine, practically and efficiently, the knowledge he had received from the Philippines."

This account was given to me in November 1992 by Edgar himself in the "back-yard" during one of my first private lessons training under Punong Guro Edgar G. Sulite at his home, when Guro Dan Inosanto's name came up in conversation during that class.

Sifu Larry Hartsell and the Lameco Eskrima System

Sifu Larry Hartsell and Debra Hartsell became private students of Punong Guro Edgar G. Sulite during 1993 by recommendation of Guro Dan Inosanto. Punong Guro Sulite would go to Sifu Larry Hartsell's home in Los Angeles and teach him there, or sometimes he would train Sifu Larry Hartsell and Guro Dan Inosanto together at the Inosanto Academy or at Guro Dan's home. Sifu Larry Hartsell came to really love both the Lameco Eskrima System and Punong Guro Edgar G. Sulite as his Instructor. It was one of his favorite things to train in, and his favorite weapon was the knife and double stick material after that.

Sifu Larry Hartsell with Punong Guro Edgar G. Sulite after a private Lameco Eskrima lesson at the home of Sifu Hartsell in Los Angeles, California circa 1994.

From 1994 until 1997, I would go with Punong Guro Edgar G. Sulite to the home of Sifu Larry Hartsell, to assist him with lessons given to both Sifu Larry Hartsell and Debra Hartsell. Punong Guro Sulite would demonstrate the techniques on me, and I would act as the training partner of Sifu Larry Hartsell, allowing him to work the material presented. After our Lameco Eskrima Class, Punong Guro Sulite and I would train in Jeet Kune Do grappling under Sifu Larry Hartsell. He would demonstrate the techniques on me, and I would act as the training partner of PG Sulite, allowing him to work the ground material. We did this for more than three years, until Punong Guro Edgar G. Sulite was sadly taken from us on April 10, 1997.

Sifu Larry Hartsell with the Author after a private Lameco Eskrima lesson at the home of Sifu Hartsell with PG Edgar G. Sulite in Los Angeles, California circa 1994.

Influenced by these training sessions, Punong Guro Edgar G. Sulite was working to create a ground fighting curriculum within the Lameco Eskrima System. The majority of the techniques, concepts, and principles Punong Guro Sulite received from these sessions were primarily adapted to the knife curriculum and used when the fight would force you to the ground. From time to time, Erik Paulson would drop by, and he and Sifu Larry would have a blast rolling on the ground and grappling with one another. A lot of times after Edgar would leave to go home, I hung back to watch Sifu Larry Hartsell and Erik Paulson trying out various ways to best the other on the ground. They truly enjoyed each other's company, and both respected the other greatly, and that was obvious by their exchanges with each other on the ground.

After we would train in the material with Sifu Larry Hartsell, Edgar and I would spend another hour or so attempting to translate the material, to see if it could be modified to be utilized with a knife on the ground. Some things were discovered to be beneficial, and others not so much, but Edgar always tried to assess and refine the combative value of everything he had learned. Some great things came out of this ground curriculum, which was never officially launched within the Lameco Eskrima System, but Edgar was getting closer and closer with every session that we had with Sifu Larry Hartsell. Unfortunately, Edgar passed away before he was ready to implement this new sub-system of the Lameco Eskrima System which never made it to fruition, sadly for the world, since his ideas were quite remarkable regarding that genre of fighting and, with knife in hand, it made it that much more dangerous. I do train a lot in the ideas he came up with during this trial and research era but only with my most advanced and loyal students, and not as a part of the Lameco Eskrima System itself.

After the Death of Punong Guro Edgar G. Sulite, Sifu Larry Hartsell requested I continue to come to his home and further advance his knowledge of the Lameco Eskrima System, which I humbly agreed to do. I would go over to Sifu Larry Hartsell's home about twice a week for further instruction in Lameco Eskrima. Sifu Larry always gave everything he had when he would train, and so it was always an enjoyable experience; and, after class, we would hang out for a couple of hours, talking about Lameco Eskrima, Punong Guro Edgar G, Sulite, Bruce Lee, Jeet Kune Do and JKD grappling, and so much more. Whether training or just talking, it was always interesting to spend quality time with him at his home

One thing I would like to share with readers is what Sifu Larry Hartsell told me in 1995, comparing Punong Guro Edgar G. Sulite with his instructor in Jeet Kune Do, Bruce Lee. He said Edgar reminded him so much of Bruce Lee in the way that he analyzed the combative equation, how he moved when he was sparring or fighting, the manner in which he established his system, his views on refining his combative prowess, his stance on eliminating excessive, wasted motion, his views of embracing reality regarding the combative equation, his understanding of minimizing center line infractions and violations, and how he held center or recovered center once center had been violated during the fight, as well as developing non-telegraphic strikes or counter strikes. Sifu Larry Hartsell really loved both Punong Guro Edgar G. Sulite and the Lameco Eskrima System, and I was really fortunate to have been placed in such a position as I was. It was without a doubt one of the highlights of my life and something that I will always reflect on with fond memories and cherish for life.

In all honesty I was not the first to be offered this opportunity. Punong Guro Edgar G. Sulite first approached my senior Lameco brother Hans Tan to see if he would be interested in doing it, and Hans told him that he could not. Punong Guro Sulite next approached Bong Hebia, and he was not able to find the time to do it, either. Then, Edgar approached Felix Valencia, and again Edgar's offer was declined. So, I was asked and, without any hesitation, I said yes right away, as I saw what an awesome opportunity this would be for me to grow better in the Lameco Eskrima System as well as to learn from Sifu Larry Hartsell, at the same time.

I always found the time to go, regardless of my schedule. Edgar would call to let me know the training was confirmed for that day, and I would meet him over at Sifu Larry Hartsell's home in Los Angeles, where the three of us would train together for about three hours on average per session. Afterward, we would hang out for another hour or two, talking about one subject or the other. In addition to training privately twice a week with Punong Guro Edgar G. Sulite at his home, training with him at Sifu Larry Hartsell's home twice a week and training in the Lameco Eskrima "backyard" class at his home, I would sometimes train with Edgar three to five times a week. It was great spending so much quality time with him privately, and I miss having that time with him dearly. We never know

The last photo taken together of Sifu Larry Hartsell, Punong Guro Edgar G. Sulite and the Author at the Home of Sifu Hartsell in Los Angeles, California on March 7, 1997 just days before Edgar would suffer his stroke in the Philippines from which he would pass away.

Sifu Larry Hartsell with the Author during a training session circa 1997.

what the future holds for any of us, so I have learned not to have idle feet regarding those things that I desire the most. Take advantage of them today as the opportunity may not still be available tomorrow.

Sifu Larry Hartsell with the Author after each taught their portion of the Jun-Fan / Jeet-Kune-Do Fighting Arts Workshop at the Inosanto Academy in Los Angeles, California in 1998.

The last class that Punong Guro Edgar G. Sulite, Sifu Larry Hartsell and I had together at his home was on Friday, March 7, 1997. Punong Guro Sulite left for the Philippines three days later, on Monday, March 10, 1997, to host the "Kali, Arnis & Eskrima Masters Tour" in Manila, Philippines, where he suffered his stroke and passed away. Neither of us knew, at that time, that the three of us would never again assemble together and train, that this would be our very last occasion. As far as we were concerned, it was just the end of another class, with many more to come. How sad this would not be the case.

In later years, Sifu Larry Hartsell and I would reflect back on that last day and talk about it with both of us always getting choked up. Punong Guro Sulite's whole family showed up that day, Felisa and all five of their children, which was a rare thing, but, on that day, it seemed as if something were a little different and, for whatever reason, Edgar did bring along his entire family. We all took plenty of photos on the front lawn of Sifu Larry Hartsell's home after we had completed our training, as if somehow we did know that this might be the last time we would see each other again, and be allowed to train together. I am glad we did because those would be the last photos that were taken of Edgar with his entire family, as well as the last photos taken of us three together.

I have to say that it was an absolute privilege to consistently be in the presence of two living legends of the Martial Arts World at the same time and place, absorbing all that each had to offer in their respective fields of expertise. But, like so many great things in life, it all had to come to an end sometime. Needless to say, I miss them both more than words can express. Both were highly noble in expressing their passion for what they did, and this passed onto their students. I think of them both fondly almost on a daily basis. They are both dearly missed.

I have heard it said: "The modern Eskrimador's life is like walking a path of knowledge. You join that path with all of the others whom walk it with you. You follow those in front of you, and you lead and inspire those behind you. You just keep on going until you reach your destination. It's the journey that matters, not the landmarks that you pass along the way." I would like to believe that this is true of all of us regarding our own individual journey's through the Martial Arts. It certainly was true regarding Punong Guro Edgar G. Sulite as well as Sifu Larry Hartsell, whom we would tragically lose just ten years later, in 2007, when he succumbed after a long fight with cancer.

An Award issued to the Author from Sifu Larry Hartsell in appreciation for him sharing his knowledge regarding the Lameco Eskrima System with Sifu Larry Hartsell after PG Edgar G. Sulite passed away as well as for the Author's participation as one of the Instructors during the 1998 Jun-Fan / Jeet-Kune-Do Fighting Arts Workshop conducted at the Inosanto Academy in Los Angeles, California, where the Author taught aspects of the Lameco Eskrima System.

CHAPTER 7:

THE LATE PERIOD OF LAMECO ESKRIMA AND EDGAR SULITE'S LAST DAYS

Edgar G. Sulite: Focus on Training (1993)

Punong Guro Edgar G. Sulite spoke a lot about keeping one's focus on trying to reach out for the more important aspects of training in developing for the combative equation, as opposed to just going through the motions with a lack of focus or end goals to be met when you trained. In 1993, Punong Guro Sulite wrote the following about one's immediate training goals:

"A novice, a beginner in martial arts, is considered to be in darkness, for his mind is not yet aware of the possibilities he has to protect and defend himself and his loved ones. Once he commences his study, then he begins to understand his true potential and lethal capabilities. Knowledge is power – but a little knowledge can be extremely dangerous. We should always strive to be thorough in our learning, for the advantage any technique or skill gives also has hidden disadvantages that must also be learned."

Punong Guro Sulite used to warn us quite often about learning just enough to get ourselves hurt. About the pitfall of developing just enough understanding about something that what we miss may get us severely injured, or worse yet, killed in an actual fight. This is why he would always tell us to verify everything in an effort to understand what will work for us and what will not.

Punong Guro Edgar G. Sulite circa 1994 at Alta Dena, California

Punong Guro Sulite went on to write: "Techniques represent knowledge; and each technique learned is like a ray of light that adds clarity and vision to what used to be unknown, strange, and formidable. Every technique that one learns and understands reduces the darkness within us. Eskrimador, how bright is your light? Can you see clearly and far? Or are you happy with just focusing a small beam on the path where your foot is about to be set on? Be honest and evaluate yourself. Consider the numerous and probably countless techniques you have learned. Which and how many of them do you consider most important and essential to you? So vital that you have the confidence that these techniques and skills are yours, a part of your repertoire and armor, ready to face any challenge or attack."

Punong Guro Sulite wanted us to take each technique, each combative concept, and each combative principle and verify these things in sparring or fighting, as only in an environment where you could face harm and are held fully accountable for your actions or inactions can you truly learn from all that you do. Consequences are attached to every decision that we make and to every action that we choose to perpetuate in motion or fail to perpetuate in motion regarding a real fight. Punong Guro Sulite wanted to make sure that we were held accountable for all that we do and for all that we refuse to do in a fight, in like manner. "Mistakes have consequences," Punong Guro Sulite often said, and he wanted to make sure that we, his students, understood this clearly, as it is better to be shown these consequences in training, where there will be a chance to correct them, as opposed to recognizing them in the street while fighting for life and limb and not being offered the chance to redeem yourself, as the consequences for mistakes made in the streets may be paid with your life.

Punong Guro Sulite would tell us that the worse place you can be when you realize that something may not work for you is when you are using it to defend your life in an actual fight because, in defeat, you end up on your back, looking up at your attacker as he decides if you will live or die. You have no more say in the matter because you gave your best effort, and your best effort was obviously not good enough. He would say that none of us could ever afford to find ourselves in this position at any time, so we were to train diligently and for full effect because, if we cannot keep our attacker from killing us, no one else will.

Punong Guro Sulite went on to write: "Do you feel that you are enveloped in a protective, bright aura of confidence in your techniques and skills? Or is it a narrow beam of light that can track only one thing at a time and unsteadily, at that? If you have the slightest doubt – then you have neither understood nor mastered the techniques you rely on. You have lost the brightness of the flame that was passed on to you, for you have not devoted time and effort to feed the demanding flame of dedication and discipline necessary to turn your knowledge into formidable weapons. We have likened training to the forging of a blade, for that is what it takes to create a perfect technique, a lethal and sharp weapon, a combat ready warrior."

One thing in specific that Punong Guro Sulite always did was demand, as our teacher, that we train daily and that we train with full intention. He got up very early every morning and trained for a couple of hours by himself, and he trained again at night for a couple of hours before going to bed. He felt it was the daily training which gave us our edge over our opponents. He, as the head of the Lameco Eskrima System, found the time to train daily, and, thusly, he expected no less from us, his students. He led by example, and he expected us to follow that example step for step.

I once asked Punong Guro Sulite how a warrior was created. This is how he responded: "We teach, encourage, guide, and train a man of great potential and of the right character. After he has realized his fullest potential, we then introduce him to the harsh realities of combat and allow the combative equation itself to become his teacher. As each fight that he wages chisels away everything not of a warrior, anything weak or uncharacteristic of a warrior will be burned away by the scorching hot flame that is combative truth. What survives and is left standing tall and strong after this process is a warrior in every meaning of the word."

I will end this segment of the book in Punong Guro Edgar G. Sulite's own words:

> "Lameco Eskrimador, how bright is the light of confidence around you? If it is but a small beam, don't you think it's time to feed that flickering flame?
>
> —*Punong Guro Edgar G. Sulite circa 1993.*

Punong Guro Edgar G. Sulite's Concerns with Flying in an Aircraft

When Punong Guro Sulite started getting more and more popular in the United States, he was being flown in to different cities across the country to conduct Lameco Eskrima Seminars. His schedule had begun to be very busy as more and more people were introduced to him, and word of mouth regarding the Lameco Eskrima System started to flow in a positive direction. This attracted a lot of attention to both Edgar and the Lameco Eskrima System, and his International Association grew by great numbers, especially from 1990—1995, when people from all over

Lameco Eskrima Seminar Poster featuring PG Edgar G. Sulite on November 19, 1995 in Orange County, California.

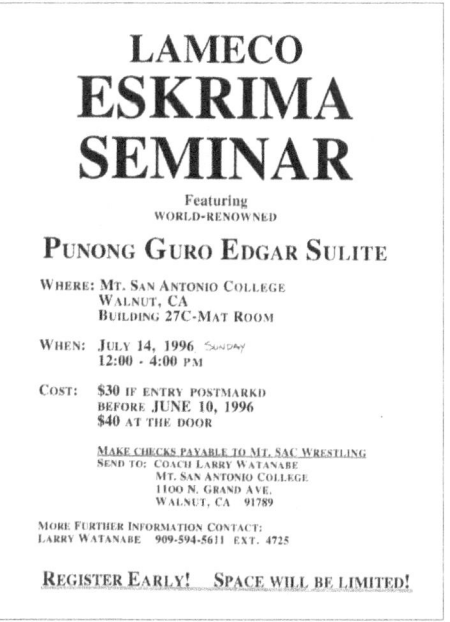

Lameco Eskrima Seminar Poster featuring PG Edgar G. Sulite on July 14, 1996 in Walnut, California at Mt. San Antonio College.

Punong Guro Edgar G. Sulite being assisted by the Author during a Lameco Eskrima Seminar in Orange, California at Mt. San Antonio College circa 1996.

the world would write him to try and get him to come to their respective countries to teach the Lameco Eskrima System to them and their students.

This was a good time for Edgar as he was starting to save a little bit of the money with which he could soon realize his dream of buying his first home. Edgar would fly out of Los Angeles on most Fridays to conduct seminars, then fly back on Sunday nights, ready to teach his classes the rest of the week. One morning I received a phone call, it was Edgar, and he was very shaken up about something. I asked him what was the matter, and he said his flight had almost crashed. He was so shaken up that I could hear his voice trembling as he spoke.

He said that, as they were returning from the east coast to Los Angeles, they hit some very bad turbulence, and the plane went into a sharp dive which lifted him from his seat, hit the top of his head against the ceiling of the plane, and then dumped him into the isle. Everyone on the plane around him was screaming, afraid the plane was going down. After a couple of minutes, the pilot got the plane somewhat straightened up, but the remainder of the flight was bumpy, and Edgar was uneasy until they made it onto the ground in Los Angeles.

Edgar was so shaken up from his ordeal that he swore off flying from that point forward. He went and bought a brand new mini-van with the intention of driving it from Los Angeles across the country, to where

Punong Guro Edgar G. Sulite being assisted by Hans Tan during a Lameco Eskrima Seminar in Orange, California at Mt. San Antonio College circa 1996.

he would be hosted for seminars. This went on for a few years, from the latter part of 1994 until he passed away in 1997. Edgar would pack up the mini-van on Friday and drive all night to his destination, conduct the seminar over the week-end, and then drive all night on Sunday night to be back home on Monday. The east Coast seminars were the hardest to accommodate, as often Edgar would be required to drive for 26 to 30 hours straight to reach his destination on time. Eventually, he got used to it and had started taking his family, Felisa, Andrew, and Leslie Grace with him on the road.

Punong Guro Edgar G. Sulite being assisted by Dino Flores during a Lameco Eskrima Seminar in Orange, California at Mt. San Antonio College circa 1996.

At that time I was taking a couple of private lessons from Edgar a week, on Mondays and Wednesdays, in addition to training with him in the "backyard" group and then spent at least one day assisting Edgar with Sifu Larry Hartsell's lessons at his home, which were usually held on either Thursday afternoons or Friday mornings. Sometimes, if Edgar had to drive to the east coast, we would need to cancel the Monday and Friday classes so he would have enough time to make it to his destination or else postpone those classes to other days in the week. We were always able to work around the inconvenience his driving brought to the equation.

Edgar kept on like this for a couple of years until he had to fly back to the Philippines in 1996, his first trip back home since he had relocated to Los Angeles in 1989. Edgar tolerated the flight between the Philippines and Los Angeles, but, after returning, he still refused to fly to seminars. I believe he put over 100,000 miles on that mini-van in the first two years that he had it.

Germany Seminar Flight and Conversation

Punong Guro Edgar G. Sulite, still very much shaken up by his horrific flight a few years earlier, approached me one day in early January 1997 after one of our private classes at his home at Palmdale, California. He was profoundly concerned with the increasing interest being shown about Lameco Eskrima throughout the world. He said he was happy with the interest he was generating in many countries but that he was concerned that this would require him to fly again. Since he considered his horrific flight ordeal of a few years earlier as a "near death" experience, it was something he did not want to do (unless flying back to the Philippines to see his family).

The trip that concerned him the most was the fast-approaching trip to Romerberg, Germany during the following month, in February 1997, where he would be hosted by Udo Mueller. He began the conversation by telling me that he was considering letting his most loyal and senior students fly around the world and do these seminars for him. He then asked me if I would like to conduct the seminar with Udo Mueller in Romerberg, Germany in his absence. I told him no, I thought it was a bad idea since these people did not want to train under his students, they wanted to train directly under him. I did offer to fly along with him to Germany, to assist with the seminar and to accompany him on the 12 hour flights from Los Angeles to Frankfurt and back, but he would have to go, too. He reluctantly said that he would have to think about it.

Edgar G. Sulite at the kaisars Cathedral at Speyer, Germany during a Lameco Eskrima Seminar that he and the Author were conducting in nearby Romerberg, Germany in February 1997.

I had previously scheduled a Lameco Eskrima Seminar for later in the year (July 1997) with Achim and Uli Weidle, whom I had met and trained with during a Pekiti-Tirsia Kali 10-day training camp in Negros Occidental, Visayas, Philippines taught by Tuhon Leo T. Gaje Jr. and Tuhon Jerson "Nene" Tortal at the Mambukal Mountain resort in March of 1996. I told Punong Guro Sulite to let me get in touch with them and move up the date for my seminar in Reutlingen, Germany, so we could do both of our seminars together during the same trip. He thought about it for about a week and decided that, as long as

PG Edgar G. Sulite demonstrating a technique with the Author during the Lameco Eskrima Seminar at Romerberg, Germany in February 1997.

I would fly with him and keep him company, he would go.

So we boarded the plane and went on our way. At first Punong Guro Sulite seemed very nervous just as I expected he would be, but once we were in the air and had begun talking, he seemed to settle down and forget we were flying. During the twelve-hour flight, I was able to discuss many things at length since we had each other's undivided attention for the whole duration of the flight. One of the things he told me was that he had decided to promote Guro Dan Inosanto from Senior Full Instructor to Chief Instructor in the Lameco Eskrima System. He felt that Guro Dan was doing exceptionally well in his training and was very pleased with his progress. He said that he wanted to make the promotion public and official sometime in the spring of 1997. But, as we all know, this never happened because, roughly two months later, he would suffer his fatal stroke and soon pass away in Manila on April 10, 1997.

PG Edgar G. Sulite correcting one of the participants during the Lameco Eskrima Seminar at Romerberg, Germany in February 1997.

Another thing which really fascinated me was that he had brought along five chapters of what would have become his last book. It was a book he had been writing for some months comparing the differences in training in Filipino Warrior Arts in the western world versus training in the Philippines. He would detail many differences in mindset as each culture looked upon training with different nuances and points of view. In this book, he really chronicled in great depth his experiences with each of his Masters in the Philippines, including GM Helacrio L. Sulite Sr., GM Jose Diaz Caballero, Tuhon Leo T. Gaje Jr., GM Jesus Abella, GM Pablicito "Pabling" Cabahug, and GM Antonio "Tatang" Ilustrisimo, among others.

He let me read the five chapters which he had brought with him over the course of the 10 days we were in Germany together. From what I was able to read, I have to honestly say it would have been a fantastic book. He told me that

Edgar G. Sulite in his Hotel room in Romerberg, Germany after a late night training sesssion with the Author in-between days during the Lameco Eskrima Seminar held there in February 1997.

PG Edgar G. Sulite demonstrating a technique with the Author during the Lameco Eskrima Seminar at Romerberg, Germany in February 1997.

PG Edgar G. Sulite demonstrating a technique with the Author during the Lameco Eskrima Seminar at Romerberg, Germany in February 1997.

he had completed the book in its entirety but was still in the process of having it edited. The five chapters he had brought to Germany with him had been edited and were ready for publication. I was really looking forward to the book being published and released either in late 1997 or 1998. After he passed away, I asked Mrs. Felisa Sulite what they were going to do with the book, and she told me the family had decided to neither publish it nor release it as they wanted something of Edgar that the general public did not have, something they could keep just for the family. I was saddened to hear of this decision since I really wanted to see the book get published, but I fully understood and respected her decision. I am grateful that, at a very minimum, I was able to read the first five chapters.

Upon approach to Frankfurt International Airport in Germany Punong Guro Sulite seemed to appear nervous again but once we landed he was relaxed once again. All in all, we had an easy, smooth flight to Frankfurt, Germany, arriving without complications. We were met at the Airport by Udo Mueller and were then driven by him to Romerberg, where we checked into a hotel not far from where we would conduct the seminar at Udo Mueller's school.

Punong Guro Sulite conducted the two day seminar in Romerberg, Germany using me to present and demonstrate the material to those in attendance. It was a fine seminar, and everyone was pleased with the training and looking forward to having him back the following year. My representative from Reutlingen, Germany, with whom I had my Lameco Seminar scheduled for the following weekend, arrived and participated in the Romerberg seminar and there got the chance to spend some time with Punong Guro Sulite.

Each day, during our down-time in-between seminars, Punong Guro Sulite and I often trained together at the hotel before the seminar began and then again after it ended. As well, Punong Guro Sulite, Achim Weidle, and I drove into neighboring Speyer, Germany and had a great time walking around the old city and visiting the famous "Kaisars Cathedral" where the majority of the German Kaisars were buried as well as a couple of Popes who were of German origin. It was a pleasant experience, and Punong Guro Sulite seemed to enjoy everything, too, especially German food, which he could not seem to get enough of. It was good to spend so much quality time along with Edgar, which allowed me to become closer friends with him.

The flight back with Punong Guro Sulite from Frankfurt, Germany to Los Angeles, California in late February 1997 was also great and full of wonderful memories of some fine conversations. We discussed Lameco Eskrima in depth, as well as what his expectations were for its future. We also spent a good portion of the flight discussing the JKD grappling we were training in under Sifu Larry Hartsell, and how the ground fighting curriculum was

Edgar G. Sulite and the Author posing in front of the kaisars Cathedral in Speyer, Germany during a day outing in February 1997.

coming along as applied to knife-fighting. For the remainder of the flight, we were discussing his upcoming trip to the Philippines, where he would be conducting the "Kali, Arnis & Eskrima Masters Tour" in Manila, Philippines beginning in only a few weeks from then scheduled from March 11, 1997 - March 31, 1997. He was really excited about the prospect of his Masters having a chance to meet and train some of his students, which also made him a little nervous because Punong Guro Sulite wanted his Lameco Eskrima students from Los Angeles to make a good impression. The twelve-hour flight from Frankfurt, Germany was otherwise uneventful, with no turbulence to speak of, and we were on the ground in Los Angeles in no time at all.

PG Edgar G. Sulite demonstrating a technique with the Author during the Lameco Eskrima Seminar at Romerberg, Germany in February 1997.

The Author demonstrating techniques with his student Patrick Schlichting during the Lameco Eskrima Seminar in Reutlingen, Germany in February 1997.

Punong Guro Edgar G. Sulite's Medical Condition and Demise

In the summer of 1996, Punong Guro Edgar G. Sulite was diagnosed with an enlarged heart due to a lifetime of high blood pressure which had never been medically monitored or treated. He and his family did not have a lot of money when he was a child growing up in the Philippines and were not able to accommodate the condition. So, over his lifetime, damage was being done to his heart year after year until it had become so enlarged it began to palpitate against his chest cavity when it would beat and became beyond painful for him, and this was combined with frequent dizzy spells which eventually forced him to schedule a doctor's appointment and have it checked out.

The diagnoses he received from the doctor was that the left side of his heart was twice the size of the right, which increasingly became too large for the confines of the chest cavity, forcing it to beat against the chest cavity at a faster and faster rate than normal, for lack of space. When he was given the test results and told of his diagnosis, he was deeply shocked and dismayed, as would be expected. After he had returned from the doctor's office, he reluctantly told quite a few of us in his inner circle, and the news was devastating for all of us. It was a very difficult time for us but for none more so than his wife Felisa who was deeply concerned and justifiably so.

The last photo taken of PG Edgar G. Sulite and the Author on March 7, 1997 at the home of Sifu Larry Hartsell in Los Angeles, California just three days before Edgar would leave on his flight to the Philippines where he would suffer his stroke and soon pass away.

Interestingly enough, a good friend of Punong Guro Sulite's, as well as a very close friend of mine, Guro Ted Lucay-lucay, had passed away almost a year before Edgar suffered his stroke, and both of them experienced almost the same symptoms and condition. I remember talking to Edgar about Guro Teddy just a day or so after Guro Teddy had passed away. Edgar told me he had heard, about three months previously, that Teddy had passed out in the bathroom while conducting a seminar,

Guro Ted Lucay-lucay with the Author taken in January 1996, less than three months before he passed away. The Author was assisting him with a Lucay-lucay Kali seminar he was conducting at Tom Belts School in Alta Dena, California.

and that the host had found him blacked-out and lying on the bath room floor. Teddy soon came-to but did not realize he had blacked out. Teddy had suffered the same problem, frequently complaining of chest pains and a tingling of his left arm, but he chose to ignore the symptoms, and he just shook the whole thing off by claiming it was stress and never had it checked out until it was too late. He suddenly passed away late one night at his home while he was sleeping, although he was awakened by a terrible pain and was later found by his sister Beverly, dead on the floor with his hand reaching for the door.

Edgar told me then that he would not want to go in the same manner, but, no more than a few months later, Edgar was diagnosed with almost the exact same condition as Guro Ted Lucay-lucay. His doctor told Edgar that his chances were not good. They could perform a surgery and cut some of the enlarged heart away, but it was extremely dangerous, and his chances of waking up and surviving the operation were slim. Meanwhile, the doctor placed him on an immediate low sodium diet and prohibited him from eating anything which would continue to raise his blood pressure. It was by no means a cure, just damage control.

The Kali-Arnis-Eskrima Masters Tour Training Camp Flyer which was conducted in Manila, Philippines and was scheduled from March 11, 1997 - March 30, 1997. This event was hosted by PG Edgar G. Sulite and it was during this event that Edgar G. Sulite was felled by his stroke and weeks later passed away.

Edgar loved to eat, and he loved Filipino food the most, and there were several local restaurants he liked to frequent more than others after our training. Filipino food is very high in sodium as well as acids, and it was Edgar's favorite, so the doctor had to forbid numerous items from that specific diet. I remember Felisa often asking Bong Hebia and I to keep an eye on what he ate and to make sure he stayed on a good low-sodium diet when he was out with us, not allowing him to have high-fat, high-cholesterol, and high-sodium foods, which we mostly did for her.

Since Edgar had decided against the surgery, he thought he could manage his condition by practicing Tai Chi and Hsing-I, which he had trained in for quite a while in the Philippines while he was younger. So, he would get up early every morning and, in addition to his typical Eskrima workout, he would finish up with a Tai Chi or Hsing-I session and also meditate to lower his blood pressure. He was hopeful this would not only control his condition and prevent it from getting worse, but maybe somehow it could also reverse the condition itself. But, with an enlarged heart, the physical damage has already been done once the actual organ has grown in size, and even though meditation could lower the blood pressure, at that point it became like treating the symptom instead of the damage which had already been long established.

Lameco "SOG" Member, Rodney Wilson, Vince Bollozos, Lameco "SOG" Member, Steve Tarani and PG Edgar G. Sulite taken the day before he suffered his stroke and soon passed away while training in Manila, Philippines during the Kali-Arnis-Eskrima Masters Tour which was scheduled from March 11, 1997 - March 30, 1997.

So on March 10, 1997 Punong Guro Sulite boarded his flight to the Philippines, taking with him two of our Lameco Eskrima "backyard" brothers, Steve Tarani and Rodney Wilson, to train with some of his Masters in the Philippines during the "Kali, Arnis & Eskrima Masters Tour" in Metro Manila scheduled from March 11, 1997 to March 30, 1997.

This tour offered training under some of the most significant names in the Filipino Warrior Arts, including Grandmaster Benjamin Luna Lema (Lightning Scientific Arnis), Grand Master Antonio "Tatang" Ilustrisimo (Kalis Ilustrisimo), Master Tony Diego (Kalis Ilustrisimo), Master Christopher Ricketts (Kalis Ilustrisimo / Bakbakan International), GM Jesus Abella and GM Pabilicito "Pabling" Cabahug (Modernos Largos), GM Ireneo "Eric" Olavides (De Campo 1-2-3 Orehenal), Guro Jun Pueblos (Lameco Eskrima System & Kali Pekiti-Tirsia), and GM Helacrio L. Sulite Sr. (Sulite-Rapelon), among others.

As everyone knows, Punong Guro Edgar G. Sulite was felled by his stroke not long after he arrived in the Philippines as host of this grand event. This would be his last opportunity to teach the Lameco Eskrima System. Our Lameco Eskrima brother, Steve Tarani, who was standing right next to him when he was felled by his stroke, later told me that Edgar had been telling a joke and was very happy, smiling and laughing with everyone in attendance as if nothing were wrong, and then he said Edgar began to mumble that he was not feeling well, that he was dizzy. As he tried to lean up against a table for support, he went limp and fell to the floor and never regained consciousness.

Edgar had suffered a severe stroke as a result of his chronic medical condition. Edgar, in a deep coma, was rushed to the hospital and admitted. There he was treated and remained unconscious for some weeks after being placed on life support by his wife Felisa, who had flown from Los Angeles to Manila as soon as she received the news, remaining faithfully by his side the whole time. While lying in a coma, Edgar suffered two more strokes which severely damaged his brain. On April 10, 1997, Punong Guro Edgar G. Sulite was pronounced dead, and the news soon shook the world, deeply affecting all of us who were closest to him. Punong Guro Edgar G. Sulite was laid to rest in a cemetery in the Paranaque area of Metro Manila just five months before his 40th birthday. He was way too young to die.

I remember first getting a phone call from my Lameco Eskrima brother Hans Tan telling me the sad news. Only minutes after that I received a call from Felix Valencia and then a call from Sifu Larry Hartsell telling me the same thing. He himself had only minutes earlier found out from Eric Paulson. Even though we knew of the stroke which he had suffered weeks before and that he was in a coma on life-support for weeks, there was still a small hope in the back of our minds that he would wake up and fully recover, but such was not the case. To say I was sad to hear this tragic news would be an understatement. I had lost someone of extreme importance in my life, and things would never be the same again.

I lost my mentor, my teacher, and one of my closest friends, all in one day. I can honestly say that there has not been a day that has passed since Edgar G. Sulite was taken from us that I have not thought of him or reflected on his memory, which is profoundly imprinted on the deepest recesses of my heart and mind. Edgar can no longer speak for himself because he now belongs to the ages, so it is up to us, those who were closest to him in life, to now speak for him in death and to continue to spread his original vision of the Lameco Eskrima System to all those who would seek it out, the world over, in addition to protecting the integrity of his rich legacy for countless future generations to come. As long as I and my Lameco Eskrima brothers live, people will know who Punong Guro Edgar G. Sulite was and what a profound positive effect that he had on all of us who knew him best.

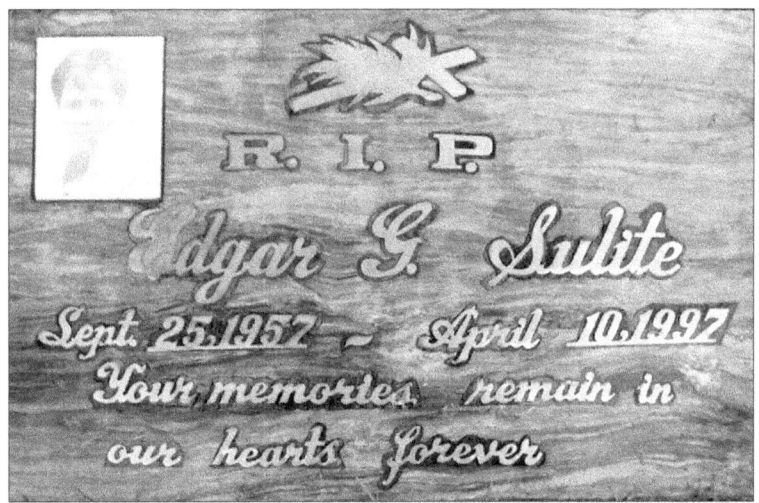

The Gravestone of Edgar G. Sulite located at a Cemetery in the Paranaque area of Metro Manila, Philippines

CHAPTER 8:

EDGAR G. SULITE'S INVITATION-ONLY "BACKYARD" LAMECO ESKRIMA GROUP

"Sulite Orehenal Group": Edgar G. Sulite's Private "Backyard" Group

The "Sulite Orehenal Group" was the private invitation-only "backyard" group of Punong Guro Edgar G. Sulite located in the Los Feliz area of Los Angeles, California. We were his personal Lameco Eskrima group, the ones who spent the most time with Punong Guro Edgar G. Sulite in training in all aspects of the Lameco Eskrima System. Within this group, there were twenty-five students who were specifically chosen by him to train solely for combative effect, as opposed to training for recognition with the intent of teaching one day, or seeking certification to that end. Function over form was the intention of the group from the very beginning.

Within this group were numerous seniors of the system and, quite frankly, some of the best students Punong Guro Edgar G. Sulite ever produced. I would recommend that anyone who has an interest in the Lameco Eskrima System train with any of the members of this group,

Various members of the "Sulite Orehenal Group" after a Lameco Eskrima training session in the "Backyard" circa 1994, Los Angeles, California.

be they Standard Bearers of the system or not, as they are the most knowledgeable within our ranks regarding the system itself.

The "Sulite Orehenal Group" was comprised of these 25 Lameco Eskrima Practitioners:

1. Eric Koh
2. Marc F. Denny
3. Mar Elepano
4. Hospecio "Bud" Balani, Jr.
5. Rem V. Cruz
6. Hans Anton Tan
7. Elmer "Bong" Hebia
8. Guro Lowell Pueblos
9. Jason Ancheta
10. Roger Agbulos
11. Steve Grody
12. Phil Rapagna
13. Felix Valencia
14. David E. Gould
15. Ron Balicki
16. Sung Han Kim
17. Bryant Emerson
18. Dino Flores
19. Choy Flores
20. Arnold A. Noche
21. Steve Tarani
22. Gary Quan
23. Pantaleon R. Revilles, Jr.
24. Rodney Wilson
25. Joel Adriatico

*Names are listed in order of appearance as based on date of membership. Out of eighty-eight registered members in Los Angeles, California, only twenty-five were personally selected and invited by Punong Guro Edgar G. Sulite to join the Private "backyard" Lameco Eskrima Group.

PG Edgar G. Sulite, Dino Flores and Guro Lowell Pueblos after a Lameco Eskrima training session in the "Backyard" circa 1994, Los Angeles, California.

I view this specific group of Lameco Eskrima practitioners as being instrumental in the future growth and propagation of the Lameco Eskrima System. As one of the members of this prestigious group, I have nothing but great things to say about each and every one of my brothers from the "backyard," and I highly recommend that any of you make yourselves available to train with any or all of them who may wish to openly share and impart their knowledge regarding the Lameco Eskrima System.

When I think of the Lameco Eskrima System, I think first and foremost of Punong Guro Edgar G. Sulite and then of the founding influences of the system under whom Punong Guro Sulite received his knowledge. Then I think of my brothers of the "Sulite Orehenal Group," to me this

PG Edgar G. Sulite and the Author in the "Backyard" after a Lameco Eskrima training session in Los Angeles, California in March 1994.

group epitomizes the very essence of what Lameco Eskrima is and was ever intended to be. If Lameco Eskrima could be characterized as being the beating heart of Punong Guro Edgar G. Sulite, then this group would have to be the blood which aggressively courses through its arteries, keeping that heart beating strongly. We were his identity in the United States, and, based on how we moved and performed in both training and fighting, directly reflected on him as our

Group photo of PG Edgar G. Sulite and the "Sulite Orehenal Group" after one of our "Sunday fight Days" in the "Backyard" circa 1995 in Los Angeles, California.

Punong Guro Edgar G. Sulite demonstrating a technique on Felix Valencia circa 1995.

Dino Flores, PG Edgar G. Sulite and Choy Flores with Roger Agbulos kneeling after a training session in the "Backyard" circa 1994 in Los Angeles, California.

instructor, which reflected on his instructors in like manner.

Punong Guro Edgar G. Sulite wanted a group of his own, something with only his fingerprints on it, so when people wanted to see what Lameco Eskrima was, no holds barred, they could see it represented within the "Sulite Orehenal Group" Every member was handpicked and selected personally by Edgar himself, and the training within this group was by invitation only. The idea was to have a group which was placed together to represent all that Edgar believed in, taught, and expected from every aspect of fighting adhering solely to combative truth. This group was more about fighting than anything else, and how we performed while fighting was of utmost importance to us as members of this prestigious group and more importantly to Punong Guro Edgar G. Sulite.

In essence, this group was formed with the intention of holding Edgar's students in Los Angeles, California to the same strict expectations as

Steve tarani and Dino Flores sparring in PG Sulites "Backyard" with the rest of us watching on circa 1994 in Los Angeles, California.

that of native Filipinos who trained in their ancestral Warrior Arts in the Philippines. Edgar noticed right away, when he relocated to Los Angeles, California in 1989, the vast difference in established training goals between native Filipinos who trained in the Philippines and western students who trained in the United States of America. The differences were quite apparent to him, so he wanted a group which he could hold to the same standards as he was held too when training back home, where all training in the Warrior Arts of the Philippines came heavily laced with discipline and intention. He wanted for us to exemplify the strict and stringent standards as were set and established by his teachers in the Philippines and for us to be role models for his other Lameco Eskrima students in the United States who were not members of this prestigious group.

Punong Guro Sulite felt that his personal "backyard" group represented his teaching better than any other and that we were the epitome of what he taught and stood for. We were trained to fight, and all of us were able to do that very well, and he knew that, if someone would come to his home and disrespect him or disrespect the Lameco Eskrima System, they would have a hard time proving themselves over anyone of

Punong Guro Edgar G. Sulite training with solo garote in the "Backyard" circa 1994 in Los Angeles, California.

Steve Grody, PG Edgar G. Sulite and the Author posing for a photo in the "Backyard" circa 1994, Los Angeles, California after one of our "Sunday Fight Days".

us. For, in the backyard, we trained "Pilipino" style, which emphasizes function over form while verifying everything we relied on in fighting; and the more we fought, the better at fighting we became. Even though our training drew heavily on a very diverse curriculum, the emphasis was on using what we were taught in an actual fight and in finding ways to do that with the most efficient results to be gained. What we applied was more of a mindset than a system, and everything relied upon would be made to bear itself out during our frequent hard sparring sessions.

Punong Guro Edgar G. Sulite was adamant regarding the necessity of sparring or fighting as it pertained specifically to this group. He felt the blood which courses through the heart of Lameco Eskrima was fighting, and he made sure we did plenty of it. Punong Guro Sulite regarded sparring or fighting as the laboratory where everything that we trained in would

Mang Leo Revilles Jr. sparring with Dino Flores as Steve Tarani looks on in the "Backyard" circa 1994 in Los Angeles, California.

either be confirmed or refuted based solely on ability because we were all held firmly accountable to various combative truths that are profoundly anchored in that realm of reality. Punong Guro Sulite would often say of fighting – and I paraphrase – "There are no guarantees in combat, only opportunities, and either we will be able to recognize those opportunities and react with positive effect toward them, if and when they avail themselves to us in real-time, or we simply won't. The bottom line is that your abilities, only your abilities and nothing else, will dictate how the situation will be allowed to play out while it evolves from second to second in combat. The situation will dictate your most appropriate counter response, and your abilities will determine the overall performance by which to defend yourself".

Steve Tarani, the Author and Bubba after a rank test at PG Edgar G. Sulites home in Palmdale, California circa 1996.

Sparring was a very important element of our training in those early days with Punong Guro Sulite, and it still is for me personally, some 22 years, since I began training in the Lameco Eskrima System directly under the astute tutelage of Punong Guro Sulite in 1992. It simply cannot be overlooked when it comes to developing essential real-time problem-solving skills against random attacks from an unpredictable opponent. I strongly feel that sparring is the absolute barometer, or test, if you will, that best sums up one's true fighting capabilities and will more so determine how you are likely going to perform, under duress in a real situation, than any other mode of training available to us. The fact is you will be able to adapt and adjust your more essential fighting attributes and hone perception and reaction in real-time only when introduced to an arena which will allow those things to come to fruition through trial and error; and that arena is sparring. It's an integral part of the learning experience and short of actual fighting, it cannot be replaced with anything else. In my opinion, sparring and fighting are of the same creature and should be trained for in a similar manner. Sparring simply yields valuable experience to the collective efforts of your training endeavor and, over many years in the field, I've found this type of experience cannot be gained through any other medium of training, which truly makes it valuable to partake in as often as possible, to say the least!

We as a group fought against each other countless times as well as against others who would be brought in from outside of the group to fight with us on our special "fight-day Sundays" or "Sunday gatherings," as we would call them. When we would fight in the "backyard," it was no

Select members of the "Sulite Orehenal Group" after a seminar conducted by PG Edgar G. Sulite circa 1995, Los Angeles, California.

holds barred; you could close range with much aggression hitting with the "punyo" or "butt of the weapon," punch, kick, head-butt, elbow, knee, or take your opponent to the ground. We would fight "one on one," "two on one," "three on one," and "two on two" using single stick, double stick, single knife, and sword. Most of the fights were very spirited, and, on our special "fight Sundays," we would start around nine in the morning and fight sometimes until the dark of late afternoon. Then, we would gather as a family, where we would eat, talk, and just enjoy each other's company. We were a family in every sense of the word and remain as such to this very day.

I remember often that Punong Guro Edgar G. Sulite often told us, when we would spar with single stick or double sticks, to always keep a knife stashed away in the waist band

Cousins, Dino Flores and Choy Flores after a training session in the "Backyard" circa 1994 in Los Angeles, California.

of our sweats, so, if we were forced into extreme close range and found ourselves compromised or going to the ground, we could deploy the knife and gain the advantage of turning a "ground fight" into a "ground fight with a knife." This always made the sparring sessions very interesting. Because of our foot work and understanding of range, most of those who fought against us from outside of the group would not be able to get close enough to take us to the ground, but the few who did got a surprise when a knife would suddenly and repeatedly be thrust heavily into their rib cage while they were fixated on getting an arm bar or choke hold, unaware of the existence of the knife until it was already too late.

A photo taken of Lameco "SOG" Member Ron Balicki and the Author in Brussels, Belgium in 2013.

Punong Guro Sulite would always videotape our fights in the "backyard," and he would offer copies to each of us who wanted them. I would use the videos to study, not just my movements, but also to locate and identify some of the things that my fellow Lameco brothers were doing when they fought, so I could analyze their movements from afar, as it were. It is one thing to stand in front of them and fight, but you get a distinctly different perspective from videos which capture things that cannot be perceived when standing in front of one another, all geared up and trying to tear each other's heads off. During my private training with PG Sulite through the week, Edgar would always demand I spar with him after each private class, and, in those sparring sessions, he always gave me a lot of really effective pointers. Afterwards, we would go into his home, and he would break out the footage from the last few fights in the "backyard," and he would play each fight of mine and critique my performance, giving me pointers about things I could do better, or things I was doing wrong, as well as making me aware of what needed to be done to gain a better result while I fought. He truly wanted for all of us to be the best fighters that we could become.

Each one of my Lameco Eskrima brothers in the "backyard" had different strengths and weaknesses when they fought, including me. Guro Lowell Pueblos was the most senior member of the Group; he was one of Punong Guro Edgar G. Sulite's first students and sparring partners from the very founding of the Lameco Eskrima System in 1981 and even before then, when Edgar was still training with his Masters back in Ozamis City, Mindanao, Philippines. Guro

Lowell Pueblos was the nephew of Tuhon Leo T. Gaje Jr. of Pekiti-Tirsia Kali and the brother of Master Jun Pueblos, another of Edgar's most senior students and sparring partners in the Philippines, also going back with Edgar to before the founding of Lameco Eskrima. Guro Lowell Pueblos was the head of our group and was the President of the Lameco Eskrima Headquarters in Los Angeles, California, or what we just called the "backyard." When Punong Guro Sulite was out of town doing seminars, Guro Lowell Pueblos would conduct the Lameco Eskrima "backyard" classes in his absence.

Mar Elepano was one of our most senior members, and he was very well balanced in using all weapons and weapon combinations, when it came to sparring or fighting. It seems as if we all had our first fights as members of the "backyard" group with Mar Elepano. All of the stories of those first fights began and ended in the same way, with Mar handing all of us our butts. Fighting Mar Elepano for the first time was like baptism by fire! He had great timing, fast reflexes, a long reach, and he was very good at putting combinations together and making you pay when you over reacted or hesitated. Some of the best fights that I fought or witnessed in the "backyard" involved Mar Elepano to one degree or the other, especially, the "two on one" and "three on one" multi-person sparring sessions. He was a master of using the extra bodies and lining them up as shields against whoever became the active fighter.

Elmer "Bong" Hebia was always a tough fight, as well. Bay "Bong" Hebia was one of our more senior members, and he was also one of our best fighters in the "backyard." "Bong" Hebia was known for his leg shots and, man alive, could he hit hard! I had bruises left on my legs for weeks after fighting with Bay "Bong." When he cracked you in the head, it sounded like thunder shaking the heavens as his stick hit solid against the mask of your head gear or, worse yet, slammed hard against the top of the head gear, where the padding seems less dense, allowing you to feel more of the strike's power upon impact. I have felt like my head actually was splitting after Bong hit me with head gear on.

A typical sparring match in PG Sulite's "Backyard" circa 1994 in Los Angeles, California.

My most spirited fights were always against Felix Valencia. We loved each other as brothers and were the best of friends when we were not fighting each other, but when we squared off with our gear on, we just wanted to kill each other. One thing was certain; when we had to fight, either

Dino Flores and Arnold A. Noche sparring in the "Backyard" circa 1994 in Los Angeles, California.

he or I would be injured at some point. We would hit each other in the groin, head butt, punch, knee, thrust to the throat, and anything else possible. When he aggressively came in and punched to my head, I got into the habit of taking a slight side-step, to use my safety hand to grab the face mask of his head gear, and then spin him slightly to the inside and away from me while I hit him as hard as I could with the butt of my stick (punyo) to the back of the head, where there was much less padding, which would always get his attention. Once the fight was over, we would hug and become the best of friends again. It was strange, but it was always like that with him and me.

I also had some very good fights against Hans Tan, Roger Agbulos, Steve Tarani, Rem Cruz, and Dino Flores, all exceptional fighters in their own right. It is strange, as many groups spar, but they do not necessarily enjoy the experience, and they seem to look forward to finishing the fights as quickly as possible – just surviving the experience, if you will. In the "backyard," we did so much sparring and fighting that we actually enjoyed it; it was who we were as Punong Guro Edgar G. Sulite's personal group, and we epitomized all that he stood for. When we would fight, most of us did not want the fights to stop, breathing-in the experience, as it were, and cherishing the lessons learned from each and every fight. I would have to say that we as a group were at our absolute best when we were sparring or fighting, as strange as that may sound to most. It is truly what defined us in the "backyard: and still does as a group today.

The "Sulite Orehenal Group" in the Aftermath of Punong Guro Sulite's Death

After the death of Punong Guro Edgar G. Sulite on April 10, 1997, a lot of us who were private students and members of his personal "backyard" group did not really have a game plan regarding openly teaching the Lameco Eskrima System. So, for the most part, we maintained contact with each other and trained amongst ourselves in undisclosed locations, inviting very few new students into our family for many years. Each of us was doing something in our own way to keep the group viable and to preserve the legacy of both the Lameco Eskrima System and Punong Guro Edgar G. Sulite.

The author teaching Law Enforcement in Germany circa 2013

I was conducting Lameco Eskrima Seminars in addition to training elite military and law enforcement all over the world, primarily in Asia, Europe, Mexico, Central America and South America as well as having a small Lameco Eskrima group in Riverside, California. We in the "backyard" group now recognized

The Author training with Edgar "Don-don" Sulite Jr. at the home of PG Edgar G. Sulite circa 1998 in Palmdale, California.

Master Christopher Ricketts as our leader, and a few of the members of our group went on to train under him after he relocated from the Philippines to San Diego, California. Master Topher Ricketts was the second highest rank in the Lameco Eskrima System under Punong Guro Edgar G. Sulite as well as the primary sparring partner of Edgar's in the Philippines, so he had earned all of our mutual respect, and we felt he should take over the reins of the system.

The question kept coming up again and again: What would become of the Lameco Eskrima System without the direct guidance and influence of its founder? We all were unanimous in our collective desire for the eldest son of Punong Guro Sulite, Edgar "Don-don" Sulite Jr., to eventually head the system and continue his father's legacy. Before moving to the United States to be reunited with his parents in 1996, Don-don had spent time training directly under some of the Masters in the Philippines, including Master Topher Ricketts, GM Antonio "Tatang" Ilustrisimo, Master Tony Diego, Master Jun Pueblos, and others.

Edgar "Don-don" Sulite Jr. and select Members of the "Sulite Orehenal Group" training with Master Reynaldo S. Galang in Los Angeles, California circa 1999.

Several of us from the "backyard" group also advanced Don-don's knowledge of the curriculum of his father's system. I would go over to Punong Guro Sulite's home in Palmdale, California at least once a week and train Don-don,. My Lameco Eskrima brother Bong Hebia came to my home in Riverside, California once a week to train. I know Bong Hebia also spent a lot of time training Don-don as did Hospecio "Bud" Balani Jr., Dino Flores, Lowell Pueblos, and Roger Agbulos, among others in our group. We wanted for him to take over the system as soon as he felt ready to do so, and our intention was to assist him with anything in our power to do so. It was also the wish of Master Topher Ricketts that one day Don-don should take over his father's system. But Don-don chose a different career when he joined the U.S. Navy and, to this day, he proudly serves our nation in uniform. I hope, after his military career is over, he will take the position we have all

Select Members of the "Sulite Orehenal Group" during the 10th Anniversary Tribute to the Passing of PG Edgar G. Sulite in Van Nuys, California in April 2007. Back row left to right: Arnold A. Noche, Steve Tarani, Mar Elepano, Hospecio "Bud" Balani Jr., Master Christopher Ricketts and Dino Flores. Front row left to right: Roger Agbulos, Choy Flores and the Author.

The Author with Roger Agbulos, Master Christopher Ricketts and Steve Tarani during the 10th Year Tribute Seminar held to honor the memory of PG Edgar G. Sulite in 2007.

secretly hoped for him since 1997, that of being the head of Lameco Eskrima International.

So, with this in mind, we all have continued to promote and propagate the Lameco Eskrima System and to guard the legacy of Punong Guro Edgar G. Sulite. We are the watchdogs of the system and of the honor of Punong Guro Sulite in this generation, and our intent has always been to preserve the lineage and not prostitute it out for personal gain. We will continue to do this well into the future, and we will continue to seek out only the most dedicated among us who desire to learn.

On April 7-8, 2007, the "Sulite Orehenal Group" conducted a reunion seminar and tribute to honor the memory of Punong Guro Edgar G. Sulite by marking the ten-year anniversary of his death. It was organized to honor his memory and to give a few lucky individuals outside of our closed family a rare chance to train and experience the Lameco Eskrima System as seen through the eyes of PG Sulite's personal "backyard" group.

Master Christopher Ricketts, Steve Grody, Roger Agbulos, Hospecio "Bud" Balani Jr., Dino Flores, Felix Valencia, and I all taught aspects of the Lameco Eskrima System to the attendees during the two day seminar, which was held in Van Nuys, California. Our other brothers Mar Elepano, Steve Tarani, Gary Quan, Arnold Noche, Bryant Emerson, and Choy Flores came to hang out and speak of their individual experiences as members of the group but chose not to teach. Also involved were our special guest Bruce Ricketts, who assisted his father, and Master Christopher Ricketts, with his own portion of the event.

Group photo from the 2007 10th Year Memorial Tribute Seminar in honor of PG Sulite. The entire front row were members of the "Sulite Orehenal Group". Front row from Left to right: Bruce Ricketts, Gary Quan, Felix Valencia, Dino Flores, the Author, Mar Elepano, Bryant Emmerson and Roger Agbulos. In the back of the photo is Master Christopher Ricketts standing next to Master Joe Tan of Tapado.

Select Members of the "Sulite Orehenal Group" during the 2nd Tribute Seminar to honor the memory of PG Edgar G. Sulite and Master Christopher Ricketts. Left to right: Bong Hebia, Dino Flores, the Author, Steve Grody, Hospecio "Bud" Balani Jr., Gary Quan, Brandon Ricketts and Johnathan Balani taken in March 2013 in Los Angeles, California.

Day two of the 2nd Tribute Seminar to honor the memory of PG Edgar G. Sulite in 2013. Left to right: the Author, Brandon Ricketts and Dino Flores with Bong Hebia, Master Bill Arrandas and Ariel Flores Mosses in the background.

It was a great event, and everyone who attended thoroughly enjoyed the experience and the opportunity to train under so many of Edgar's personal "backyard" group, which came to be known as the "Sulite Orehenal Group." This was the first time we had united so many of our members to do something like this publically since the passing of our beloved mentor. It took us back to the early 1990s, when we would come together as brothers to train, fight, enjoy each other's company, and to eat, as we had done so many times in the past.

On March 16-17, 2013, the "Sulite Orehenal Group" reunited for a second tribute seminar in Los Angeles, California, this time to honor the memories of our fallen founder. Edgar G. Sulite and of Master Christopher Ricketts. This event promised to be as exciting as the first, held just six years before, and it exceeded all expectations. During the two day event, Hospecio "Bud" Balani Jr., Bong Hebia, Dino Flores, and I, along with special guests Brandon Ricketts and Ariel Flores Mosses, taught from the Lameco Eskrima and Kali Ilustrisimo curriculums, with special appearances made by "backyard" brothers Steve Grody, Gary Quan, and Choy Flores, who chose to attend but not teach. The first day of the event was held at Dino Flores' place, and the second day, at Bill Arrandas'

Bong Hebia demonstrating gun disarms during day one of the 2nd Tribute Seminar to honor the memories of PG Edgar G. Sulite and Master Christopher Ricketts in Los, Angeles, California (2013).

Brandon Ricketts and Dino Flores demonstrating blade technique during day one of the 2nd Tribute Seminar to honor the memories of PG Edgar G. Sulite and Master Christopher Ricketts in Los, Angeles, California (2013).

Group photo taken after the 2nd Tribute Seminar to honor the memories of PG Edgar G. Sulite and Master Christopher Ricketts in Los, Angeles, California (2013). Including Ariel Flores Mosses, Dino Flores, Bong Hebia, Choy Flores and the Author with Master Bill Arrandas and Hospecio "Bud" Balani Jr. in the front row.

Christopher Ricketts Memorial Gym in Los Angeles, California. Sadly, only a few weeks after this event, Master Bill Arrandas succumbed after his long-fought battle with cancer. This is one of the last events in which he partook, and it was a real pleasure to spend time with him there.

One of the things which has always made me extremely proud to be part of the close knit family of Lameco Eskrima has been our collective allegiance to Punong Guro Edgar G. Sulite, in always putting his purpose first, well above our own. We are not a political group, such as can be found in a lot of other FMA groups, primarily because we are not willing to drag the good name and reputation of our founder through the mud for our own profit or selfish promotion. This is one of the reasons why I am always excited to hear of my "backyard" brothers getting more and more exposure and being brought in to teach Lameco Eskrima at events around the world, to benefit both present and future generations of enthusiasts to come. Success for one of us is success for all of us, but we can only enjoy that success if we continue to place the interests of Lameco Eskrima and Punong Guro Edgar G. Sulite before our own. So far, we have managed to do just that.

Group photo of Lameco "SOG" members circa 2000. To include Hospecio "Bud" balani Jr., Roger Agbulos, Felix Valencia, Ron Balicki, Dino Flores and Arnold A. Noche. Master Joe Tan of Tapado is also the first person in the photo on the left.

I have in the past and will continue to place political matters well beneath my feet and not partake in that self-destructive practice, as all it does is divide the closest amongst us, as opposed to bringing us closer together under the same banner in a tight, cohesive family such as we are and will remain. Before all private enterprises which I consider, engage in, or partake of, I first and foremost stand back and look at how it will reflect on Lameco Eskrima, PG Sulite, and our fraternal family as a whole, and only then do I consider my own interests. Punong Guro Edgar G. Sulite told us countless times that all we do, good, bad, or indifferent, in his name will also reflect on him as our Founder and Master. If we do something good that will reflect well on Punong Guro Sulite. So, we were commanded by him to give one hundred percent in everything we did regarding public exposure of Lameco Eskrima.

If we first keep Lameco Eskrima respectable and viable, we will all prosper by its good standing in the Filipino Warrior Art Community as a whole. I am in servitude to Lameco Eskrima, as one of its chosen standard bearers, in addition to serving Punong Guro Edgar G. Sulite, neither of whom, I may add, are in servitude to me. The future looks bright for the Lameco Eskrima System and the legacy of Punong Guro Edgar G. Sulite, and I have the utmost certainty both will be around for a very long time, since each continues to grow in popularity and both are able to remain pure during the process of sharing them with the world.

CHAPTER 9

SELECT MEMBERS OF THE "SULITE OREHENAL GROUP" IN THEIR OWN WORDS

Hospecio "Bud" Balani Jr. — Lameco "SOG" Member (11LA)

Being part of the backyard was more like being with family than being in a martial arts class. Before PG Sulite had a private group at his residence, he used to say he wished to have an all Pinoy group, so he could enjoy his culture without being too American. At seminars, he had a certain curriculum he had to teach, all while speaking English, and, at times, he felt awkward when he could not find the correct English words to describe what he wanted to convey. He wanted to have a group so he could feel at home both with his culture and fellow countrymen. He also wanted a place to teach Fil-Ams (American Born Filipinos) part of their culture which they were missing.

Hospecio "Bud" Balani Jr.

What I regard as utmost value in my training is footwork and staying in your chosen range. Move too little, you get hit. Move too much, you get tired. Move too slow, your opponent is out of range, move too fast, you are out of range. Without footwork, your techniques become harder to achieve.

By 1995, when the group was in full swing, PG wanted a group where his guys could experiment. You went to class. You fought. You were critiqued and tried again and again and again. He wanted guys who could hold their ground, for his honor or your own.

Hospecio "Bud" Balani Jr. in the pinid position with his knife drawn and at the ready.

After the passing of PG Sulite, many original Backyard Group members went their separate ways. Some started claiming mastery of the system and started teaching, and others continued on with their lives as they were before they joined the group, but some continued their training and continued delving into the system that was introduced to them by PG Sulite.

Guro Dino Flores, Guro Arnold Noche and I continued our training under Master Christopher Ricketts and Master Rey Galang and Prof Ireneo Olavidez. Guro Hans Tan returned to the

Hospecio "Bud" Balani Jr. demonstrating a technique to his son Johnathan Balani.

Hospecio "Bud" Balani Jr. holding photos of his Teachers, Punong Guro Edgar G. Sulite and Master Topher Ricketts in 2013 in Los Angeles, California.

Philippines and became a top student of GM Tony Diego and would return to the US to share his knowledge of Kalis Ilustrisimo with us, his brothers from the Backyard.

In 1998, Guro Flores, Guro Noche and myself formed Kapisanang Mandirigma, to share our knowledge with the public thru the Filipino Community in Los Angeles. We taught publicly through SIPA (Search to Involve Pilipino Americans), a Los Angeles Based Community Group formed in 1971 to cater to the wellness of the Filipino Community. We started a program to teach at-risk youths the Filipino Martial Arts, using the discipline of the martial arts as an Anti-Drug Diversion Program. Our classes grew beyond teaching at-risk youth to instructing adults and younger children as well.

Our Program ran for nine years and was the longest running martial arts program in SIPA's history. Our

Organization flourished until the death of my wife, Cynthia, in 2004 from breast cancer.

After taking a four-year break, I was talked into starting up a private group by Guro Bill Aranda, to share my knowledge. I have now been teaching weekly classes since 2008 at the Aranda-Ricketts Memorial Gym in Glendale, California, where I continue to keep the spirit of the backyard alive for my students.

Hospecio "Bud" Balani Jr. posing with the Author and Bong Hebia.

Speaking for myself, I would love to see Lameco Eskrima come back into the spotlight under the reign of the Sulite Family. PG Sulite spent his life researching and formulating his acquired knowledge into the system we know as Lameco, so it would be fitting that someone with the name Sulite runs his system.

The defining characteristic of Lameco is its many drills and its focus on sparring. When PG Sulite first formed his "backyard group," class would always end with sparring. There you would learn to combine all the techniques you learned in class and try them against an opponent who is trying to hit you as well. Sparring became a very big part of our backyard training.

Roger Agbulos — Lameco Eskrima "SOG" Member (23LA)

PG Sulite was my mentor, and he was my friend. As a teacher, he shaped the way I looked at the combatives of the Filipino Martial Arts. The constant drilling of basics and concepts of Lameco Eskrima gave me an appreciation of simple and effective movement. The simplest movement performed efficiently became a guiding factor in the training methodologies and principles today.

Roger Agbulos

Techniques were constantly drilled to ensure that they were functional and effective in real-time. This constant evaluation and sparring developed into a desire to remain in fighting trim because, if you don't train in the use of your tools, the hand that guides them is less sure, and the tools themselves fall into disuse and start to corrode. The attention to detail and the methods used to train were what got me passionate and focused on the Lameco principles.

Roger Agbulos training with Master Topher Ricketts with the Ilustrisimo Blade.

When I worked with PG Sulite on the video "Advanced Laban Laro," it gave me the opportunity to get to know him as a person due to the amount of time spent with him. His passion for the FMA was so deep in his heart and subconscious! His adage and motto "Repetition is the mother of all skills" was one of the strongest and most important guiding principles I took from him.

Training with the "Sulite Orehenal Group" provided me partners/opponents whom I could test my skills against. Since we learned from the same teacher, we did what we could to frustrate and defeat the other person in order to develop our own personal sense of style within Lameco. Training with my brothers, I think, brought out the best in me. Working with them pushed me to develop and to continue to grow. Testing what we learned and practiced gave us a better idea of what was useful and what wasn't, and what we needed to practice on. The different mentalities and body types helped me to understand what worked best and helped me progress in my development and viewpoints.

There were a lot of things that were taught that were incredibly valuable. I don't think there is any one single thing that was more valuable than the rest as I found value in it all. There were quite a few things that would be considered of utmost value. 1) Development of basics to where they are done perfectly every time, which includes timing and speed. 2) Keeping things simple and functional. 3) Frequent sparring to put into practice what is learned and to remove the mistakes that are occurring. 4) Strong training ethic to maintain the fighting edge.

Roger Agbulos and the Author in 2007 in Van Nuys, California

I believe the primary function of the SOG was to train a core of functional and effective Lameco practitioners. The SOG members were the ones who were handpicked by PG Sulite to carry forward the Lameco name and methods.

Through the development and practice of the Lameco Astig Combatives, I work towards preserving the training methods and principles that were instilled during those backyard sessions. The use of sparring and intense drill work furthered the understanding and comprehension of the techniques taught. Keeping the training functional and useful in combat, while economizing motion is a perpetuation of the vision of what PG Sulite taught us. By promoting the combatives aspect, keeping movements functional and bringing a realistic view to sparring enhances the legacy that PG Sulite created.

I would like to see the SOG guys all become successful in whatever endeavors they pursue. Though I think maintaining Lameco Eskrima in the form that was taught to us would require the SOG to regroup and recollect our training experiences. This would allow us to sift what we learned from PG Sulite from what we learned later on. This way, we don't lose the techniques, principles, and concepts that we were taught to use during those sessions. I think this would help refresh us as a group by revisiting what brought us together and what gave us a strong foundation in what we do.

Having a focused goal to preserve the legacy of PG Sulite and to promote the art as he taught it would reinforce who we are now, where we have come from, and who we should thank for these opportunities.

It is the emphasis on mastering the fundamentals, such as: footwork conditioning; understanding of balance, timing, distance and speed; strength development through intensity of strikes; economy of motion (non-telegraphic hitting) using combination striking and set-ups from varying stages of the learning-curve concept to application (as in constant sparring sessions).

Steve Grody — Lameco Eskrima "SOG" Member (24LA)

I was first exposed to Lameco through what Dan Inosanto was bringing into his classes at the Inosanto Academy. It was clear that he was very impressed by the system that he was learning from Punong Guro Sulite as it was not unusual for the majority of the kali classes to be composed of the Lameco curriculum during that period of time. I liked the Lameco I was learning and very much enjoyed it when Guro Sulite did a seminar there but thought that was good enough and didn't think to seek out further training with him.

Then, one day in October, 1990, I was at Guro Inosanto's home doing some training, and he

Steve Grody with Punong Guro Edgar G. Sulite in the "Backyard" in Los Angeles, California circa 1995.

Steve Grody with the Author training at his Downtown Martial Arts Studio in Los Angeles, California in 1997.

mentioned that Edgar was coming over to give him a lesson and that he wanted to give me that time as a gift, something I will always appreciate. The technique and drill that Edgar did with me were good, but what really got to me was the quality of his feeding, and I thought: "Oh yeah, I got to have me more of this!" And that's when I arranged to start training privately on a weekly basis.

Steve Grody with the Author in Los Angeles, California n 2013.

The three questions in my mind, that make up the "Holy Trinity" when defining a superior teacher are, 1) Is the technical basis of the system and its organization sound? 2) Are the physical capabilities of the instructor superior? And last, but certainly not least, 3) Is the teacher open-hearted and actually willing and able to articulate and share what he knows? The answer to all of those questions in regard to Edgar was yes. That didn't mean you didn't have to work for the skills and knowledge, but, if you worked hard enough (and he *did* push you), it was available. I greatly appreciated his openness and candor as well as his warmth and sense of humor even in the midst of serious training.

The most emphasized issues were the development of a strike with "intention," that is, with authority, power and focus, and a sense of timing and distance. While long, medium, and close range were all addressed in training, the clearly dominant real-time interaction was long range entry and follow up at "largo at media," that is, a strike to the head or body but without checking because the opponent's hand was either smashed, or deceived and bypassed, to get to the head or body.

The curriculum was one thing, but in the sparring and spontaneous interactions during drills, principles and strategies would come out that were not necessarily part of the explicit curriculum and often of great value. If I was able to make good observations and formulate a proper question about something interesting that transpired at those moments, then Edgar would happily clarify the principle. Indeed, it was simply moving with Edgar and trying to learn from, absorb, and problem-solve his timing and energy that was most inspiring, and much of the basis for how I approach teaching weapons. He made it clear that there is a world of difference between being able to do the footwork in the curriculum, for example, and the subtle real-time application of that footwork.

Many superior practitioners of any skill, be it martial art, visual art, music etc., do much of their best execution in an intuitive way that they may not be aware of, and it is up to the people trying to learn from the highly-skilled to look beyond the given explanations for how results

Steve Grody with with the Author after training at his Downtown Martial Arts Studio in Los Angeles, California circa 1998.

Steve Grody with Punong Guro Edgar G. Sulite and the Author circa 1996 at the home of Edgar G. Sulite in Palmdale, California.

come about. That is one reason why those who study with someone privately can have such varied experiences from one another. I was honored when, one day, Edgar came to my studio and the first thing he asked was "Do you have a favorite stick?" I brought over a somewhat beat up but solid stick and handed it to him. He pulled a roll of black electrical tape out of his bag, tore off a piece of tape and wrapped a nice thick stripe around the stick and said "There, you're an instructor!" I like to think that happened because of the quality of the movement and reactions that he pressed me to develop rather than my memory of curriculum (which is not the greatest).

Edgar was constantly rethinking and revising his curriculum. Though he gave appropriate respect to all of his teachers, he was open about which ones most contributed to his development, and how he altered what he learned. In turn he expected me to think for myself. Indeed, he didn't press me to be a Lameco fundamentalist, but he wanted me to "have a home," that is, a set of base skills and strategies that I could most count on in the real world. Part of that meant understanding natural human combative instincts and how they could be taken advantage of, and common kinds of Filipino approaches and how they could be countered as well. The students I have trained that have interacted with other FMA practitioners as well as weapon-wielding non-FMA people have found this perspective to serve them very well.

As for the backyard sessions, when I came to the sparring sessions, they were always a remarkable example of the best of Filipino culture. Instead of sanctimony, when people were sparring, the others watching would shout out encouragement and would laugh while tossing out teasing jokes! The friendliness and good-heartedness was genuinely impressive. At times, school brothers would ask what I observed and what I thought could be improved, and it was always a great testing ground for us all. Afterwards, a wonderfully excessive amount of homemade Filipino food would be brought out for all to enjoy while we hung out into the afternoon.

I will always be grateful for the time Edgar spent with me and for the friendship he extended past the teacher-student relationship. He is sorely missed.

For information on Steve Grody's availability, instructional DVDs and blog, see stevegrody.com.

David E. Gould — Lameco Eskrima "SOG" Member (43LA)

I first came to train under Punong Guro Edgar G. Sulite in the Lameco Eskrima System quite by coincidence, actually. At the time I was a student training under Tuhon Leo T. Gaje Jr. in the Pekiti-Tirsia Kali system. I saw an advertisement for Lameco Eskrima in a then-recent issue of *Inside Kung-Fu* and my attention was drawn to the Lameco hand protectors and forearm guards which were advertised in the magazine.

I thought that it would be beneficial for me to purchase them and incorporate them into my personal training as well as for sparring as they looked quite sturdy, and I thought that they would offer a lot of protection, more-so than the fencing mask and hockey gloves which I had been accustomed to using in Pekiti-Tirsia Kali, which would enable me to train a little harder with more contact. In addition, I took note of some of the Lameco Eskrima videos produced by Unique Publications, in which Punong Guro Edgar G. Sulite had been featured, which were also advertised in the same magazine. That was the first time that I had been made aware of the Lameco Eskrima System per se and I was a little curious to find out more.

I called the number which was advertised in the magazine, and Punong Guro Edgar G. Sulite answered the phone. We spoke briefly and I placed my order for one hand protector, one forearm guard and one piece of head gear. I was told that they would be mailed to my home within a short period of time, and I was given the address to send my payment of $160.00.

Punong Guro Edgar G. Sulite demonstrating techniques with the Author in Santa Ana, California circa 1996.

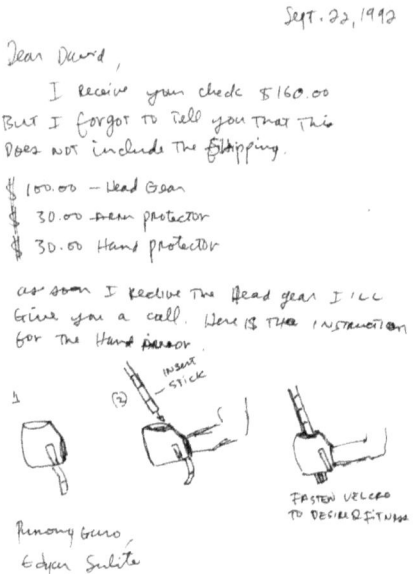

Letter Written from PG Edgar G. Sulite on September 22, 1992 to the Author which led him to train with PG Sulite and become a member of Lameco Eskrima International less than a month later.

Within the week, on September 22, 1992, I received the hand protector and the forearm guard but the head gear was not included. Punong Guro Edgar G. Sulite enclosed a letter with the training gear demonstrating how to use the hand protector with hand-drawn illustrations as well explaining that he did not charge me for the shipping and asking if I would mind paying him for that. In addition, he informed me that the head gear was not in from the Philippines yet and that he would send it on as soon as it got to the U.S.

I called him and told him that I would be glad to pay him extra for shipping and handling and that he should call me when the head gear arrives as I lived only about forty-five minutes from him outside of Los Angeles, and that I could just swing by his place and pick up the head gear when it arrived from his supplier in the Philippines. He said that he would. Meanwhile, I immediately contacted one of my students, Howard Chen, as I badly wanted to try out the hand protector and forearm guard in training. We were able to really strike hard with little of the power from the strikes going through the training equipment. I was happy and could not wait until the head gear had arrived.

After a few weeks I received a phone call from Punong Guro Sulite telling me that the head gear had arrived, and he gave me the address to his home, to come and pick it up. I left only minutes after I had gotten off the phone with him. I arrived about forty-five minutes later at his home and met him face to face for the first time on October 15, 1992. We discussed my training in the Filipino martial arts and how long I had trained and under whom I had trained. He began to tell me a little about his back ground and asked if I would like to see how to properly use the protective gear which he had sold to me. I said that I would love to.

We then went out into his yard, and he had me put on all of the gear and feed him random strikes. I did and wow! What a culture shock. He was so smooth in putting together seamless combinations but with great intensity. When he would strike, he was lightning-fast and powerful beyond belief. I could feel every strike which he threw going right through the hand and forearm protectors, clean to the bone it seemed, as well as through the head gear. I was really astonished at his accuracy and power as he was hitting my hands and wrist at will. With me feeding fast, unexpected angles, he was reacting to everything that I threw against him with no problems and countering everything with which I would counter.

To say that I was impressed would be quite an understatement at the very least. After that demonstration, I had to learn more of this. He asked what I thought about the equipment, and I responded that I loved it!, but I was really impressed with his movement, and that I was really becoming more and more curious about the Lameco Eskrima System based on seeing him move and more importantly feeling him move. He asked if I would like to schedule a private class with him, to learn more about Lameco Eskrima as well as learn more about him, and I said that I would be really interested. We scheduled that first class for five days later, on October 20, 1992, which would be a turning point in my life.

I showed up at nine o'clock on the morning of October 20, 1992 to what I would later come to know as the infamous "backyard" of Punong Guro Edgar G. Sulite, and my Lameco Eskrima Odyssey had begun. I trained with him for almost two hours that day and, before the session was complete, he had convinced me that this is what I had been looking for my entire life. On that day, before leaving his home, I officially joined the Lameco Eskrima International Association and became one of Punong Guro Edgar G. Sulite's private students.

After two months of training privately with him at his home in Los Angeles, California, I was invited by him to join the invitation only "backyard" class which years later went on to become known as the "Sulite Orehenal Group." That would be the very first time that I met my Lameco

The Author posing with a banner of his Teacher, PG Edgar G. Sulite behind him on the wall. Taken in Mexico City, Mexico circa 2012 during a Lameco Eskrima Seminar that he was conducting there.

Eskrima "backyard" brothers, and I was required to fight on the very first day against Mar Elepano, Bong Hebia, and Roger Agbulos, which I had considered to be my baptism into the "Sulite Orehenal Group." What can I say? Other than I loved it from the very first day of training with him, and I still love it to this day.

I trained with Punong Guro Edgar G. Sulite from 1992 - 1997 a couple of times a week, privately at his home, as well as in the "backyard" group. In addition to that, from 1994 – 1997, I would assist Punong Guro Edgar G. Sulite with the Lameco Eskrima lessons of Sifu Larry Hartsell and Debra Hartsell at their home in Los Angeles, California a couple of times a week until Edgar passed away on April 10, 1997.

I remember when I first began to train with Punong Guro Edgar G. Sulite that Lameco Eskrima was all that I thought about and, any free moment that I found throughout the day, I used to train either by myself or with my students, counting down the hours until I would be able to train again with Punong Guro Sulite. I actually dreamt of training Lameco Eskrima when I would sleep at night. It was on my mind twenty-four hours a day when I was awake as well as when I slept. I simply could not get enough of it then and still cannot even to this day.

To this day, I am still quite excited about it, and I feel truly fortunate to have found my way to train with the great masters under whom I have trained, including Tuhon Leo T. Gaje Jr., Guro Dan Inosanto, and Guro Ted Lucay-lucay, but meeting and training with Punong Guro Edgar G. Sulite was exactly what I had always looked for, and I am blessed to have found him and the Lameco Eskrima System. Years later it is still my greatest passion in life!

The Author assisting PG Edgar G. Sulite with a Lameco Eskrima Seminar in Orange, California circa 1995.

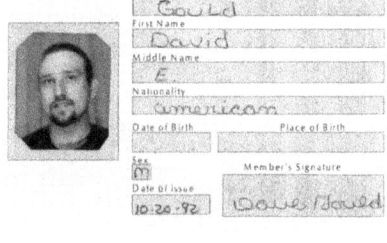

The Authors Lameco Eskrima Training Passbook and Lameco ID from 1992.

One of the Authors Lameco Eskrima ID Cards showing the rank of "Tagapagsanay" which he received from PG Edgar G. Sulite on July 29, 1996.

Below, I would like to call attention to some of the more important lessons and goals which Punong Guro Edgar G. Sulite always emphasized as being of utmost importance pertaining to the proper training and development of the Lameco Eskrima System. I do not think one can discuss what defines the Lameco Eskrima System as a combat art without going into the following subject matter in great detail. I will take them up one by one.

Lameco Eskrima Regarding the Separate Phases of Combative Development

Punong Guro Edgar G. Sulite learned very quickly in his own training that there were numerous distinctions made between learning to fight, training to fight, engaging in a fight for real, and teaching one to fight with positive effect. Therefore, in the Lameco Eskrima System, we have four separate phases of development which have to be mastered before one can become a recognized standard bearer in the system: the learning phase, the training phase, the fighting phase, and the teaching phase. All are vital in their own regard and quite necessary in reaching one's elevated combative development, with each phase of development being distinct and unique unto itself. No one phase is more important than the others, but all must be present and fully accounted for, working in unison towards the best interest of the warrior in training, for the student to advance through the system and meet the expectations and high standards as set forth and established by Punong Guro Edgar G. Sulite.

The Author doing a photo shoot for Svenska Fighter Magazine in Stockholm Sweden circa 1997.

In the "learning phase," we build an effective delivery system and instill an efficient basic foundation of combative movement. In the "training phase," we reinforce and expand on what was developed in the learning phase and actualize the student's true combative value through trial and error as we interject adversity and non-cooperation into the training model in appropriate doses. In the "fighting phase," we measure one's true combative capability while keeping our abilities aligned with combative truth in dealing with the uncertainty of a real situation that only sparring or fighting can reveal regarding the training model. In the "teaching phase," we learn how to teach all that we have learned regarding the curriculum and a lifetime of experiences while passing along those things to our students in a way they can learn with pristine clarity as we transfer to them all of our strengths and none of our weaknesses. I will address each of these one by one.

The Learning Phase — The "learning phase" of our training involves forming one's most basic foundation of combative movement, combative attributes, and, finally, combative technique, concepts, and principles. Learning can be done slowly or faster, as dictated by each student's individual capacity to learn and assimilate all combative information which has been taught and place it all in proper combative context. This is where the most important work is accomplished, and unless a strong combative foundation is established, developed, and allowed to root itself in the student's capability, all may come crashing down on top of the student the first time he is shaken and forced to defend life and limb under pressure. Punong Guro Edgar G. Sulite called this "fighting form" and that was inclusive of everything that was expected to be present and accounted for in laying a solid foundation of basics necessary for the beginning student to build confidence in his abilities.

As one develops combatively through the learning phase, the most critical areas of development are basic combative movement and instilling an effective delivery system. This is made up of the four basic attributes: speed, timing, power, and position. Then, the student learns and develops non-telegraphic striking, perception, and reaction, centerline infractions, and violations, centerline recovery, proper body mechanics in delivering one's strikes, location and re-location principles, and proper ranging principles.

After a functional working knowledge of movement and attributes have been instilled, one then begins to draw from a fully diversified curriculum of practical techniques, combative concepts, and combative principles, learning, not only the strength, but also any inherent weakness regarding any technique, concept, or principle by fully dissecting them in the training environment in search of their true combative value, which quickly becomes necessary in realizing ones fullest potential. Punong Guro Edgar G. Sulite used to warn us that it was not enough to learn just the strength of what we do but that we also had to understand and investigate the weakness attached to the other side of that strength in what we do to be successful fighters. He would say that, unless we knew the fullest extent of the weakness attached, we could not assess fair combative value to the strength itself. Being made aware of one's greatest weakness in these things directly factors into the ability to make a proper risk assessment, since sometimes the weakness is greater than the strength, making it ill-advised to use in certain circumstances.

Punong Guro Edgar G. Sulite would then instruct the beginning student in how to efficiently utilize each weapon or weapon combination found in our curriculum, including how to hold each weapon, and what parts of each weapon could actually be used to fight. Then, he would teach the starting positions and the proper fighting stance; next, the different grips, dividing them into "hard target" and "soft target" grips, and then breaking them down further into thrusting weapons, edged weapons, and impact weapons. After all of this had been accomplished, he would introduce the various basic strikes, basic foot-work, basic blocks, basic hand sectoring, basic deflections, basic disarms, and basic long range hitting options. After these things had been rehearsed and thoroughly investigated, he would introduce the Laban-laro drills for dissection. These drills allowed all that could be expected from within the combative equation to come together in training and forced the student to coordinate many things at the same time into drill format by performing each individual drill as a series of drills addressing numerous probabilities which the combative equation could bring forward at any point in time.

As the student became more and more comfortable with this training phase, Punong Guro Edgar G. Sulite would then start inserting adversity in mild doses into his feed on occasions. If he were going over one of the Laban-laro drills, for example, with the student, every once in a while he would do something that was not part of the drill, something unexpected by the student, to start training the student that, when people fight, they often strike back when the opportunity presents itself, which indicates that the student always

The Author training at home in Riverside, California circa 1996

had to be prepared to deal with uncertainty and the unexpected counter attack at any time during their training, and how they responded to this uncertainty when it presented itself in training became the more important lesson learned. Punong Guro Edgar G. Sulite used to tell us that fighting was about reacting to what your opponent "actually" does, not what you think he is "supposed" to do. So, he always held us to realistic expectations even in the earliest stages of development regarding our training in the learning phase.

All of the drills which we have in the Lameco Eskrima System serve one purpose, and that is to package a specific function in drill format, with the desired intention being to transfer that function to the student in such a way that he fully comprehends every detail involved in its implementation, so he then can assimilate that function into his combative movement, thereby allowing the drill to achieve its original intent of transferring that function to the student. Punong Guro Sulite felt the function was more important than the drill in which it was packaged. He felt that every drill was important and possessed great value in the learning phase, but his end goal was transferring the function to the student, since the student relied on each specific function when he was expected to fight and not necessarily the drill, which was only used to deliver that function.

I saw the Laban-laro drills change several times from 1992 - 1997 when I was training directly under the astute tutelage of Punong Guro Sulite, the reason being that he was occasionally somewhat dissatisfied with how the function was being transferred to the student and was always looking for a better way to package the function in drill format in a manner where it could be transferred with more clarity. This is why, in the "backyard," the Lameco Eskrima System was defined and taught to us as "function over form," and that is how we perceived it to be and practiced it amongst ourselves. The sooner we could master the function, the quicker we could acquire, assemble, assimilate, and actualize each specific function into our combative movement, so that we could then verify its potential and assess fair combative value through sparring or fighting.

The Author with one of his students, Byron Fairchild in Riverside, California training aspects of the Ilustrisimo Blade circa 1999.

The learning phase was the most basic phase of the Lameco Eskrima System and, as such, Punong Guro Sulite would not interject too much uncertainty into the training model early on for fear of possibly disrupting the balance of the beginning student as he formed his most basic foundation and delivery system. The goal of the learning phase was just "to learn," and that is what Punong Guro Sulite allowed to take place, as opposed to fighting or resisting heavily, and inserting a lot of counter-to-counter activity when he would exchange strikes with his beginning students.

The most important aspect of the learning phase is developing a clear and concise understanding of material learned and developing a functional basic foundation of combative movement and attributes by which to deliver ones deadly intent when

Punong Guro Edgar G. Sulite being assisted by the Author during a Lameco Eskrima Seminar in Orange, California circa 1995.

opportunity presents itself. At which time, the very relationship between movement, range, counter response, recovery, and technical expertise are delved into for proper combative development, and the results found there-in unified for optimum effect.

The Training Phase — The "training phase" should be geared toward testing one's true combative capability in an actual combative experience while facing all consequences and risks involved in that endeavor. In this phase, aggression, non-cooperation, counter-to-counter skills, perception, reaction and recovery principles are all introduced and become key to proper development. In this phase, more and more of the training is done either at or close to real-time speed, to enhance all things combative, as the laws of cause and effect govern them when staying close to combative truth. This phase is the first phase when you start facing true consequences for your actions or failure to act. Yes, the failure or hesitation to act is a willful act, not a very wise one, but an act nonetheless. In this phase, the student is held accountable for all things that he chooses or refuses to do in a fight. This is accountability, and the transition from martial artist to warrior cannot be made without being held accountable for one's actions or failure to act.

The "training phase" should not be confused with the "learning phase" because the desired effect sought in each phase is quite different. In the training phase, you simply investigate, experiment, assimilate, and utilize all that was encouraged, learned, and developed in the learning phase. In Lameco Eskrima, "little" is always seen as being "more," as the most effective warriors will train to perform with the intent to maximize effect while minimizing risk. The more simple and economical by nature the approach with intention is, the more effective the results gained will be.

One of the more important parts of the training phase is the reality of training to prepare for both failure and success. Punong Guro Sulite used to warn us that, if we only train to succeed in a complacent training environment where there is no natural resistance against what we train, then we will only learn to merely succeed. But when we will be forced to defend life and limb in the streets, we cannot expect to succeed with one-hundred percent of what we would expect to do. Eventually, we will fail in our attempt to strike our opponent, or fail in defense against our opponent's strikes, and, if we have never failed before, then we will not know how to turn those failures into successes when we encounter them in a real fight.

So Punong Guro Edgar G. Sulite would often resist or counter his student's responses during the training phase when the student least expected it in real-time, just to see how the student would react when confronted with uncertainty and adversity in training. He would say that "one" successful recovery from a failed attempt on target was more valuable than "one hundred" complete and uncontested successes in a complacent environment where failure is neither forced on nor experienced by the student. So, if Punong Guro Sulite were practicing disarms with his student, in this phase, he would resist, disrupt, or counter the student's efforts to disarm him, forcing the student to transition from what he was told to do to doing what was dictated by uncertainty and non-cooperation on the part of Punong Guro Sulite. Likewise, if they were training any drill, Punong Guro Sulite would find a place to "break out of the drill," again countering unexpectedly with something that did not belong in the drill and forcing failure on the student. Then, either the student would recover, turning that failure into a success by giving an adequate counter response to the unexpected intrusion from Punong Guro Sulite, or he would not and would be forced to admit failure due to his lack of awareness and inadequate response.

The Author doing a photo shoot for Svenska Fighter Magazine in Stockholm Sweden circa 1997.

Punong Guro Sulite used to tell us that, for what we do to be effective in fighting, the way we train has to resemble as much as possible the very thing for which we train. Meaning, if uncertainty, unexpected counter attacks, strikes thrown in real-time speed, and aggression were all part of the combative equation (fight) which we are training to engage, then those things at some point in time also had to be present and addressed in our training environment in like manner. Punong Guro Sulite would go on to say that, when we train with weakness and compromise in our training environment, both would follow us onto the streets and present themselves in our response when we would be forced to fight for our lives. He would say we respond the way we train, and for us to be effective in fighting, at some point in time, our training had to brush up against reality, to allow the situation itself to dictate our counter response and to let our overall capability govern both how long the fight would be allowed to continue and its outcome.

In the training phase, the intent of proper combative development is always to question the combative environment and, in doing so, adequately prepare ourselves to deal honestly with any answers received. We begin to act out of necessity as opposed to acting by

The Author with one of his students, Patrick Schlichting in Reutlingen, Germany training aspects of the Ilustrisimo Blade circa 1997 during a Lameco Eskrima Seminar there.

choice. The situation and training environment start to reflect the realities of the actual combat environment which serves as the very model for our training environment, all for the sake of keeping one's training environment as closely aligned with reality as possible. If something can happen for real on the street, then it also must be addressed in one's training environment – an environment where reacting under duress amidst chaos, mayhem, and uncertainty replaces merely responding out of convenience and comfort while being given an unrealistic amount of time in which to respond.

Another element of the training phase which is not included in the learning phase is validating that which we train in an attempt to know for sure that what we were training would hold up against hard, aggressive strikes thrown with full speed and power on impact. Punong Guro Edgar G. Sulite would have us gear up as though we were sparring for this validation process. We would don all protective equipment – head gear, hand guards, and fore arm guards – and then Punong Guro Sulite would throw several random strikes at us in real-time speed with full power while allowing us an opportunity to test our ability to block, deflect, counter, disarm, close range or evade each threat as it was coming toward us with full speed and power. Since we were wearing protective equipment, he would really try and hit us with full power, making it all but impossible for us to do what we wanted against him, which, in turn, forced us to do what we had to do, instead. Remember that, in the learning phase, the student was allowed the opportunity to learn without much resistance or disruption to interfere with that learning process. In the training phase, disruption and interference *were* the learning process, and what was being taught was how to adapt to it and recover from it when it would unexpectedly present

The Author training at home in Riverside, California circa 1996.

itself in a random exchange. Furthermore, in the training phase, the significance of the training was shifted from learning to validating what has already been learned, and part of that validation was to adapt and adjust to the unexpected element as well as dealing with more and more strikes thrown in real time speed with full power.

Punong Guro Sulite would tell us to block his strikes when he threw a series of strikes to the head, without announcing intent, with full speed and power, but, if we were not completely prepared, he would collapse our block back on our head gear and strike through with full power, hitting us in the head. This would happen because most practice blocks against strikes which are thrown at a much-reduced speed, in order not to hurt the training partner, so it appears easier than it actually is. You find out quickly and realistically the amount of time that you actually have to respond, as well as the speed and strength required to block such a strike when thrown with full intention, power, and speed. Then, he would tell the student to deflect the strikes, with the majority of his attempts pushing through and crashing into the student's head gear. Then, he would test the student's ability to grab his hand out of mid-air and disarm him of his weapon at real-time speed, which would lead to the same result: the student failing miserably and getting hit hard in the head as a result. Literally everything that was trained in the "backyard" was validated in this manner, and it revealed and cast a bright light of combative truth onto everything that we were learning. If something worked for you against him, in this training phase, it was not because he allowed you to make it work, but because you did what was required and made it work on your own merits. That was the significance of the training phase: to make something work, even if it was not that which was initially expected.

The one approach that I always subscribe to in training is to better the techniques, concepts, and principles in order to make them whole and more effective in the combative equation. I do this by simply introducing into training a realistic environment where the student is expected to utilize my training while defending life and limb someday. Reality seems to detect and bring attention to even the smallest flaws and weaknesses found within our overall combative structure. Fighting is serious, so our training should be, as well, to reflect and underscore this reality. A wise man once said: "The warrior who thinks that he will live and the warrior who thinks that he will die in combat are both right" The more pertinent question that I pose to you is, which of those two warriors are you? Life or death hangs in the balance of your answer. Only the way you train can prepare you for which of these two outcomes will become your reality in combat. Train for one mind, one body, one life, and one goal… that being survival, and you will be well prepared for any eventual conflict in the streets while everyone else is running around in a fog of confusion and anxiety.

The Fighting Phase —The "fighting phase" of our training really puts everything into clear perspective and verifies all that you were taught in the "learning phase" and have diligently refined in the "training phase.", It allows pure uncertainty to realistically govern and dictate combative response better than any other medium available to you except experiencing and surviving an actual life-threatening crisis situation itself. Combative truth speaks loudly to us in this phase of development because one's true combative abilities, sure to come forth in this phase, will literally allow us to bring order out of chaos while revealing any deception in our own capabilities as governed by the rules of engagement and allowed to evolve in accordance with the natural laws pertaining to cause and effect.

In this phase of training, sparring and fighting becomes the combative gauge by which to best monitor one's actual combative effect. The actual event itself and our collective experiences within that environment become our most valid advisors and pertinent teachers in this realm of reality. For, in this environment, we are only as effective as our abilities, and only our abilities will determine if we will win or lose a fight. In this phase of training, you no longer rely on things you were told would work for you in your time of need. Rather, you verify for real what will actually work for you and what will not work against a non-cooperative opponent who is trying to hit you as hard as you are trying to hit him, with consequences attached to everything that you do or refuse to do during the fight.

This was the phase of training that all of us in the "backyard" loved to find ourselves in and experience most of all. It was up to each of us to move and react in accordance to what we perceived during each fight against one another, and, if we did well or if we did poorly, it was one-hundred percent on us. As individuals we owned our success, or we owned our failures, in these fights. We could blame no one but ourselves if we performed poorly. Punong Guro Edgar G. Sulite regarded the fighting phase to be the laboratory where everything we were taught in the "backyard" would bear itself out. He would say that, in

The Author with one of his students, Johnny Arias in Riverside, California training the Lameco Blade circa 2001.

this environment, what we learned would either be confirmed or refuted, depending on our individual capabilities as we moved against each other in earnest, trying to soundly defeat the other. I absolutely loved this time in my life!!! When I reflect back on my training with Punong Guro Edgar G. Sulite, this is where my mind almost always takes me back to.

One of the more important lessons which fighting forces you to deal with and try to figure out are the various ranges and the consequences of each range as they are allowed to play out during a fight. Fighting forces you to respond to threats perceived in the long range, medium range, and the close range. Then there are the hybrid ranges in-between those three: the distance between close and medium ranges, and the distance between medium and long ranges. Also, there is the extreme close range, where the fight could very well go to the ground if you are not careful, or else devolve into chaos from the clinch. The fight evolves best on its own merits when it is allowed to breathe and expand in and out of all of these ranges at will; and, if you cannot contend with your opponent wherever you may find him, then you will have difficulties which give your opponent a considerable advantage. Learn to fight wherever the fight may take you and not just expect to fight within your preference. Every good fighter knows better than to fight against one's strength; instead, he will fight against one's weakness, as he knows he has a better chance of defeating his opponent at a range where his opponent feels most uncomfortable, not strongest or, dare I say it, invincible. Hence, Punong Guro Sulite would always tell us to play to our strength and not our weakness and vice-versa: to play to our opponent's weakness and not his strength.

Punong Guro Edgar G. Sulite being assisted by the Author during a Lameco Eskrima Seminar in Orange, California circa 1995.

Bong Hebia and the Author training Lameco "dos manos largos" material at his home in Riverside, California circa 1998.

As you continue to develop and learn from sparring or fighting, you will be forced to address certain realities, and one of those is transitioning from one range to another while evolving with the fight as it is allowed to naturally breathe and expand. Sometimes you will be successful in protecting one body part by removing it from the reach of your opponent, but then you may unknowingly expose another in the process. When fighting with edged and impact weapons, you fight with greater effect using hand and body evasions in medium and close ranges. In Lameco Eskrima, we are taught to maintain the line of engagement, leaving us standing just outside of our opponent's reach, where we will readily wait for or manufacture opportunities. Most people would categorize this as being just outside of medium range, or, as Punong Guro Edgar G. Sulite would refer to it, as "medio-largo."

In "medio-largo" range, while positioning yourself just outside of your opponent's ability to strike your head or body, you are still in range for strikes to your hands. Therefore, there is a great need to develop and use hand evasions for defense against strikes primarily to the weapon hand and, secondarily, to the safety hand. Even if the hands are not specifically targeted in this range, they are accessible by happenstance en route to or away from the head or body and, therefore, must be protected. When hand evasions are done properly, they can be used to positive effect in counter-to-counter activity just after you make your opponent miss big, since now he is forced to recover his center line or be hit. This will always be your greatest opportunity, as you have less distance to travel to take advantage of his exposed centerline than he has adequate time to recover his centerline.

Punong Guro Edgar G. Sulite demonstrating knife techniques on Howard Chen one of his students at Santa Ana, California circa 1996.

Most people, myself included, who fought or sparred against Punong Guro Edgar G. Sulite always thought he was too close to them, and this made them nervous because they realized that, the closer they were to him, the greater the chance they would be hit. Yet, when they struck, they found out that Punong Guro Sulite was just outside of their range as he made them miss by minimal or maximum margins. As soon as they grossly violated center, Punong Guro Sulite only had inches to move forward to capitalize on any and all opportunities, and only inches to move back to take himself out of harm's way just beyond their weapon's reach. This is also a well-known feature of GM Jose D. Caballero of De Campo 1-2-3 Orehenal, and he used it with great success for numerous decades, eventually retiring as the undefeated "Juego todo" champion of his region of Barrio Ibo, Toledo City, Cebu, Philippines.

As dictated by the threat faced, Punong Guro Sulite would use either hand or body evasions in dealing with the initial strike and any counter strikes that might follow, while he negotiated in and out of range, randomly targeting opportunities revealed or created as a direct result of those evasions. The closer to the line of engagement, the greater the need for hand and body evasions because his body stayed just outside of the reach of his opponent's weapon, but his hands were still within range. When sparring or fighting against Punong Guro Sulite, he seemed to be always just where he needed to be for only as long as he needed to be there, and then he was gone. The majority of the time, you would not even know you were exposed and vulnerable until you had already been hit and, by that time, it was too late. When you struck at his weapon hand, you were initially convinced it would be easy, but, as soon as you threw your strike, he would respond with one of his hand evasions, making you miss by a wide margin and, left without time to react, he hit you before you could recover your position.

Punong Guro Sulite considered hand evasions to be paramount in successful fighting; in sparring, too, although to a lesser degree. In the Lameco Eskrima curriculum, we have numerous variations of hand and body evasions and subsequent counters and counter-to-counter measures used in a wide variety of circumstances. But, more important is one's ability to perceive and react to immediate threats faced quickly. It is not enough only to recognize the threat, you must also move against it as soon as it is perceived, and, if you cannot do this quickly, then you will heavily pay the consequences for your indecisiveness. We train to develop on both sides of this equation in the Lameco Eskrima System. On one side, non-telegraphic strikes were practiced, and the more proficiently you were able to use them, the less movement there was for your opponent to react to. On the other side of the equation was the ability to perceive and react, and the more your opponent wasted movement, the sooner you could evade his strikes since he would announce his intent beforehand. One attribute is woven into the other. The less wasted motion when striking, the greater your success in hitting your target; and the better you are at perceiving the threat and reacting to it by evading, the less you get hit by your opponent. Both attributes are equally necessary for fighting.

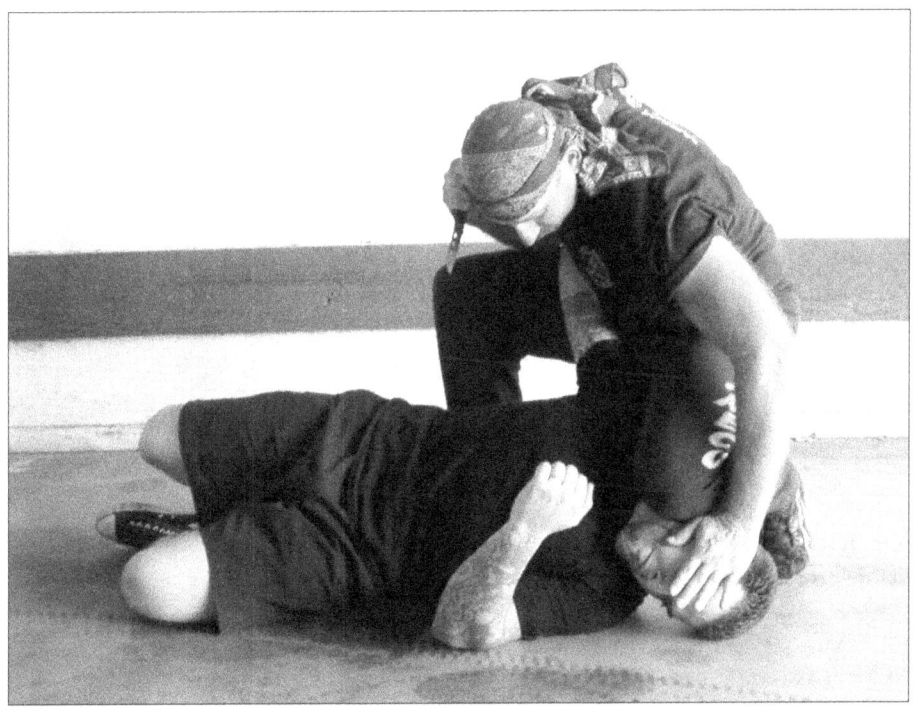

Student Johnny Arias being taken to the ground and trained in the Lameco Blade by the Author at his home in Riverside, California circa 2005.

Punong Guro Sulite always trained his students to have a clear understanding that combat changes dynamically, and one has to learn to adapt and adjust to the circumstances as they change in each fight. The "fighting phase" of our training places you squarely in this environment. Only when we are able to adapt and adjust to the situation as it happens in combat have we truly mastered combative movement in general. The secret to fighting isn't to blindly learn a thousand different techniques, but rather to master the combative equation itself and all of its variables in order to be able to change with it as it evolves from second to second. The ability to perceive and react against your opponent's attack will take you a long way.

In our training to fight, we want to be effective, but, for this to be realized, we have to train with intention in real-time and be left to face all consequences of our actions, both good and bad. Most people seem to want to become great warriors without having to fight or challenge themselves in the process. This is all but impossible because only through adversity and experiencing the harsh realities of combat itself can we truly transform from martial artist to warrior. Punong Guro Sulite used to say that there were no short cuts to fighting as fighting itself was the path way to fighting. The more of it you do, the better at it you will become. And the best way to get started is to begin sparring with your training partner, and then begin to experiment with all that is found within your arsenal in order to verify what works for you and what does not. If something does not work well, then you must attempt to re-engineer or adjust it until you find a workable solution and make it viable. If it still does not work, then ditch it in favor of something that will work.

There is a huge distinction between "knowing" how to fight and actually "being able" to fight. Many people know how to fight, but very few of those who claim to be in the know actually will be able to do so with any measurable effect, should their lives be called upon one night in the cold, hard streets. There are no easy ways to success, no short cuts; you have to sweat and work diligently through an enormous amount of adversity while challenging yourself daily in an effort to realize your fullest potential during each training session. Remember that integrity is doing what is expected of you even when no one is watching, so we must train for the right reasons, not to impress but rather to develop our combative capability to high proficiency while being held to numerous combative truths. It is up to the Instructor to convey this to the student and to guide the student out of ignorance about their overall combat effectiveness.

In the final analysis, it comes down to perception versus reality. The simple reality of a combative situation must be prepared for. Too many of us perceive that reality based only on training drills, word of mouth, or conceptual points of view rooted in assumptions and anticipation. The truth is a combative situation will evolve and advance on its own terms and will dictate how we best can deal with it, if at all. We have no choice but to accept it on its own terms, not ours.

The problem as I see it is that too many of us get stuck in the learning phase and never leave it, thereby prohibiting ourselves from evolving in our training. It seems we all get too caught up in doing the drills, disarms, locks, and other things solely for the sake of doing them.

Student Tad Waltman being placed in a choke hold by the Author while using his garote in Forest, Mississippi circa 2013.

Their functions are lost on us, making it very hard for us to transcend ourselves and grow as warriors. The training phase was designed to shake you out of your comfort zones and place you in the real world. The fighting phase allows you to reformulate your understanding of that environment and develop to the point where you can react with positive effect and strong purpose. Again I repeat Punong Guro Edgar G. Sulite's famous motto: "An ounce of experience is worth a pound of speculation."

Just as you quench a blade in cold water when it is scorching hot, to establish its integrity and capture its character, the quenching process for the warrior is combat. This establishes the integrity and captures the character of the warrior. At the very heart of the warrior is his willingness to fight, even when faced with insurmountable odds. A true warrior controls his emotions, never allowing them to control him. Punong Guro Edgar G. Sulite told us many times that we should claim combat as our teacher and the field of battle as our home.

The Author teaching a Lameco Eskrima Seminar in Reutlingen, Germany in February 1997 for Uli Weidle and Achim Weidle.

The Teaching Phase — The "teaching phase" of our training allows us to learn how to best get across to others by our example how we do what we do to make us great fighters. The ultimate goal of any instructor is to teach what is needed to pass along all of his strengths to the student and none of his weaknesses. More important still is for the instructor to assist the student to discover and enhance his own unique strengths and fighting ability. It is said that a great instructor will show the student where to look, but not what to see.

My goal as an instructor is to prepare my students for the reality of combat and reveal to them combative truth and introduce all consequences faced, while also holding them fully accountable for all of their actions or inactions done in the heat of the fight. However, being a good teacher is not enough; it is actually only half of the equation because, equally, the student must also be a good student and want to learn. He has to be willing to do whatever is required and make an earnest attempt to learn. This is important because, as a teacher, you quickly learn, if someone truly does not have any interest in learning, it will be almost impossible to teach this person, and the results will be poor.

On October 20, 1992, when I began training under Punong Guro Edgar G. Sulite, he told me: "Dabe, I wish that I could connect a rubber hose from my head to your head and transfer the knowledge that way, but I cannot. So, you will have to learn everything as I did and pay with your lessons not only with money but with blood, sweat, and black and blue marks all over your body."

I hold myself responsible, not only for each of my student's overall combative effectiveness, but also for any signs of arrogance or lack of confidence in their abilities. They need to be made aware of what their true abilities are and not be misled into think they are some sort of invincible demi-god. An inflated ego has no place on the streets. As soon as you start thinking you are better than everyone else on the planet, you are assured of meeting the one person or group of people who will prove you wrong. On the street, you will not be fighting on your own terms but on someone else's terms instead. So, get it into your head now that, if you are required to defend yourself, expect the worst-case scenario, because this will be closer to reality.

Punong Guro Edgar G. Sulite was a very good judge of character, and he would not let just anyone into his organization. Period. All of us in the "backyard" group were handpicked by him, and the training was by invitation only, meaning if you were not invited into the group, you did not train in the group. So, we had to earn his trust just as he had earned ours. He trusted us to keep his secrets and promote the system as he wanted it promoted. Punong Guro Sulite wanted us to become, not just good, but as proficient as he was. In fact, he wanted us to become better than he was. He understood that the better the students, the harder he himself would have to train to keep up with us. So, he trained by himself early every morning and late every night, to stay sharp and to stay well ahead.

Punong Guro Edgar G. Sulite being assisted by the Author during a Lameco Eskrima Seminar in Orange, California at Mt. San Antonio College circa 1995.

The Author taking his host, Achim Weidle, down to the ground with the blade during a Lameco Eskrima Seminar that he was conducting in Reutlingen, Germany in February 1997.

PG Sulite often told me he would never overwhelm his students. He always positioned himself just slightly above his students level of proficiency, enough to keep us challenged in our training but never so far ahead of us we would just give up and want to quit due to frustration. This is the sign of a very capable Instructor. Punong Guro Sulite knew, not only how to make us proficient, but how to keep us motivated and hungry for more of his teachings. He did not want to break our spirit, rather he wanted to ignite a passion within us and make us challenge ourselves in training, fighting, or teaching.

Punong Guro Edgar G. Sulite left us, his appointed standard bearers and Certified Instructors, a very diverse curriculum, and he broke it down into what would be taught and when it should be taught to basic, intermediate, advanced, apprentice Instructors, Certified Instructor/Trainers, and Full Credentialed Instructors. But, for you to be considered for promotion to an Instructor level, you had to prove your worth and spend time in the Apprentice Instructor program learning to become an Instructor and standard bearer.

Many years ago in the spring of 1993, Punong Guro Edgar G. Sulite and I were discussing what inherent qualities were necessary for a great teacher. What he told me, based on his personal opinion, has stuck with me ever since. He stated that a great teacher should possess three very important qualities:

1) He should possess great technical skill. This person knows his system's curriculum inside and out. In other words, he is able to evolve the student through growth within the system. He should be very fluent yet effective with all aspects of his system. But,

he has to understand the difference between doing a technique for show and doing it for combat. He should always move with intention, meaning he's gonna' be able to hit whom he's striking at and be able to bring him to the ground with power and accuracy. He should have good speed, timing, power, position, non-telegraphic striking, and recovery measures – all of the attributes required to be effective in a possible life-threatening situation.

2) He should have the ability to impart his knowledge in such a way as to connect with his students. Be able to give them a clear and concise understanding of whatever points he is trying to convey to them. The Instructor's clear understanding of the material to be presented is key to learning well, and a lot of patience on both sides of the teacher/student equation is required. He should also understand that, for students to learn well, a fine balance must be struck. The student also has to want to learn and be willing to apply himself one-hundred percent in their training together. By understanding this, a great teacher can motivate his students to want to learn, to continue coming to class, and, most importantly, train daily on their own in his absence.

3) He should be a great fighter. This is insignificant when it comes to his ability to teach but valid nonetheless. It gives the student first-hand information about what will work and what won't, as opposed to "I know it will work because my instructor said his instructor said it would." The fact is, if you haven't been there first-hand, there will always be some doubt, you will only be able to speculate, and, to this point, experience speaks volumes. Functional knowledge is more valuable in combat than speculative knowledge. Moreover, a great teacher imparts the need to seek this verified "knowledge" over streams of speculative "information."

Very rare is the Instructor who possesses all three qualities. Some may be great teachers, but their mindset is off, and they're not great fighters, or have no technical skill. Or, some may even be great fighters, but their ability to teach you to move the way they do is weak or non-existent. They can do it themselves, but they can't tell you what they're doing that makes them so effective. Some can show you a thousand techniques that might end any situation, but they won't have intention in their techniques, meaning: there is only technique minus the power, speed, position, and timing which is required on the street. I strive to possess all three qualities, and I hope more and more will do the same.

Lameco Eskrima Regarding Adversity in Training

Punong Guro Edgar G. Sulite once made a brilliant analogy between the development of a warrior in training and an oyster as it creates, in pure anguish, a pearl. He began by explaining that an oyster makes a pearl when a single grain of sand accidentally gets trapped between the muscle and the shell. The grain of sand aggravates the muscle, and the oyster struggles to push the grain out of its shell. However, because of the shape of the shell and the limitations in movement of the muscle, this is all but impossible.

As it fights daily against the grain of sand, through relentless maneuvering and moving around in anguish, it constantly grinds the grain of sand against the inside of the shell, from which the grain scrapes, collects, and builds up around itself layers of "Mother of Pearl," growing in size daily. The longer and more extensively it labors and fights, the more its intruder grows. Finally, after a life of aggravation, turmoil and struggle, a pearl is born as a direct result of the oyster's misery.

Punong Guro Sulite used to tell me that, as my Instructor, his duty was to become that "grain of sand" which would aggravate me in training and, as a direct result, force me to create a pearl from whatever suffering I experienced during our training together. The pearl might be a specific function, technique, concept, or principle learned, applied, and actualized when he inserted adversity into the training model, which, in turn, forced me to recover and create success from failures.

Punong Guro Sulite believed "failure" was a much better teacher than "success." When success is consistent and uncontested by resistance and adversity, there is never a reason to plan beyond a projected initial technique because our expectation is that it will succeed, and so we never prepare for the possibility of failure. We need to train for both failure and success, to become fully prepared to contend with both. Without adversity in training there can be no challenge to keep ones skills honed and combat-ready. Simply stated, failure is the window through which we glimpse success.

Punong Guro Sulite often told us that, at the intermediate and advanced levels of the Lameco Eskrima System, we needed to include the possibility of failure, either in our reactions or because of hesitating to act at some crucial point in a fight. Consequences are attached to everything we do or hesitate to do, and, when we add adversity to our training sessions, we create a healthy training environment based purely on cause and effect and not mere speculation.

The Author training at home in Riverside, California circa 1996.

Too many of us buy into the hype that "once a Master always a Master," and, speaking frankly, this could not be farther from the truth. When we reach a point in our combative development where few can keep us challenged, we tend to become lazy in our training, thinking we have evolved into some sort of demi-god or, to a lesser degree, something simply amazing. But, when we cease to challenge ourselves, we will, at best, maintain our skills at their current level or, at worst, diminish in ability due to neglect and inactivity. Only when we challenge ourselves in training, and prepare for both success and failure, do we have the potential for further growth as Warriors in training.

Punong Guro Sulite used to tell us, until we became so fast that lightning was challenged to match our speed, or when we hit our opponent, thunder bellows as we break the sound barrier, we will always have room for improvement. None of us of whom I am aware meets either criterion so, being human, we have a long way to go towards achieving those ideals.

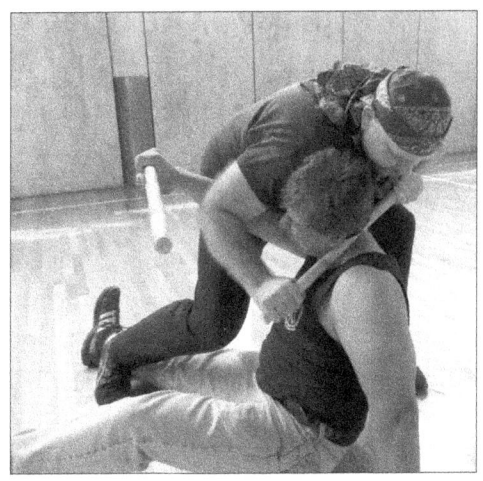

The Author taking his student down to the ground with a neck crank during a Lameco Eskrima Seminar that he was conducting in Mexico City, Mexico in 2010.

Punong Guro Edgar G. Sulite once commented to me that, in training, he would rather aggravate and annoy his training partner than compliment everything thing his training partner does or comes to expect. What he meant was that, if you only agree with and systematically echo everything presented to you in training without first thoroughly testing its actual combative worth in a noncompliant training environment, how can you honestly gauge its effect? By being disruptive and not just echoing sentiment, you are keeping your training partner challenged to adapt and adjust to the unexpected attack or counter attacks. When we resist our training partners in earnest during training, it annoys, distracts, and requires greater alertness on their part. If we allow complacency and a lack of resistance to become the standard in training, this quickly dilutes response and ability.

I demand my students constantly challenge me when opportunities become available to do so in training. Only this will hone my combative abilities and keep them sharp against an unexpected random attack. My students or training partners resisting me in training keeps me honest. Most importantly, it keeps me challenged and kept on a heightened level of awareness. Unless we thoroughly challenge ourselves, we will remain only martial artists without the possibility of ever moving onwards to achieve Warrior status.

During an actual fight, Lameco Eskrima becomes more of a mindset than a system. Nothing is more important than mindset; mindset trumps technique. A huge part of developing a proper mindset is maintaining under pressure the ability to keep your mind focused like a laser beam while everything is coming apart around you. At this point, no distraction can be great enough to break your focus and diminish your efforts to win.

Lameco Eskrima Regarding Acting on Available Opportunity

In actual fighting, spotting the "window of opportunity" becomes absolutely essential to taking full advantage of existing opportunities as they are either revealed to you or created by you. The problem Punong Guro Edgar G. Sulite saw was that most training exaggerates the window of opportunity, so students respond to attacks at an unrealistic speed which allows more time for countering than what would actually be possible during a real street fight. Therefore, it is absolutely necessary that a realistic "window of opportunity" must be created and addressed in one's training environment, in order to best recognize fleeting opportunity for what it is in its natural environment. In fact, Punong Guro Sulite taught us, not to operate in the window of opportunity per se, rather in the "crack" in the window revealed as the window quickly closes shut.

Moreover, the ramifications of two totally different types of strikes require two totally different recovery measures and methods of counter activity toward any available target. Let's face reality here: when dealing with slow, compliant strikes, and when given more than adequate time to think and counter, anything is possible, albeit not probable. But, when faced with full speed and power unleashed by raw aggression in real-time, the "window of opportunity" naturally becomes smaller, and any opportunity to counter becomes increasingly difficult and must be seized in the smallest measurable amount of time. Hence, Punong Guro Edgar G. Sulite told us that, in training, when you extend your hand and leave it hanging in dead space for an unrealistic amount of time, your training partner can do magic, but throw a strike with full power and speed while following it through the intended target without stopping midway, and then you will see what your training partner can really do.

In Lameco Eskrima there are no advanced techniques per se. Punong Guro Sulite explained that everything we would be expected to use in a real fight would be basic in nature, so basics were what we were required to master. In Lameco Eskrima, an advanced technique is a basic technique that works well in its current form but further refined and made more efficient, not by doing "more," but rather by doing "less," in such a way that it has the same effect or greater while limiting and presenting less risk in the process. Advanced methodology in Lameco Eskrima is defined as becoming simpler in one's approach, not more complex, as a narrowing down rather than expanding outwards, becoming smaller, not larger, and by looking inward as opposed to looking outward.

Punong Guro Sulite used to tell us that, if we wanted to know whether or not a technique could be effective in a fight, we needed to try it out while we were fighting. In theory, everything works as it was designed to do, but, in application, theory is mere speculation, and the reality of the fight itself will reveal to you what will work for you best and what will not. If you want to understand what it takes to become a better fighter, do not speculate – fight.

When I spar or fight, I don't count how many times I hit my opponent, I count how many times I myself get hit. This was something that Punong Guro Sulite demanded of us. He would say that in the streets, when we are forced to fight, it will not be for a trophy or accolades, but

Training Equipment which was used in the "Backyard" for sparring and training so that the training could be pushed to the maximum in order to gain the best results. Available for purchase at LamecoEskrima.com.

rather for the right to continue living. If I hit my opponent ten times, and I get hit five times in the process, I don't consider this a victory because five times my life was placed in danger. The best fight I can hope for is to break the head of my opponent with only one strike, without ever tasting the tip of his blade in turn, in which case, I distance myself while remaining at the ready. Take one calculated step at a time.

Bong Hebia and the Author training Kalis Ilustrisimo blade at his home in Riverside, California, circa 1999.

Timing is definitely one of the most essential attributes of an effective delivery system, and if one cannot time a stroke against a threat in real-time through the smallest "window of opportunity," that opportunity will be lost, and, subsequently, so may life and limb as a direct result. In order to verify our timing, we must spar or fight against unexpected attacks and counter attacks, fully aware of every angle of attack that can possibly be made in real-time from a three-hundred-sixty degree circle.

Lameco Eskrima Regarding an Effective Delivery System

Punong Guro Edgar G. Sulite taught that an effective delivery system was of utmost importance to any warrior art. This is especially true in Lameco Eskrima, where it is fused into the core structure of our most fundamental combative foundation. The way we move, and how effectively we apply ourselves when fighting, speaks volumes about our combative capability. These things also speak poorly of our abilities if we fail to apply ourselves seriously enough while developing these essential skills in training. Combative truth bends to no man's arrogance and needs no interpretation. It is what it is, and either you are effective, or you are not, it truly is just this simple.

How well the delivery system is understood, developed, and applied in one's most dire time of need will directly reveal one's true combative capability. Whatever technique we learn is of little use to us without the ability to deliver our deadly intent on-target and with positive effect. We as Warriors in-training are charged with the daunting task of learning a combative technique, concept, or principle, and we must assimilate their finer qualities in training, and then actualize their true effect while fighting. This is a simple-enough formula for success but one often neglected in training due to one's misguided, confused, or misdirected training goals. Most people these days seem to train only with the intent of impressing large crowds at staged demonstrations as opposed to conditioning themselves to deal with the harsh realities of senseless violence in the streets. If you are not training for combative effect against non-compliant opponents, with your end goal being survival, then I dare say you are not training for the right reasons. Only when you train as if your life depends on it will you then fight as if it does. Punong Guro Edgar G. Sulite said, when you win a fight in the street, you do not win a trophy, you just get one more day to go home and spend time with your family.

The delivery system in Lameco Eskrima incorporates numerous essential components which all must come together and work in unison for optimum effect in delivering one's deadly intent on-target. Basically, the delivery system in its entirety is relentlessly held to the natural laws of physics while being governed by simple geometry, resulting in cause-and-effect abilities gained solely through economy of motion. Only secondarily does one's combative effect rely on technique or technical knowledge to any degree. The fact is any technique is useless unless it can be successfully delivered on-target with positive effect in a timely manner; and finding the proper distance has everything to do with achieving that goal. Anything that complicates the combative equation results in the bastardization of motion and is destined to end in failure while leaving you to face severe consequences for your bad judgment or failure to act, as the case may be. Without an effective delivery system, even the most destructive techniques will be of little use simply because, if you cannot touch your opponent with your weapon when opportunities are made available, then you cannot hurt him.

All components of an effective delivery system are essential, but some do stand out in terms of importance. One of these exceptions is ranging or "bridging the gap," as Punong Guro Edgar G. Sulite commonly referred to it. This ability comes from proper positioning, specifically as pertaining to monitoring the line of engagement. Until the line of engagement has been fully understood, mastered, and applied with effect against a non-compliant opponent, ranging can never be completely functional or realized with positive effect. In Lameco Eskrima, we have a saying: "Less is more." What this means is the less distance traversed, the less distance required to recover centerline infractions and correct any vulnerabilities exposed to your opponent, should he decide to further impose his will on you by claiming your center. Fighting efficiently is about adopting a risk-versus-reward mentality, since the less you leave yourself vulnerable, the fewer opportunities your opponent has and, as an additional reward, the less distance you will need to move to recover your center line once violated.

In the higher levels of Lameco Eskrima, everything works on this concept of less being more. For example, a basic technique is one that works well albeit on a very rudimentary level. An advanced technique is nothing more than that same basic technique reduced to greater simplicity in an effort to minimize risk as it maximizes gain. The advanced technique remains a basic concept in theory but, being heavily governed by the laws of economy of motion, it results in a more effective outcome achieved with less mechanical intervention. Simply put, it is the shortest route between the point of perception and the point of contact. Less risk results in greater gain. The simpler the approach, the more successful the outcome; the more complex the approach, the greater the chance of compromise and eventual failure.

By definition, the line of engagement is an invisible line, which evenly separates you from your opponent at all times. This line constantly changes while the fight moves freely around the field of battle, requiring constant monitoring and adjustment if the line is to be properly maintained. If maintained correctly, the line of engagement should always leave you just outside of your opponent's reach. This requires you to only move inches forward in order to be able to attack your opponent, or move only inches backward to get just outside of his reach again. The longest reaching weapon of either opponent establishes the line of engagement. If this line is not constantly monitored and maintained, you may find yourself either too far from your opponent to take advantage of a fleeting opportunity when it is revealed, or else too close, thereby leaving yourself vulnerable to his deadly intent whenever he chooses to impose his will on you.

You should develop a sense or feel for this line at all times, but only through countless hours of practice, where you are held accountable for your actions, will you be able to accomplish this task. On a subconscious level, we must constantly monitor the distance between our opponent and ourselves for the duration of the fight. We must adapt and adjust to this line in our efforts to maintain proper fighting distance while the situation is allowed to naturally breathe and expand. Any time too much distance has separated you from your opponent, footwork is required to regain the line. This is a bad thing because, if you are forced to use excessive footwork just to get back to the line of engagement, you have already made mistakes due to not monitoring the line closely enough, to begin with. To reiterate: the greater the distance to be traversed, the greater the chance of compromise and eventual failure in combat. Less is more, with simplicity leading the way.

Once mastered, fully understood, and thoroughly commanded, the line of engagement can become your greatest ally. It allows you to always be right where you need to be for as long as you need to be there, and then it allows you to range back across the line of engagement, placing you just outside of your opponent's reach, while still leaving you in a position to counter attack with precision against any measurable threat. Again, advanced status in Lameco Eskrima is obtained only through utilizing less movement resulting in greater gain, not by "weighing down" or "complicating" the combative equation by adding more movements which can only be considered wasted motion. Simplicity in its purest state is the quickest route to success.

Lameco Eskrima Regarding Weapons of Opportunity

In Lameco Eskrima, not only do we find it important to identify weapons of opportunity, we attempt to get hands-on experience with all things, big and small, that can be found in our immediate environment and spend countless hours training with these things. One task Punong Guro Edgar G. Sulite set for us was to constantly control and monitor our personal space. Since a lot of people may not carry weapons on their persons, they need to get into the

Some Backyard Lameco Eskrima students of Dino Flores in Los Angeles training hard with proper training gear.

habit of casually scanning their environment for weapons of opportunity with which they can defend themselves should they find themselves accosted on the streets late one night while they are otherwise minding their own business.

Punong Guro Sulite would have us train with boards, axe handles, metal pipes, baseball bats, screw drivers, hammers, tennis racquets, brief cases, bandanas, belts, bottles, a shard of broken glass wrapped in a piece of cloth, ice picks, and numerous similar items. The reason for this was to always have access to a weapon should you require one in your time of need. Anything becomes a weapon when your mind makes it a weapon. Punong Guro Sulite always told us the Lameco Eskrima System was not a "knife" fighting system, or a "stick" fighting system or a "sword" fighting system, but rather a "fighting" system that could utilize anything you could lift from the ground and place in the human hand. Punong Guro Edgar G. Sulite spoke of you being the weapon and not the object which you held in your hand. Most people view a weapon as an extension of the hand; Punong Guro Sulite took it one step further. He felt that weapons are not so much an extension of the hand but rather an extension of the mind. He felt the real weapon was the mind, since it controls everything. To him, your hands, feet, elbows, and knees were all extensions of the mind, and anything that was in your hand was also, by default, an extension of the mind.

It is a different world when you are getting attacked with a knife, machete, or stick, and all you are armed with is a small rock or some other little object with which you must defend your life. Only by experiencing these things first hand will you be adequately prepared to deal with this reality, should it become your reality one day. Experience speaks with a loud, resounding voice and finds weakness or strength, advantage or disadvantage, where it was not obvious before. The only way to make these determinations regarding each probable weapon of opportunity is actual physical training with such objects, and the more time you spend exploring the

Punong Guro Edgar G. Sulite demonstrating knife techniques on his and the Authors student, Howard Chen at Santa Ana, California circa 1996.

advantages and disadvantages of each one, the more you will fully come to understand and appreciate what can be relied upon and what cannot be relied upon in your time of need.

It is better to gain these insights while in your training environment, not being held to realistic consequences, as you would be on the street using them for real, but, at that time, you will not have the opportunity to improve upon your mistakes. I trained with a lot of different common items under Punong Guro Sulite. On his advice, I would train with items I found in my immediate environment at work, at home, or anywhere else I spent time. Also, he would make me scan my immediate environment in an effort to recognize the weapon-potential of anything found within my grasp, should I need to obtain it to defend my life.

In some of the photo sequences, you may notice I am using a fireplace poker and a fireplace shovel to demonstrate this aspect of our training. The reality is I actually do train with these items for real at my home in case I am surprised there and not able to access my other weapons. I have to say that the fire place poker is quite a weapon and can be used to create numerous difficulties for a would-be attacker. It really feels good in the hand as well as being extremely effective on impact. In addition, I spend a lot of time training with loose boards I picked up from the yard of my home, as well as screw drivers, chisels, hammers, ink pens, and an axe for splitting firewood. All these make nice weapons of opportunity. Be creative, and see what you have lying about your home or workplace, and then, more importantly, train with these items.

Lameco Eskrima Regarding Training Safely

Punong Guro Edgar G. Sulite always spoke of training with intention and of allowing one's training to brush up as close as possible to reality, but he was also concerned about safety when training at more advanced levels. He felt the better your training gear, the harder you could push your training without concern of harm or injury, remaining able to adjust to real-time speed and power while being held strictly accountable for all your combat decisions by being made to face all the consequences associated with those decisions.

As discussed in a previous chapter, Punong Guro Edgar G. Sulite was inspired to develop the concept of the hand protector and forearm guard in Ozamis City, Mindanao, Philippines after proposing a friendly fight with Mang Eric Olavides in De Campo 1-2-3 Orehenal. This resulted in Edgar pulling off his sandals and wrapping one around his wrist and forming the other to cover the outside of his fist, tying both securely in place, to offer some protection from strikes thrown at those targets.

Punong Guro Edgar G. Sulite later took this idea and improved upon it by creating his Lameco forearm protectors and Lameco hand guards, as we know them today. These allowed us, his students, to really push ourselves, to align our training model with reality by permitting strikes thrown with full intention, speed, and power without having to be overly concerned about getting injured.

During an interview given years ago, Punong Guro Sulite shared his thoughts on using protective training gear: "I wanted to preserve the ancient teachings, but bleeding knuckles, and forearms, and bumps on the top of the head, are not a good way because there is no safety. So, a good compromise is using safety equipment. As the student becomes more proficient, he can slowly remove the safety equipment a little at a time, so he can wean himself from the training gear and face real consequences for his actions in training." By the time a student reaches the advanced levels, his movements have become proficient enough for him to rely on his ability to perceive and react to his opponent's strikes.

Shown are two early versions of the Lameco Eskrima Hand Protector with one of the early Lameco Eskrima Logos from the mid 80's belonging to long time Kalis Ilustrisimo, Bakbakan and Lameco Eskrima Student, Doran Sordo in Metro Manila Philippines.

Punong Guro Sulite also had us wear headgear, so we could, not only spar with full intention, speed, and power, but also test and verify our ability to block or deflect strikes thrown on our position in real-time speed; and, if we were unsuccessful in our attempts to do either, then the headgear protected us. Thanks to headgear, the training partner need not hold back and would deliver each strike with full speed and power as he did not have to worry about hurting his training partner.

What I have written above are but a few of the more important attributes and necessary components of training which Punong Guro Edgar G. Sulite felt were important to the Lameco Eskrima System. There were many more, and our curriculum is full of such things in dire need of being addressed and developed, one after another, in one's training environment in order to reach proficiency. At least, what is written above gives some idea of a few of the more important training aspects and the mindset which must be adopted and developed in order to accommodate such training.

Lameco Eskrima Regarding Established Training Goals

I can see no more fitting way to end my contributed chapter to this book than by quoting Punong Guro Edgar G. Sulite himself. The following is what Edgar wrote regarding the proper goals to be established and met in training the Lameco Eskrima System.

"It is my true goal, and the goal of the Lameco Eskrima International Association, to promote goodwill to mankind throughout the world. Regardless of race, nationality, and language, all must be treated equally in order to encourage brotherhood, not only in the Filipino Martial Arts, but all other martial arts as well.

"Pride and the feeling of superiority over another has no place in the heart of a true Lameco Eskrima practitioner, nor does the feeling of inferiority.

"A true Lameco Eskrima practitioner must be humble, courteous, helpful, kind, and polite. A true Lameco Eskrima practitioner does not criticize the people, systems, and styles of other martial arts schools.

"A person who does not have the above qualities does not have a place in the Lameco Eskrima Brotherhood.

"As the leader of this prestigious association, any and all good or bad actions done by my students reflect upon me. If you do something that will either uplift or mar the Association, it will reflect on me as your head instructor and on the whole Lameco Eskrima International Association as well.

"A question which you need to ask of yourself daily: How do you represent the Association outside your class? Encourage your friend, and he will become your brother, so always dig up reasons to applaud, and never scratch around for excuses to gossip. When you are tempted to

The Author holding photos of Punong Guro Edgar G. Sulite and Master Topher Ricketts to honor their memories at the 2nd Tribute Seminar in Los Angeles, California (2013).

criticize – bite your tongue. When you are moved to praise – shout from your rooftop. If you encourage this kind of character within yourself, then you will be making friends, not enemies.

"If you honestly feel you do not have this kind of character yet, go home and swing your garote for twenty-four hours a day, until you become a refined person whom the Lameco Eskrima International Association will be proud of." – *Punong Guro Edgar G. Sulite (1995)*

Dino Flores — Lameco Eskrima "SOG" Member (60LA)

Punong Guro Edgar G. Sulite being assisted by Dino Flores during a Lameco Eskrima Seminar in Orange, California at Mt. San Antonio College circa 1995.

Being a student of Punong Guro Edgar Sulite elevated me to a new level of understanding the Warrior Arts. More importantly, my experience with him set my whole path in a new and positive direction. Punong Guro's teaching method expanded my skill and ability to analyze, compare/contrast, test and experiment. To this day, his method of dissecting an idea and studying it further by using progressions is still one of my most effective learning tools. These elements have proven to be just as important for me as memorizing terminology, drills, and techniques. Regarding the delivery of a technique – his lessons on intensity, focus, intention, function, and honest combativeness will always be a part of the equation. Punong Guro's teachings will always be reflected in my approach to the Warrior Arts.

When Punong Guro put the Los Angeles Backyard Group together, his original intention was to create a group based on what he had experienced with his training partners in Manila. He missed the close friendships and brotherhood. He wanted an environment where you could train among friends with no concern for politics or ill intention, a place where he could share combat secrets reserved for the few, somewhere he could experiment with theories and test them through various levels of sparring with no concern for trophies. Punong Guro wanted a refuge where he could once again train out of pure passion because his tireless seminar schedule and the business side of things were starting to take its toll on his love for the art. Forming a dedicated and passionate group that respected the old ways of learning was his solution.

After the creation of the group, several "disagreements" with outsiders led to a number of not so friendly challenges. These situations focused the Backyard Group in an even more combative direction. Sparring took center stage. This was fine with me as, at the time when Punong Guro asked me if I wanted to teach, I told him I only wanted to learn to fight using our system in the most textbook manner possible. In my mind at the time, I was planning to just be his student forever. My love was the love of learning. Thus, his primary focus with me became increasing my ability to accept a challenge and win. It was very important for Punong Guro to bring the group to a level where we could accept a real fight challenge with minimal concern about us losing. It was a tall order, but as far as we were concerned at the time, we had the rest of our lives to achieve it. Punong Guro wanted us to be able to defend the system and do so without getting hurt. Our focus was on real function over theories and fancy drills.

Dino Flores with punta-y-daga

My first day in the Backyard, I was first required to fight my senior, Mar Elepano, full-blast with no holding back. This set the tone for the group the entire time. Sparring was done with all manner of weapons in the Lameco arsenal, be it single stick, double stick, knife, or empty hands. Sometime we sparred with padded sticks, and sometime we sparred with live sticks. Frequently, it was one-on-one; however, we also sparred against multiple opponents. The degrees of intensity also varied widely, from the finese of hand sparring to taking someone down hard on concrete and continuing from there. For the most part punches, elbows, kicks,

Punong Guro Edgar G. Sulite demonstrating a technique on Dino Flores circa 1996.

Dino Flores demonstrating Ilustrisimo Double Blade work in Los Angeles, California (2013)

knees, takedowns, and grappling were permitted. More often than not, it was intense, and more than once I remember people going over the fence or getting slammed into the garage door and other objects. Injuries were frequent, but this was still our idea of fun.

The roots of the sparring concepts were developed through trial and error in the Philippines. Punong Guro Sulite, Master Christopher Ricketts, Master Rey Galang, Master Yuli Romo, and Master Tony Diego developed a method of sparring training. Innovations included the creation of the forearm guard, hand armor, and the invention of the now popular "hand sparring" method. The original group in the Philippines initially started sparring with live stick but found out the injuries took too long to heal and detracted from training. They needed to keep up the realism without injuring each other too much. They wanted to maintain respect for the weapon, which they felt was being lost in many of the tournaments of the time.

Another aspect of training in the Backyard was the video tapes. Punong Guro would have us analyze our own fights as well those of possible opponents. This was another powerful tool for learning that Punong Guro and his training partners in the Philippines took seriously. When I first trained with Master Christopher Ricketts in the Philippines, almost immediately upon entering the door, he made me spar two of his seniors, Dodong Sta. Iglesia and Boy Garcia – both tough and experienced pro fighters. Having to spar seniors reminded me of my first day in the Lameco Backyard. Because I was at Master Ricketts' to learn, I thought I would act like a new fighter, so I wouldn't possibly offend anyone and thereby affect the lessons I was seeking. After the fights, Master Ricketts told me, "I know you are holding back. You do not usually fight like that. I have watched many fights of yours that your Punong Guro has sent me on VHS. Do not hold back!" I was totally busted. Apparently, even though they lived in other countries, they were still sharing and analyzing fight tapes, to come up with fight solutions. When we had challenges from other systems, Punong Guro would give me tapes of those systems for me to study. Although there was a deep and reverent respect for the old ways and traditions, they were not adverse to technology and innovation in the art.

In the United States, the sparring method evolved to suit the environment. There was a greater possibility of lawsuits due to injury in the United States as compared to the Philippines. So, this was taken into account. Additionally, it was the early 1990s, and most of the group started to have a deeper knowledge of grappling and Muay Thai and the possibility of an opponent using these arts. So, we found counter techniques that already existed in our arsenal. These factors and more contributed to the growth of the training method.

The group consisted of a wide variety of ages, skill levels, experiences, backgrounds, and personalities. As well as fighting each other, we always had visitors from the Lameco International organization and elsewhere. Naturally, we had to spar them as well. Each and every one of my fights was an education. There are certain sparring memories that stick to my mind from those days. I recall sparring Arnold Noche, who was left-handed, which required me to change my usual strategies. Hans Tan was very clever and analytical. Bud Balani did not like to retreat and always went for the kill. Fighting Steve Tarani was like facing a much taller version of myself. Dave Gould was very clinical in his approach. M'ang Leo Revilles was one of my favorites, with his superb timing and elegant movements. Fighting Mar Elepano was like fighting a "Lameco Machine." Ron Balicki was versatile and quick. Briant Emerson was very

Punong Guro Edgar G. Sulite demonstrating a technique on Dino Flores circa 1995.

determined and strong. Roger Agbulos was light on his feet. Sung Han Kim was adaptable and persistent.

Choy Flores moved like an athlete with a quick temper. Eric Koh methodically stalked his opponent like an assassin, while Bong Hebia had unhindered raw power. Naturally, however, the most profound lessons I ever obtained during this period came from sparring Punong Guro Sulite himself. Each and every attack and defense he implemented spoke volumes to me. I will never forget them and rarely share the secrets that were revealed as per his request… These are a few memories of sparring in the Lameco Backyard.

In retrospect, I can say that the whole experience was of accelerated growth. Looking back at videos, my personal style evolved from an aggressive and instinctive energy to one that was more refined and precise. I came out a different person from the one who entered. This was all due to Punong Guro Sulite's guidance, as well as the teachers he would send me to. To this day, I am still on the path of growth that began when I entered the Lameco Backyard.

Our teacher, Punong Guro Sulite was a person of remarkable long-term vision. As the groups fighting ability moved forward, he was already planning the next phase of our training. He truly wanted what was best for us. He was setting-up training for us with his teacher Grandmaster Ilustrisimo himself. As well, he wanted us to train with his fellow Five Pillars of Ilustrisimo, namely Grandmaster Christopher Ricketts, Grandmaster Rey Galang, Grandmaster Yuli Romo, and Grandmaster Tony Diego. He also mentioned that, if I ever had the chance, I should train with Professor Olavides of Eskrima De Campo, although, he added, this would be highly unlikely since the Professor was very secretive and did not teach the public. Now that some years have passed, I have a better understanding of his intentions. I did not embrace them at the time, as I was already overwhelmed by Punong Guro's incredible level of knowledge. In my

Dino Flores demonstrating the Ilustrisimo Blade with Alex Garduno in Morelos, Mexico (2012).

Punong Guro Edgar G. Sulite demonstrating a technique on Dino Flores circa 1995.

twenty-something mind, I was content with his deep well of wisdom. I felt there was no way I could truly absorb and master all his lessons, let alone train with other icons of the art. I thought I was going to be his student and train under him until I was old and gray.

Punong Guro Sulite was in love with the Philippine Warrior Arts. He was very attentive and respectful of the proper form and function of the fundamental and original movements as taught to him. From my first day to my last day of training with them, we always began with the basic foundations. He wanted them ingrained within us, and, now more than ever, I understand why. He had concluded that real fighting must be kept as simple as permissible. Focusing too much on looking good during training could get you hurt in a real-life situation.

The lessons my teacher shared with me guide me to this day. Thus, one of my objectives is to do my part in preserving his legacy in an honorable and respectful manner. Additionally, I do my best to pass these treasures on to a small but dedicated next generation, in the way it was taught to me. In this mission, I am fortunate to be working with my brothers from the Original Lameco Backyard Group, select members of the extended family lineage, and the various teachers Punong Guro Sulite sent me to.

More about Guro Dino Flores

A glimpse into Guro Dino's family tree finds a lineage as diverse as the Philippines itself. His ancestors ranged from Katipuneros in Bicol serving under General Simeón Ola y Arboleda, the last General to surrender to American forces during the Philippine-American War; "Tulisan" in Luzon who never surrendered; Datus in Tanawan Batangas; Traditional Healers using methods such as Orasyon and Anting-Anting in Laguna; Filipino-Spanish Hacienda owners who migrated from Seville, Spain via the Visayas to settle at the foot of Mayon Volcano in the early 1900s; World War Two American Colonial Army officers fighting under General Douglas Macarthur in Bataan and Corregidor who survived the infamous "death march," as well as University Scholars in the 1970s, reluctantly leaving the country to escape martial law.

Guro Dino was first introduced to the concept of "Arnis" and Philippine Warrior history by his father Dr. A. S. Flores in the mid-1970s. This was done through the oral tradition, classic Pilipino Komiks, and hard-to-find publications during martial law. His first exposure to physical training was in the early 1980s in Laguna Province, Philippines. Older relatives and neighbors in family ancestral lands of many generations introduced him, in backyard sessions, to basic street applications and the strategy of the balisong blade during his stays in the Philippines.

Cousins, Ariel Flores Mosses and Dino Flores.

Guro Dino trained for several years with Grandmaster Conrad A. Manaois in Ninoy Cinco Teros Arnis and Master Henry Bio in Sikaran Arnis in the 1980s along with his cousins Ariel Flores Mosses and Choy Flores. In the early 1990s, he was accepted as an initial member of Punong Guro Edgar Sulite's newly forming Backyard Group, a.k.a the Sulite Orehenal Group. At the strong request of Punong Guro Sulite, Guro Dino first visited Grandmaster Christopher Ricketts in the Philippines in 1995 and was introduced to his perspective on the Warrior Arts. Since the passing of Punong Guro Sulite, he has continuously trained in Kali Ilustrisimo under Grandmaster Christopher Ricketts, who gave Guro Dino permission to teach his method in 2010. Guro Dino was the Lameco representative for Grandmaster Ricketts and a member of Bakbakan Philippines sponsored by Grandmaster Ricketts. Guro Dino continues in Grandmaster Ricketts' method of training along with the Grandmaster's two sons, young Masters Bruce and Brandon Ricketts. Additionally, at the Grandmaster's suggestion before his passing, Guro Dino also continues his studies in Kalis Ilustrisimo under Grandmaster Antonio Diego. In 2013, Guro Dino was honored with certification to teach by Grandmaster Antonio Diego.

In addition, Guro Dino had the good fortune to experience training in Kali Ilustrisimo with Dodong Sta. Iglesia, Arnold Narzo, Peachie Baron, Grandmaster Rey Galang, and Grandmaster Yuli Romo. He also trained in Kali Ilustrisimo with one of his training partners and fellow Lameco Backyard member Guro Hans Tan, who was also certified to teach Kali Ilustrisimo under Grandmaster Tony Diego. What's more, Guro Dino trained privately for several years in California and the Philippines with Professor Ireneo L. Olavides in Eskrima De Campo JDC-IO. Guro Dino also cites the importance in his growth of his training partners in Lameco SOG and Kapisanang Mandirigma.

One of Guro Dino's primary objectives is to honorably preserve what he has learned from his teachers. More information can be found at: http//backyardeskrima.com and http//mandirigma.org

Arnold A. Noche — Lameco Eskrima "SOG" Member (62LA)

On a professional side, Arnold A. Noche is a seasoned information-technology leader with a substantial business in consulting, implementation, and project management, working with various Fortune 1000 companies and government agencies in mapping people, process, and technology with best-of-breed, best-of-class, state-of-the-art solutions in mission-critical environments throughout six countries.

Arnold A. Noche in the bukas fighting position with his blade drawn and at the ready.

On a personal side, Arnold is one of the remaining survivors of Lameco SOG under the late Punong Guro Edgar G. Sulite of Lameco Eskrima International and a descendant of General Pantaleon Garcia, one of the trusted Cavitenyos appointed by General Emilio Aguinaldo as commanding general of all Filipino forces in Central Luzon during the time of the Katipunan and the Revolution.

An "economic mercenary" who considers himself a member of the "warrior" class, he was last seen floating around Houston, Texas, working with a small energy company, and he took time out to reminisce.

I have been involved with the martial arts since I was eight years old. That was back in 1974. My first exposure to ancient traditional arts from the Philippines came about in 1978, through my eldest cousin on my father's side of the family Kuya Roland M. Noche was part of the fourth or fifth wave of immigrants, coming to the US with his parents and two younger brothers and temporarily residing in Los Angeles, California prior to relocating to Stockton, California. Though I continued to dabble in other traditional martial art disciplines, I have always felt a connection with the ancient arts from the Philippines and continued to seek it

Arnold A. Noche and Punong Guro Edgar G. Sulite eating after training.

out in whatever shape or form that was available throughout my years in junior high school, high school, and college.

I met Punong Guro Edgar G. Sulite from Lameco Eskrima for the first time on November 14, 1992 at Master Ner Reodica's Laban Tulisan Seminar in Oxnard, California, which was put together by the Ventura County Eskrima Group. On June 18, 1993, the City of Los Angeles, along with FilAm ARTS, honored the Living Treasures of the Filipino Martial Arts by putting together a presentation at downtown City Hall in collaboration with the Kali Association of America, whom I was currently under while studying the Villabrille-Largusa Kali System with Professor Greg Lontayao and Guro Al Galius. Although Punong Guro was out of town that weekend conducting a seminar in some part of the world, I was fortunate to have met three key individuals who would later become my colleagues in the infamous "backyard" group: Guro Lowell Pueblos, Hospecio "Bud" Balani, Jr., and Roger Agbulos. A week later, at Guro Lowell's residence in Glendale, California, I met Elmer "Bong" Hebia, Rem V. Cruz, and Jason Ancheta. I still remember Guro Lowell explaining to me that, though many individuals wanted to train, very few individuals will allow themselves to be trained. Roger was instrumental in finding an additional place to train on Monday and Wednesday evenings at Grandmaster Conrad Manaois' school in Hollywood, California; and this is where I would later meet Hans Anton Tan, Venicio "Choy" Flores, Arturo "Dino" Flores, and the rest is pure history.

I saw Punong Guro for the last time on March 9, 1997 at his residence in Palmdale, California prior to his departure for Manila, Philippines on March 11 to participate in 1997 Masters Tour. This special event, which was to be held from March 12 to March 26, was a rare opportunity for individuals to train with the original colleagues, masters, and grandmasters under whom Punong Guro started his journey: Grandmaster Jesus Abella, Grandmaster Pablicito Cabahug, Grandmaster Benjamin Luna Lema, Grandmaster Antonio "Tatang" Ilustrisimo, Grandmaster Ireneo Olavides, Grandmaster Helacrio Sulite, Sr., Master Antonio Diego, Master Christopher Ricketts, Master Helacrio Sulite, Jr., and Guro Benjamin S. Pueblos.

Since his untimely passing on April 10, 1997 at the young age of thirty-nine, I have been fortunate to have been able to continue my training in the various ranges of combat Lameco Eskrima is known for:

- Long Range – Eskrima de Campo through Professor Ireneo L. Olavides
- Medium Range – Bakbakan Kali Ilustrisimo through Master Reynaldo S. Galang and Kali Ilustrisimo through Master Christopher N. Ricketts

- Close Range – Teovel Balintawak Arnis through Master Nonato "Nene" Gaabucayan

General Pantaleon Garcia.

Though I never met Master Antonio Diego personally, I was able to further supplement my training in Kalis Ilustrisimo through Guro Hans Anton Tan.

I have three rules: I never walk into a place I don't know how to get out of, I'm not interested in things that don't concern me, and, three, I always finish what I started, and, if I can't, I'll bury it so deep, it will become a figment of your imagination. These rules, which I developed over time in my martial arts training, have helped me greatly in everyday life, as I continue to satisfy my personal, financial, and creative needs.

I lost my father, Orlando L. Noche, in April 1995, my grandfather, Atty. Pio S. Noche in October 1995, my teacher, Punong Guro Edgar G. Sulite in April 1997, and his teacher, Grandmaster Antonio "Tatang" Ilustrisimo, in October 1997.

It was quite painful, and there is only so much one can take. I could have easily buried this traditional art form, at that time, and pretend that it never existed, or perhaps take the commercial route. I chose none of these. Instead, I grounded myself in the Filipino American community for the benefit of the Filipino American community – to nurture leaders who would make my job easier as I got older by helping continue to support, develop, and propagate this ancient traditional art form of the Philippines, in an effort to keep it alive with integrity for future generations.

This traditional art form has kept me out of trouble by keeping me balanced and focused in everything I do. From my rise and fall in Corporate America, to struggling to build my own company, I have learned to be humble, accept humility, and to be grateful for the little things that I have, instead of being the powerful executive I once was. It has provided me with constant direction and a stable foundation in a world of change. It has also brought me closer to my "roots," while trying to understand the complexities of being Filipino American.

Though things sometimes just don't happen fast enough for me, I have no complaints, looking back over the past sixteen years since 1997. And, quoting a good friend, Grandmaster Bobby Taboada from Balintawak Eskrima Cuentada out of Charlotte, North Carolina: "Martial arts most powerful and enduring legacy is the bond of friendship."

This traditional art form is one of the rare treasures left which links us to a past we can be highly proud of. It is a true Filipino activity which deserves the support of our people, not only for its preservation, but also for its continued propagation and development. Like other self-defense techniques, this is both an art and a science that must be studied and learned not solely for its practical values. One cannot be an expert unless he or she undergoes a daily regimen of rigid physical and mental exercises that test one's mettle and strength as it develops in him or her positive character traits.

Of the eighty-eight registered members of the Los Angeles Chapter of Lameco Eskrima International, I am probably one of the few, if not the only, left-handed practitioner of Lameco Eskrima. There was a time when I would do everything right-handed, in an effort to perform the techniques correctly and to try to keep up with everyone in the backyard, but, when it came down to fighting, I would switch hands and do everything left-handed. I guess you could say that I practiced right-handed, taught right-handed, but fought left-handed. Though I have developed my right hand to be stronger than most people's left hand, Punong Guro insisted that I stick with the left hand and just have everyone work around me.

With that said, I still teach public and private classes and seminars with my left hand. I teach primarily with my left hand and will only switch to my right hand when absolutely necessary. I face the class and instruct them to follow me as in a mirror (i.e., salamin) from head-to-toe. Even my fighting position is reversed. Come to think of it, I've only had a total of four left-handed students since 1999, with the rest of them being right-handed.

This traditional art form offers a broad range of educational services, whether it be physical, mental, or spiritual, which aim to allow all people in our cultural community to take advantage of understanding one aspect of their culture through the ancient arts of the Philippines, which, in turn, serve as a vessel carrying understanding of their roots and identity as Filipino/Filipina persons.

Quoting Punong Guro: "A person must have LAMECO goals in life. LA for long-range plans establishing and targeting future goals. ME for medium-range plans that assess and prepare for the goals of the near future. And CO for close-range plans and actions that meet intermediate needs. Set your LAMECO goal, visualize it, dream it, plan it, and work on it. Once you have reached your goal, your success is not the end of your vision but merely the stepping stone to your next goal, for the next higher level. A person without LAMECO goals is like a ship sailing in the vast ocean with neither direction nor destination."

Quoting my teacher's teacher, the late Grandmaster Antonio "Tatang" Ilustrisimo: "There is no unexpected attack, only an unaware and unprepared warrior."

Very few traditional art forms combine so many elements in such a short amount of time.

- Alertness and Awareness
- Confidence
- Coordination and Concentration
- Determination
- Focus
- Proper Delivery of Strikes
- Speed
- Stamina and Endurance
- Technique
- Timing

Some of the hardest fights I fought were in the backyard, perhaps due to the fact that we all had the same foundation, system, and teacher. We had all the personalities in the backyard, and they were all strong. When I took it outside, I was well-prepared.

I've come to realize that it's not about how well you fight when everything is going right, but how well you react when everything is going wrong.

Being left-handed, I had to focus more on offense rather than defense, and I never saved anything for my second strike. I've also come to realize there is a fine line between being coordinated and being combative.

Arnold A. Noche and Master Christopher Ricketts.

Lameco Eskrima was a combative system, and the backyard group was a fighting school.

And, quoting another teacher, the late Grandmaster Christopher "Topher" Ricketts: "I will never hesitate, not even for a minute, to settle things like Eskrimadors if you refuse to settle things like gentlemen."

When Punong Guro Edgar G. Sulite of Lameco Eskrima passed away in 1997, he left behind his wife Felisa, two sons – Edgar Jr., and Edgar Andrew – and three daughters: me, Glady Lea, and Leslie Grace. He also left behind Lameco Eskrima International, an organization of over 2000 members both here and abroad, which was broken up into Clubs, Chapters and Affiliates throughout Australia, Canada, Germany, Philippines, and USA – California, Illinois, Indiana, Maryland, New Jersey, Michigan, New Mexico, Ohio, Oregon, Pennsylvania, Texas, Washington, D.C, and Virginia.

Punong Guro did all this on his own during the analog age and long before the days of electronic mail, internet, social media marketing, and social networking... simple things that we now take for granted in the digital age.

Some things have not changed, though. I have learned in my constant travels that there are teachers, fighters, and those who are a combination of the two. Some of the best teachers don't know how to fight. Some of the best fighters don't know how to teach. Rarely, you will find those exceptional individuals who can do a combination of the two, but even that can get exhausting at times. One day you want to teach, and then the next day you want to fight. And so the cycle continues. Anyway, the latter are exceptional individuals, and those are who you want in your network. The backyard group was Punong Guro's core group. We were his infrastructure. We were his support structure.

In all sincere honesty, I think Punong Guro was grooming the backyard group to help him to continue the support, preservation, and propagation of Lameco Eskrima. We were also being groomed to help him continue the expansion, cultivation, and development of Lameco

Arnold A. Noche and Dino Flores training Ilustrisimo Blade.

Eskrima International. Perhaps, one day, to even have groups of our own while continuing to maintain the high standard, high integrity, and fraternal spirit he had established and nurtured within the organization. It was definitely an accelerated growth process. We had already been assisting him in his various projects pertaining to print, video, and web. It was just a matter of time until we were exposed to the masses.

In 1998, a few of my colleagues from Lameco SOG and I formed Kapisanang Mandirigma (i.e. Federation of Warriors) and took it upon ourselves to continue the support, development, and propagation of the Warrior Arts of the Philippines, in an effort to keep them alive with integrity for future generations. Though we did not expect to do it all, we just wanted to do our part or, at least, meet like-minded organizations and people halfway. It has been an interesting ride so far…

Kapisanang Mandirigma is not a style, nor a representation of any singular style, but rather a federation of practitioners with similar goals, a vehicle to provide for growth and personal discovery through continued training in a combat realistic, non-commercial, and non-political environment. Founded in 1998 by Guro Hospecio "Bud" Balani, Jr., Guro Arturo "Dino" Flores, Guro Arnold A. Noche, and Guro Hans Anton Tan from Lameco SOG (Sulite Orihinal Group), this unique federation has an ever-growing but extremely selective membership representing numerous progressive fighting styles. The ideas is that interchange between the diverse styles and dedicated members creates a dynamic foundation for continuously improving the Warrior Arts of the Philippines.

Kali Klub, an award-winning project of Kapisanang Mandirigma, initially started as a positive diversion against drugs and gangs for youths in the Temple-Beverly corridor, now known as Historic Filipinotown. Since our inception in 1999, we have expanded to teaching children (ages five-twelve), youths (ages thirteen-seventeen), adults (ages eighteen and over), and elders (ages forty and over) the Warrior Arts of the Philippines in a non-commercial, non-political, combat-realistic environment where art, culture, and heritage are integrated into our curriculum.

It is important to note that I am still extremely selective about who I choose to take under my wing, as I do not commercially teach this traditional art form. My involvement with the Kali Klub was merely a vehicle for the community to get to know me, if they had not already known me on a personal or social level, and to get a taste of what I've endured that led me to where I am today. Outside of the Kali Klub, I have participated in demonstrations, presented lectures, and taught seminars at colleges and universities both here and abroad… all for the promotion of this traditional art form.

For the late Punong Guro Edgar G. Sulite of Lameco Eskrima, it was never about him but solely for the Filipino Martial Arts itself. He always gave credit where credit was due. If he couldn't promote the Filipino Martial Arts, he would promote his teachers and his teachers' teachers, and did so with passion. He was blessed to have learned from so many prominent grandmasters and masters, whom he would acknowledge by stating all martial arts were good, and it was truly the individuals that made them superior. It was through him I realized there were probably more similarities than there were differences.

I would like to see Lameco Eskrima become a household name in all of its combative essence and glory. Though I would not want to see it get commercialized, I would like to see the awareness level increase for both practitioners and non-practitioners, Filipinos and non-Filipinos – that it does exist, that it's very much alive and well, and that it's fully understood by only a selected few.

This traditional art form is a complete martial art that is basically a product of Filipino creativity, and there is no doubt whatsoever it is Filipino. Banned for nearly four hundred years, it is a complete system of self-defense techniques which utilizes Filipino weaponry as extensions of the hands for maximum impact and reach.

What makes this traditional art form unique is that it begins its training with the use of weaponry and then progresses to empty-hand techniques. The training does not regress, since it is believed that proficiency in weaponry first will mean perfection in empty hand techniques later.

It was greatly developed and refined, and the evolution still continues…

"The ancient Filipinos had army and navy with artillery and other implements of warfare. Their prized krises and kampilans, for their magnificent temper, are worthy of admiration, and some of them are richly damascened. Their coats of mail and helmets, of which there are specimens in various European museums, attest to their great achievement in this industry."
–Jose P. Mercado Rizal (1861-1896)

Lameco Eskrima is a dynamic system of martial arts representing some of the best of the Warrior Arts of the Philippines. It acts as the focal point or vortex of these proven and effective arts of defense, harnessing and combining their individual strength and power, creating a dynamic system of combat, both armed and unarmed.

Lameco Eskrima is a composition of five major systems and six minor systems from the Philippines and is a perfectly-balanced synthesis of the many effective teachings and styles which the late Punong Guro Edgar G. Sulite had come to master in the span of his life.

There are some systems which specialize in long range fighting (Largo), while others specialize in medium range fighting (Medio), and still others which specialize in close range fighting

(Corto). An acronym was made from these three ranges of combat in order to name Lameco Eskrima.

What separates Lameco Eskrima from all other contemporary systems is its emphasis on the totality of the human being – mind, body, and spirit – not just the physical elements alone. Attention, Intention, Visualization, and Complete Focus are the integral components of the Lameco System.

I have come to realize that, if you want to be the best, you have to train like the best. Training is measured not by the quantity of your training but by the quality of your training. You have to train both harder and smarter. You have to create both the intensity and the drive. How much is entirely up to you. What works for one individual may not work for another. But you have to keep working on it.

Lameco SOG (Sulite Orihinal Group) trained like the best in Lameco Eskrima, and I am forever grateful to have had experienced this as an integral part of my journey.

"Life is a journey, not a destination." –*Ralph Waldo Emerson (1803 - 1882)*

Gary Quan — Lameco Eskrima "SOG" Member (77LA)

I first learned about Lameco Eskrima and Punong Guro Edgar Sulite through my good friend and training partner Phil Rapagna. Phil was training privately with Punong Guro, and he would often rave to me about his Punong Guro's skills and training methods. At that time, I was training FMA under Guro Dan Inosanto, and it was at the Inosanto Academy where I got to first experience a few classes with Punong Guro. I really enjoyed those classes and hoped to train with him again.

Gary Quan with his Lameco "SOG" Brothers in the back ground, Bong Hebia, Dino Flores, the Author, Steve Grody and Hospecio "Bud" Balami at Los Angeles, California (2013)

A few months later, Phil called me and told me that Punong Guro was going to be holding classes in Altadena and asked if I was interested in training with him. I told him for sure I was interested. And through Phil I was accepted as a LAMECO student.

At my first LAMECO class, I remember being warmly greeted by Punong Guro. From then on, I was in Kali/Eskrima heaven. Even though I had previous training in FMA, I felt like I was a beginner again. I even had to relearn how to do my angle one and two strikes. Footwork was heavily emphasized in class. We always started classes with footwork drills, and I remember huffing and puffing after we were done. Also, the LAMECO stick progressions and drills were so well thought out.

One of the most important martial art lessons I learned from Punong Gruo was that, whenever we train, we must always strike with "INTENTION." I can still hear his voice in my head: "Gary, you must strike with INTENTION!" Even now I continue to apply that lesson to whatever martial art I am training in.

Classes eventually resumed back at Punong Guro's home in Glendale, and I was very honored to be invited to train with the "backyard" group. Unfortunately, I did not get

Gary Quan (center) with Ariel Flores Mosses and Dino Flores.

to train with him at his Palmdale home. The last time I spoke with Punong Guro was when he called me to invite me to train with him in Palmdale. I told him I would train with him after

Gary Quan relaxing in a chair while his "SOG" Brothers take the wall, Bong Hebia, Brandon Ricketts and Dino Flores at Los Angeles, California (2013).

he returns from the Philippines. Unfortunately, with great sadness, I would never get to train with Punong Guro again.

I am very thankful that I had the opportunity to train with Punong Guro Edgar. His teachings will always have a special place in my heart.

Pantaleon R. Revilles Jr. — Lameco Eskrima "SOG" Member (79LA)

"We just called him "Mang Leo," but his friends and family knew him best as "Mildo" back in Bohol, Philippines where he came from. Mang Leo was the eldest member of our backyard group, around the age of fifty when he joined us, I believe, in late 1994.

Mang Leo Revilles Jr. grew up on the Island of Bohol, Philippines in the vicinity of the Chocolate Mountains and trained under GM Momoy Canete in the San Miguel System. He also trained under GM Eulogio Canete in the Doce Pares System at their headquarters in neighboring Cebu. Also, M'ang Leo was the long-time training partner of Guro Arnulfo "Dong" Cuesta in the Doce Pares System during those early years.

Mang Pantaleon R. Revilles Jr. taken in the Authors Garage after training at Riverside, California circa 2001.

Mang Leo Revilles Jr. gained much respect from all of us in the backyard group, as he always gave one-hundred percent in everything he did and never complaining. He may have been limited somewhat by his age, but he more than made up for it in determination and persistence. Some of my fondest memories of Mang Leo were regarding his countless fights against a much younger Eric Koh. Eric would start out fast and hard but, within a short time, he would get winded and start to slow down for the remainder of the round. You would see Mang Leo weather the storm for the first minute of the fight, and, as Eric would begin to slow, or as PG Sulite would say: "No wind," then M'ang Leo would light into him with everything he had and would, for the most part, dominate the fight from that point forward. It was something to see, and, for whatever reason, PG Sulite always arranged for the two to fight at least once during our "fight Sundays," as well as having him fight with the rest of us periodically.

After PG Sulite passed away, Mang Leo, who lived close to me in Fontana, would come over to my house and train with me a couple of days a week in my Garage at Riverside, California. As well, M'ang Leo would come over to my house or meet me and Bong Hebia at PG Sulites' home in Palmdale, to help train "Don-don" Sulite in his father's system once a week, usually on Sundays. Don-don is the eldest son of PG Sulite.

Mang Leo and I trained a few times a week in the garage of my house, from 1997 to 2001, before he had taken ill and eventually passed away. I really greatly admired Mang Leo Revilles Jr., not just as one of my Lameco Eskrima "backyard" brothers, but as a person and a very good friend as well. M'ang Leo said something that really made me think about the value of life and the need to place things in proper perspective. Then in his late fifties, when asked if he felt old, he would reply: "I am young, only my knees are old." Or, "I am young, only my body is old." He would always consider himself to be a young man imprisoned in the body of an increasingly older man.

Mang Leo Revilles Jr. and the Author during Lameco Eskrima training at Riverside, California circa 1998.

Mang Leo Revilles Jr. said that he felt young, and that, in his mind, he could still run up and down the basketball court, and play all day long, like he could when he was a much younger man. However, his body told a different story. M'ang Leo said that, even though he was aging physically, in his mind he was still the same person he always was when he was younger, in accordance with the way he felt in his spirit, but, he said, when he looked in the mirror, he would see his grandfather's reflection looking back at him, and he could not understand how that happened, and where all of that time went.

This made me reflect on my own life, and how fleeting time is for all of us. I gleaned from his wisdom that we should live life to the fullest because, one day, if we all live long enough, we will start to see our own grandfather's reflection staring back at us when we glance in the mirror, and any plans to do things that may require a physical effort or conditioning may well be placed just beyond our reach. Time waits for no man, and, as we get older, it seems as if life speeds up, with weeks and months passing before our very eyes as if they were days. For, when we are old, regardless of how bad we may want to slow down life, it is all but impossible, as time moves at its own speed, and it moves us right along with it." –*David E. Gould.*

Below is what our Lameco "backyard" brother Dino Flores wrote in remembrance of M'ang Leo Revilles about his own reflections of him; and I quote:

"I first met Mang Leo in Punong Guro Sulites' Backyard Group. He had a previous background under Filemon "Momoy" Cañete in San Miguel Eskrima in Cebu, Philippines. I remember him being a true gentleman in the traditional sense. I admired his excellent manners, kindness, and humility.

Mang Leo was at least twenty years older than most of us. However, regardless of his many years of experience, he was open-minded and always eager to learn. Even though he was much older, he clearly treated us as seniors, since he joined the group a little later than most of us. Even with his advanced years, he was always excited to spar and mix it up with his much younger classmates.

I learned much from these encounters, and appreciated it more as I got older. What he lacked in power and stamina was made-up in timing, patience, and distancing. It was elegance in motion and wonderful to behold. Punong Guro taught us to appreciate text book applications of techniques in real-time. Mang Leo had a knack for them. At the time, I was young and full of bravado after doing well in a number of live stick fights. Mang Leo was great at bringing me down a notch or two. It pushed me to train even harder, and I appreciate him for that. I still see those moments in my mind's eye to this day.

After Punong Guro passed away, Mang Leo still thirsted to learn more and continued training with some of his classmates, such as myself and Dave Gould. After returning from one of his trips to the Philippines, he presented me with a pinute sword from Cebu. I was slightly confused and asked him why he was giving me such a fine gift. He said it was for taking the time to teach him after Punong Guro passed away. I was deeply touched and humbled. He tragically passed away soon after that day. The sword is one of my prized possessions. It sits on my wall along with swords I obtained from my Grandfather, Punong Guro Sulite, Grandmaster Ricketts, and various other ancestors. He is truly missed. I have not met another like him since" *Dino Flores.*

Below is what our Lameco "backyard" brother, Arnold A. Noche had to say in remembrance of Mang Leo Revilles; and I quote:

Mang Leo was the oldest member of the group and also the youngest at heart.

From what I remember, Mang Leo had very close ties with the Canete family in Cebu. He was also a training partner of Guro Arnulfo "Dong" Cuesta in the early days. I met Guro Dong out in Jersey City, New Jersey back in 2004, and he was saddened to hear that M'ang Leo had passed away. He, too, had fond memories of his former classmate in Doce Pares.

Aside from being the oldest member of the group and the youngest at heart, M'ang Leo was also the wisest, having lived the life of an eskrimador.

Mang Leo Revilles Jr. and the Author during Lameco Eskrima training at Riverside, California circa 1998.

Focusing solely on his individual training in the backyard, he held his ground with the best of them. He was already in his fifties, while most of us were in our twenties. He pretty much kept to himself but would not hesitate, not even for a minute, to share some of his lifelong experiences if you asked nicely. I should have asked more often, but, just like everyone else, we were all focused on our individual training at that time.

I honestly cannot remember the last time I saw M'ang Leo, but I am forever grateful for having him allow me to be a part of his journey"–*Arnold A. Noche*

Mang Pantaleon R. Revilles Jr. (1945–2001) rest in peace brother!!! Rest assured that you will continue to be missed and appreciated by all of your Lameco Eskrima "backyard" brothers, and you will always be thought of with much fondness as a deeply-respected member of our family.

Mang Leo Revilles Jr. and the Author after trainng Lameco Eskrima at Riverside, California circa 2001.

CHAPTER 10:

THE LAMECO ESKRIMA SYSTEM IN APPLICATION

Hospecio "Bud" Balani Jr. Photo Sequence

Hospecio "Bud" Balani Jr. and Johnathan Balani square off with their blades drawn and at the ready in the "bukas" (open) position.

JB initiates a high forehand strike against HBB who steps forward and intercepts with "panipis" which is an immediate counter strike meaning to "slice thinly", down the center line of JB.

HBB then continues to pass the blade of JB with "waslik" (throwing the hand) as he positions to counter to center.

As HBB clears center by fully passing the blade of JB he then begins his counter using "bagsak" which is a vertical strike along the centerline.

JB reacts by intercepting the attack with his safety hand and checks the weapon hand of HBB as he attempts to counter with "bagsak".

HBB reacts quickly to clear the obstruction with "patibong" (trapping) by pulling the safety hand of JB from his own weapon hand.

HBB then pulls the hand of JB forward in an attempt to imbalance him as he prepares to counter.

As HBB initiates his counter attack to the head, JB recognizes and counters the attempt by straightening his arm forward thereby jamming his forearm into the pathway of HBB as he attempts to counter, creating another obstruction.

HBB clears the obstruction with a technique known as "dukot" which allows him to drop the butt of his weapon allowing it to dip down and to the inside of JB which will allow him the opportunity to re-engage with a counter strike.

HBB then moves forward with the left leg as he breaches into close range and grabs for the back of the head of JB.

Hospecio "Bud" Balani Jr. forces the head of Johnathan Balani down driving him into the tip of his "pinute" to end the situation.

Steve Grody Photo Sequence

Application of Lameco Eskrima Drill #3

Steve Grody and Petar Sardelich square off with one another in the open position.

PS steps forward to strike, and SG drops back with Illustrisimo Retirada foot work while dropping his weight into his strike down to Petar's weapon hand.

As PS follows through with his strike, SG retracts his stick back and up while he prepares to advance forward.

Steve Grody advances forward and follows up with a circular strike (paikot) striking Petar Sardelich in the top of the head. Note that even though Steve is doing a strike early (before Petar's extension) that he is still moving back to the farthest distance from which he can strike.

Notes from Steve Grody regarding his photo sequences: Though I am illustrating "techniques" here, they are meaningless without the training process through which choices are made on the fly and fluidly changing from moment to moment. It is crucial that each individual works to "own" the material and know what he or she can do in real time.

Application of Lameco Eskrima Drill #3

Steve Grody and Petar Sardelich square off with one another in the open position.

SG feints a strike (enganyo) to PS to draw a counter-strike from him.

PS takes the bait and strikes for the hand. SG stops his feint short to allow the strike of PS to pass missing his hand.

Steve Grody then advances forward before Petar Sardelich can recover his missed strike and Steve hits him in the hand with a circular strike (paikot). The important points here are to fake with conviction but without moving in too close, and then to strike at the earliest point after his strike passes. Additionally, Steve has to take into account the reach of the opponent, which in this case is considerable.

Application of Lameco Eskrima Drill #9

Steve Grody and Petar Sardelich square off with one another in the open position.

PS steps forward with an attack and SG steps back and strikes horizontal (plansada) hitting his hand.

As the strike of PS follows its natural course SG pushes his counter strike through to the inside as he prepares to advance forward.

SG then advances forward as he initiates his counter strike to the head of PS before he can recover his center line.

Steve Grody then completes his counter with a circular strike (paikot) to the head of Petar Sardelich ending the situation.

Application of Lameco Eskrima Drill #9

Steve Grody and Petar Sardelich square off with one another in the open position with their knives drawn.

SG slashes horizontally at the wrist of PS who evades back in response to the attack.

PS then takes a step back and tries to cut down on the passed hand of SG who then "centers" his hand being evasive and not allowing his hand to be cut by PS.

Steve Grody then times the opportunity and follows through with an immediate downward circular cut (paikot) to the hand of Petar Sardelich in an effort to get to him first.

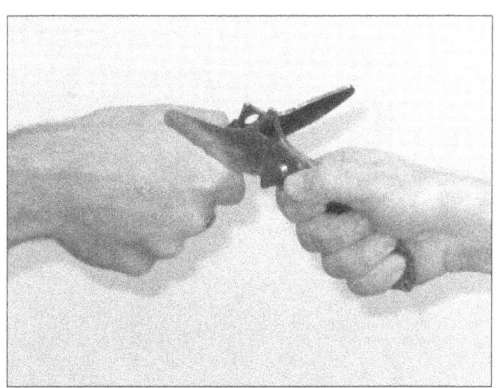

Close up of the cut to the hand. "Centering," is bringing the weapon back to the center for offense or defense (and not "over stroking"), it is a primary principle in Lameco. If Steve's cut traveled too far past the center, there is no way that he could beat Petar to the cut.

Application of Lameco Eskrima Drill #12 with "panipis"

Steve Grody with an axe handle and Petar Sardelich with a base-ball bat square off with one another in the open position.

PS initiates an attack at SG, who feels he's not quite far enough away to counter at "largo" (long range strike to the incoming hand while evading), so he intercepts the bat with his axe handle as he prepares for an immediate counter.

SG after intercepting and coming into contact with the bat then immediately slides (dalinas) his axe handle down the length of the bat and strikes the hand of PS which is also known as a "reverse sweep".

As the strike of PS follows its natural course SG retracts his axe handle back and up as he prepares to counter.

SG then advances forward as he initiates his counter toward the head of PS.

Steve Grody completes his counter striking Petar Sardelich on the top of his head with the axe handle ending the situation.

Application of Lameco Eskrima Drill #12

Steve Grody with an axe handle and Petar Sardelich with a base-ball bat square off with one another in the open position.

PS initiates an attack but telegraphs his intent as he winds up before striking as he leads with his elbow (the most common telegraph with two-handed bat-like weapons) which allows SG to capitalize by smashing the elbow of PS with a downward circular strike (paikot).

SG following through his strike forces the base-ball bat of PS downward

Seeing an opportunity SG steps forward as he initiates his counter strike towards the shoulder of PS.

Steve Grody completes his counter striking Petar Sardelich in the right collar bone with a high back hand strike.

Example of the Evasive Hand:

Steve Grody with a knife and Petar Sardelich with a baseball bat square off with one another in the open position. SG Counting on his opponent to be a regular knuckle-head and telegraph his strike so that he can evade the strike, SG leaves his hand out far enough to (hopefully) draw a strike to it

As designed PS takes the bait and swings for the awaiting hand of SG who quickly disengages under the bat to evade the strike.

Timing the opportunity perfectly as the base-ball bat follows its natural course SG advances forward and initiates his counter strike with the knife.

SG quickly cuts into the brachialis of PS

Continuing to press the counter attack forward SG traps the arm of PS as he moves in even closer still iniating his finishing strike.

Steve Grody completes his counter with a precise cut to the chest severing the pectoralis major in an effort to disable Petar Sardelich to end the situation.

David E. Gould Photo Sequence

David E. Gould and Michael Frazier square off with one another in the "bukas" (open) position.

MF throws a high forehand strike and DEG responds simultaneously with "panipis", which is an immediate counter strike meaning to "slice thinly", down the center line of MF.

DEG completes his narrow counter strike following it all the way down the center line of MF.

DEG then continues to push the weapon hand of MF until it has past his own centerline and simultaneously counters again with a vertical strike to the center mass of MF cutting deep into his head.

Then DEG continues the narrow vertical strike downward as he cuts the arm of MF in an attempt to keep him from coming back with a counter strike.

David E. Gould then closes distance while checking the back of the arm as he thrusts deeply with the tip of his "pinute" into the side of Michael Frazier to end the situation.

David E. Gould and Michael Frazier square off with one another in the "bukas" (open) position.

MF throws a high forehand strike and DEG responds simultaneously with "cruzada" which is a counter strike resembling a "Cross" when completed. DEG intercepts the weapon hand and as he repositions himself he strikes a horizontal strike to the stomach of MF.

MF follows through with his initial strike and then sets himself up for a counter strike as DEG recognizes what is happening and moves his blade upward to intercept the counter strike once it is thrown.

MF comes back with a high back hand counter strike and DEG intercepts it with a vertical strike down center cutting into the arm of MF as he simultaneously checks the back of the arm to prevent the strike to follow through.

DEG then passes the weapon hand of MF as he repositions himself more to the inside and thrusts deep into the heart of MF with his "pinute".

DEG then cuts upward with his blade, "hiwang paakyat" catching MF in the center of his jaw.

DEG follows through with his upward cut, "hiwang paakyat" forcing the head of MF to be lifted up.

Then David E. Gould checks the inside of the weapon hand as he simultaneously counters deep into the heart of Michael Frazier thereby finishing the situation.

David E. Gould and Michael Frazier square off with one another in the "bukas" (open) position.

MF throws a high forehand strike and DEG responds simultaneously with "tala bartikal" (vertical block) impeding the strike of MF.

DEG then secures the weapon hand of MF in "bantay kamay kuwatro" (hand placement) as he just takes the sword offline while he simultaneously counters with "plansada" (horizontal slash) to the ribs of MF.

DEG then following through with his cut to the side transfers the blade of MF high while he makes contact with his forearm and the flat of the blade of MF preparing for a disarm.

DEG then disarms MF of his blade as he simultaneously cuts deeply into the head of MF with "bagsak" (vertical slash) as MF drops his blade to the ground.

MF seeing an opportunity punches at DEG with his left hand as DEG perceives the threat and intercepts the punch while he simultaneously counters with "plansada" (horizontal slash) to the stomach of MF.

DEG then slightly pulls the left hand of MF down as he simultaneously thrusts with "tusok taub" (palm down thrust) to the temple and eyes of MF.

David E. Gould then follows through with his "tusok taub" across the eyes of Michael Frazier as he finishes the situation.

David E. Gould and Michael Frazier square off with one another in the "bukas" (open) position.

MF throws a high fore hand strike and DEG responds simultaneously as he intercepts the blade of MF utilizing the inside of his "pinute" initiating a counter action known as "florete".

After intercepting the blade DEG continues executing the counter action known as "florete", which glides on top of the blade of MF as it follows and redirects it safely past center.

DEG continues the "florete" counter action as he moves the blade of MF past his own center line.

DEG now seizes an opportunity which was created as a direct result of the "florete" counter action and thrusts deeply into the side of MF.

MF prepares to counter with a high back hand strike with his blade and DEG perceiving this threat immediately turns the blade of his "pinute" upwards towards the threat with the intent to intercept the blade of MF.

MF initiates his counter attack and DEG simultaneously checks with his left hand and intercepts the strike with "trankada" as he cuts deeply into the forearm of MF.

MF throws a left punch and DEG immediately counters that action with "a la contra" which allows him to intercept the threat with his forearm as he simultaneously strikes deeply into the neck of MF.

David E. Gould pushes through his strike thereby ending the situation.

David E. Gould and Michael Frazier square off with one another in the "pinid" (closed) position.

MF throws a high back hand strike and DEG simultaneously steps forward and responds with "bagsak", a vertical strike thrown down the center as he intercepts and cuts deeply into the forearm of MF while checking his arm with the left hand.

DEG then uses "dukot" with his left hand in an attempt to contain and pass the blade of MF past his centerline.

As DEG passes the blade of MF to the outside he then checks with his left hand as he simultaneously thrusts deep into the stomach of MF.

MF throws a punch with his left hand and DEG counters that action with "sumbrada bartikal" which is an upward block with the "pinute" of DEG as he cuts into the arm of MF.

As DEG pulls the left hand down of MF and prepares to thrust into the chest, MF immediately prepares to counter with a high forehand strike.

MF counters with a high fore hand strike as DEG passes with his left hand and simultaneously counters with a thrust into the heart of MF.

DEG then turns the blade of his "pinute" down as he pushes his blade along the chest and stomach of MF.

David E. Gould continues to push his opponents blade outside of reach as he follows through with his slash to the stomach of Michael Frazier.

David E. Gould and Tad Waltman square off with one another in the "bukas" (open) position.

TW throws a high fore hand strike and DEG simultaneously responds intercepting his blade with "florete" using the flat of his "pinute" as they make contact with their blades.

DEG continues to pass the blade of TW with the flat of his own blade past his center line.

DEG perceiving an opportunity then thrusts deep into the heart of TW with "tusok taub" (palm down thrust).

TW tries to counter by coming in with a back hand strike but DEG perceives the threat and immediately turns his blade down cutting into the forearm of TW as he intercepts the counter attack.

DEG then follows through with his slash as he checks the weapon arm of TW and prepares to counter to center.

DEG then pushes his thrust deep into the stomach of TW as he continues to check his weapon arm.

DEG then turns his "pinute" to the side and slashes the stomach of TW.

David E. Gould completes his slash as he pulls the strike through the stomach of Tad Waltman.

David E. Gould and Tad Waltman square off with one another in the "bukas" (open) position.

TW attempts to throw a high fore hand strike and DEG perceiving the threat simultaneously counters to the left hand of TW as he passes the weapon hand.

DEG pulls his blade through as he positions for a counter strike while continuing to pass the weapon hand of TW past center.

DEG now counters with the tip of his "pinute" to the right eye of TW with "tusok tihaya" (palm up thrust).

DEG then follows through his thrust to the eye and then checks the blade of TW with the back of his "pinute" while he simultaneously checks the weapon arm.

DEG then cuts back into the left arm of TW as he steps out.

DEG perceives that TW is attempting a horizontal counter strike and he immediately intercepts the strike of TW cutting him into the arm.

DEG then continues to push and follow the blade of TW past center and to the outside.

DEG then slashes back to the body of TW as he moves to the inside and grabs the left hand.

DEG then pulls the left hand down to prevent TW from being able to counter from the other side with his blade as he follows through with his slash to the Stomach of TW.

DEG then thrusts with "tusok taub" to the left eye of TW.

David E. Gould completes the situation as he pushes his thrust through the left eye of Tad Waltman.

David E. Gould and Tad Waltman square off with one another, TW in the "bukas" (open) position and DEG with his "pinute" still in its scabbard.

TW attempts to throw a high fore hand strike and DEG perceiving the threat simultaneously counters by drawing his "pinute" free from its scabbard.

DEG strikes up catching TW in the jaw as he clears his "pinute" from its scabbard.

DEG then passes the weapon hand of TW past center as he simultaneously retracts his "pinute" in preparation for a counter strike.

DEG then counters into the chest of TW with a thrust as he continues to pass the weapon hand of TW away from his body.

DEG then turns his blade down and begins to cut through the body of TW.

David E. Gould then completes his cut through the stomach and across the weapon arm of Tad Waltman as he completes the situation.

David E. Gould and Tad Waltman square off with one another, TW in a low "bukas" (open) position and DEG with his "pinute" still in its scabbard.

TW telegraphs an attempt to throw a high fore hand strike and DEG perceiving the threat simultaneously counters with the scabbard while the "pinute" is still inside as he hits TW hard in the face.

DEG perceiving that TW is continuing with his strike responds by deploying his "pinute" from its scabbard

DEG then pulls his "pinute" completely free from the scabbard as he simultaneously intercepts the strike of TW with the scabbard.

DEG then thrusts deep into the throat of TW with the tip of his blade as he checks the blade of TW.

DEG then passes through the strike of TW as he immediately turns his blade down and inside of the throat of TW while he steps back.

DEG then steps back in as he turns his "pinute" up and begins to cut into the chin of TW.

DEG then follows through with his slash with strong purpose.

DEG then thrusts back into the throat of TW.

DEG turns his blade down and cuts downward from the chest to the stomach.

David E. Gould completes his downward slash as he cuts across the weapon arm of Tad Waltman.

David E. Gould and Tad Waltman square off with one another, TW in a high "bukas" (open) position and DEG with his "pinute" still in its scabbard.

TW attempts to throw a high fore hand strike and DEG perceiving the threat simultaneously passes the blade of TW with his scabbard with his "pinute" still inside.

DEG then begins to deploy his "pinute" from the scabbard as he continues to control the weapon hand of TW.

DEG pushes his scabbard down checking the weapon hand of TW as he successfully frees his "pinute" and is ready to counter strike.

DEG immediately counters with a fore hand strike to the neck of TW just as TW is preparing to counter with his own fore hand strike.

DEG then pushes his strike through the throat of TW and into his weapon hand as TW continues to counter.

DEG immediately counters behind the counter strike of TW to the neck.

DEG pushes though his strike through the neck of TW and into the back of his weapon hand.

David E. Gould then thrusts straight into the throat of Tad Waltman ending the situation.

Tad Waltman pulls a knife on David E. Gould who is without a weapon of his own.

DEG perceiving the threat immediately initiates by reaching his hand out making contact with the left hand of TW as he jams it backward.

DEG then continues to quickly jam the left hand of TW until it is slammed hard up against his left eye as TW counters with a thrust to the head of DEG with his knife.

DEG then intercepts the knife attack as he grabs the weapon hand of TW still aggresively jamming the left hand of TW into his eye.

DEG then secures the weapon hand of TW with both hands in "bantay kamay" (hand sectoring) as he prepares to disarm TW of his knife.

DEG then disarms the knife as TW counters with a left punch to the head as DEG intercepts the punch with the knife cutting into the forearm of TW.

DEG then pulls the left arm of TW down as he thrusts upward with the knife into the throat of TW.

DEG pulls the arm of TW a little forward as he slashes to his stomach with the knife.

DEG then thrusts into the temple of the head of TW.

DEG continues the thrust through the temple and slashes across the left eye of TW.

DEG then places the blade of the knife into the side of the neck and braces the back of the head with his left hand as he prepares to cut deep into the neck of TW.

DEG then pulls the blade back and across the neck of TW securing a deep cut as he pushes the head of TW down and away from his body.

DEG continues to push TW to the ground as he stabs him into the kidney.

David E. Gould drives the knife deeper into the kidney of Tad Waltman to finish the situation.

Tad Waltman pulls a knife on David E. Gould who is without a weapon of his own.

TW then initiates with a high forehand slash to the head and DEG perceiving the threat simultaneously intercepts the slash with his left hand as he drives his right thumb into the eye of TW for pain distraction.

DEG then pushes the knife hand down as he secures the knife with "bantay kamay" preparing to disarm TW of his knife.

DEG lifts the knife up to the inside and with his forearm against the flat of the blade applies pressure to disarm the knife.

As DEG completes the disarm TW throws his left hand up in pain.

TW begins to throw a left punch as DEG perceives the threat with the knife of TW in hand.

TW continues his punch to the head of DEG as he intercepts the punch with his left hand as he simultaneously drives the blade into the chest of TW.

DEG then pulls the left arm of TW down and cuts into a very dangerous artery under the armpit as he slashes up with the knife.

DEG then pulls the arm of TW positioning him forward and downward to off balance him as he prepares to counter.

David E. Gould then slams his blade down into the back of the head of Tad Waltman making him buckle at his knees in an effort to finish the situation.

Tad Waltman pulls a knife as David E. Gould deploys one of his own.

TW then initiates with a high forehand slash to the head and DEG perceiving the threat simultaneously intercepts the weapon hand of TW with the forearm of his own knife hand.

DEG not wanting to go force to force with TW passes the knife through past his center line leaving TW vulnerable and susceptible to a counter attack.

DEG seeing an opportunity quickly closes range as he grabs and pulls the back of the arm of TW while slamming hard into the side of the face of TW with a head but.

DEG pushes the knife hand of TW forward as he closes in deep taking control of his back.

DEG continues to turn TW further to the inside and grabs the knife hand of TW with his left hand bringing him closer into the embrace of DEG.

DEG then pulls the knife hand to secure a more preferable position as he slams his blade into the throat of TW forcing him to begin to collapse deeper into the embrace of DEG.

David E. Gould then tightens his control of TW as he sinks his knife deeper into the throat of Tad Waltman as he brings him closer to the ground to finish the situation.

Tad Waltman pulls a knife as David E. Gould deploys one of his own.

TW then initiates with a high forehand slash to the head and DEG perceiving the threat intercepts with "wasay" (hack) into the right wrist of TW.

TW seeing that he may be in trouble quickly throws a left punch as DEG intercepts the punch with another "wasay" (hack) as he secures the weapon hand of TW with his one left hand grabbing the thumb and index.

As TW drops his left hand in pain DEG prepares to disarm the knife of TW with his knife hand.

DEG disarms the knife of TW as he simultaneously slams his knife forward and deep into the sternum of TW.

Tad Waltman looking down as he watches the knife enter into his sternum David E. Gould then lifts the tip of his blade and stabs into the underside of the jaw of TW.

Larry Ingle reaches into the back of his waist band for his knife as David E. Gould is currently without a weapon of his own.

LI then pulls his knife from the waist band into view as DEG perceives the threat and becomes operational.

LI then thrusts forward with an attack to the stomach as DEG grabs and secures the knife hand of LI as he prepares to punch.

DEG then punches with his right hand hard into the bicep of LI in an attempt to utilize pain distraction.

DEG taking advantage of the pain distraction gained by the punch to the bicep closes range as he delivers an upward elbow into the jaw of LI which turns his head.

DEG drops his right hand down and passes the blade to the inside of his body and past center as he checks the back of the arm of LI to make sure that he can not cut back with the knife as DEG closes range.

DEG then seeing an opportunity rushes forward to distance himself from the knife of LI as he tries to get to his back.

DEG then suddenly turns his body and pushes LI forward and off balanced long enough for him to deploy his own folding knife.

LI quickly recovers and turns back toward DEG slashing to the throat as DEG intercepts the slash and fully opens his folder as he checks the knife arm of LI.

DEG then thrusts into the stomach of LI with his knife as he aggressively moves forward closing range.

DEG then collapses the knife hand of LI back and downward against his body with his left arm as he prepares to finish the situation.

David E. Gould now seeing an opportunity to finish the situation he buries his knife deep into the chest of Larry Ingle as he continues to check the knife against his body.

The Lameco Eskrima System in Application

Larry Ingle reaches into the back of his waist band for his knife as David E. Gould is without a weapon of his own.

LI then pulls his knife from the waist band into view as DEG perceives the threat and becomes operational.

LI presents and brandishes his knife in full view of DEG as he makes demands.

DEG suddenly reaches for, grabs and secures the knife hand of LI as he applies cohesion with the blade of his hand against the flat of the blade in an attempt to disarm the knife.

DEG failing in his attempt to disarm LI of his knife secures the weapon hand with a two handed grab and pulls LI forward and off balance.

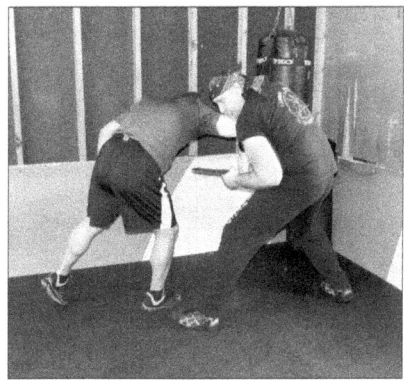

DEG then continues to pull LI forward keeping him unbalanced as he turns the knife back on LI.

DEG continues his thrust deep into the side of LI using his momentum against him.

David E. Gould then steps back and withdraws the knife from the body of Larry Ingle as DEG disarms him of his knife and ends the situation.

David E. Gould and Tad Waltman square off with one another using "espada-y-daga" (sword and knife), both starting in the "bukas" (open) position.

TW attempts to throw a high fore hand strike and DEG perceiving the threat simultaneously counters with "estrella" intercepting the attack with the flat of his blade to protect the edge as he cuts the weapon hand of TW with his knife.

DEG then counters with "kadena reyal" as he simultaneously comes around the blade of TW and cuts into the neck with his "pinute" and simultaneously thrusts into the ribs of TW with his knife.

DEG then passes through as he guides the sword of TW down and to the outside while he slashes into the stomach with his "pinute".

TW thrusts with his knife and DEG perceiving the threat intercepts the knife arm of TW with his "pinute" as he simultaneously thrusts to the body with his knife.

DEG then lowers the blade of his "pinute" slashing into the mid section of TW as he checks the knife hand of TW with his knife.

DEG then passes the knife hand down and to the outside with his own knife as he slashes deep to the side of the neck of TW.

TW attempts a high forehand slash with his sword and DEG intercepts it with his knife as he slashes down the body of TW with "bagsak".

David E. Gould steps back out of harms way as he delivers the final blow of the situation cutting deep across the eyes of Tad Waltman.

David E. Gould and Tad Waltman square off with one another using "espada-y-daga" (sword and knife), both starting in the "bukas" (open) position.

TW attempts to throw a high fore hand strike and DEG perceiving the threat simultaneously counters with "florete" as he makes contact with the flat of his blade in an effort to guide the blade of TW down and past center.

DEG continues to guide the blade of TW past center and then perceives the opportunity for a counter strike to the body of TW.

DEG then closes range just enough to thrust deep into the chest of TW.

TW counters with his knife as he attempts to thrust DEG perceives the threat and moves to the side as he intercepts the knife attack as he cuts deep into the knife arm of TW with his "pinute".

DEG then collapses the left arm of TW as he steps forward to close range and thrusts into the top of the chest of TW with his "pinute" in an attempt to collapse a lung.

David E. Gould seeing that TW may try and counter with his blade steps back just out of range as he cuts down the body of Tad Waltman and into his right arm.

David E. Gould and Tad Waltman square off with one another using "espada-y-daga" (sword and knife), both starting in the "bukas" (open) position.

TW attempts to throw a high fore hand strike and DEG perceiving the threat simultaneously counters with "florete" as he makes contact with the flat of his blade in an effort to guide the blade of TW down and past center.

DEG continues to guide the blade of TW past center and then turns his blade upward underneath the wrist of TW.

DEG then cuts into the underside of the weapon hand of TW with his "pinute".

TW counters with a knife thrust and DEG perceiving the threat side steps as he simultaneously counters with "bagsak" cutting into the arm of TW.

DEG then closes range as he collapses the knife arm of TW pushing it downward with his forearm and simultaneously slams the tip of his "pinute" deep into the head of TW.

DEG then follows through with his thrust to the head of TW as he continues to check the knife hand with his own knife.

David E. Gould then steps back with a cross step as he delivers the final blow to the throat of Tad Waltman.

David E. Gould and Tad Waltman square off with one another using "espada-y-daga" (sword and knife), both starting in the "pinid" (closed) position.

TW attempts to throw a high back hand strike and DEG perceiving the threat simultaneously counters with "florete" as he makes contact with the flat of his blade in an effort to guide the blade of TW down and past center.

DEG continues to guide the blade of TW past center as he cuts into the hand of TW upon the completion of the "florete".

As DEG begins to push his blade forward toward the chest he perceives that TW is preparing to counter with a knife thrust so he shifts focus from offense to defense and takes his eyes off of the chest of his opponent onto the shoulder of his opponent.

Just as TW begins to execute his knife thrust DEG redirects the tip of his "pinute" from the chest and drives it deep into the shoulder of TW.

TW in pain still pushes out the thrust with the knife and DEG side steps off line and intercepts the knife counter with "sumbrada bartikal".

DEG then passes the knife hand of TW down with his own knife as he simultaneously pushes the tip of his "pinute" deep into the neck of TW.

DEG then turns the blade down and slashes through the body of TW.

DEG perceives that the leg is accessible he quickly cuts deep into the leg.

David E. Gould then steps back just outside of the reach of Tad Waltman and delivers the final blow with a deep thrust into the stomach.

David E. Gould and Tad Waltman square off with one another using "espada-y-daga" (sword and knife), both starting in the "bukas" (open) position.

TW attempts to throw a high fore hand strike and DEG perceiving the threat simultaneously counters with "panipis" (to slice thin) as he intercepts the sword strike with his knife and simultaneously counters with a very narrow vertical strike down the center line of TW with his "pinute".

DEG then immediately counters with "dukot" as he collapses the sword arm of TW down and to the inside as he simultaneously stabs into the chest of TW with his knife.

TW counters with a knife thrust with his left hand and DEG perceiving the threat steps outside and intercepts the knife thrust with his blade using "a la contra" cutting TW deeply to the side of the neck.

DEG not wanting to take any chances with the knife hand of TW uses his wrist to push the knife away and to the outside of the body as DEG slashes to the other side of the neck with his "pinute".

DEG then closes range as he slams his knife deeply into the stomach of TW.

DEG then turns to the side as he slashes through the other side of the neck in an effort to end the situation.

David E. Gould then continues his final slash completely pulling it through the neck of Tad Waltman as the power from the strike knocks him back and out of range to continue.

Tad Waltman pulls a knife on David E. Gould who is without a weapon of his own.

TW then initiates with a straight thrust towards the stomach and DEG perceiving the threat simultaneously intercepts the slash with his forearm using "praksyon" which is a sudden counter meant to contain unexpected surprise attacks.

DEG then pushes his hand forward as he continues to check the knife hand of TW with his forearm and makes contact with the chest of TW.

DEG then temporarily pushes TW out of range and scans his environment for a weapon of opportunity with which he can use to defend the on-going knife attack. DEG then reaches for the closest thing to him with combative value, being a fireplace poker right next to him.

TW having recovered his position from the previous push out of range continues his attack with the knife and DEG with Fire Poker in hand prepares to defend himself with the weapon of opportunity.

As TW pushes his knife forward DEG immediately side steps and hits TW in the head with the fire poker using "combate heneral".

DEG immediately allows the extension of his first strike to follow through past the head and make contact with the weapon hand of TW.

DEG then checks the weapon hand of TW as he simultaneously strikes a horizontal strike to the head hitting with the hook of the fire poker.

DEG then counters back to the opposite side of the head hitting TW in the temple with the fire poker.

David E. Gould completely follows through with his final strike to the head of Tad Waltman ending the situation.

Tad Waltman pulls a knife on David E. Gould who has just grabbed a nearby fire poker using it as a weapon of opportunity with which to defend against the knife attack.

TW then initiates with a straight thrust towards the stomach and DEG perceiving the threat simultaneously intercepts with "florete" dropping the fire poker on top of the knife hand of TW as he prepares to guide the knife threat down and past center.

DEG guides the knife hand of TW past center using the hook of the fire poker to dig into the hand.

DEG then perceiving an opportunity checks the back of the weapon arm of TW as he prepares to counter.

DEG immediately counters with a thrust using the tip of the fire poker into the stomach of TW.

DEG then positions back outside of the reach of TW as he continues to check his weapon arm and prepares to strike.

DEG then counters with "bagsak" as he drives the hook of the fire poker deep into the head of TW.

TW counters to the stomach with a horizontal slash and perceiving the threat DEG then continues his strike down center as he hits the knife hand of TW.

DEG then directs the tip of the fire poker into the left eye of TW.

David E. Gould then side steps as he drives a hard strike into the right temple of Tad Waltman using the hook of the fire poker to make contact with the final strike of the situation.

Tad Waltman pulls a knife on David E. Gould who has just grabbed a nearby fire poker using it as a weapon of opportunity with which to defend against the knife attack.

TW then initiates with a straight thrust towards the stomach and DEG perceiving the threat slightly steps back as he simultaneously counters by striking to the weapon hand of TW making hard contact with the hook of the fire poker.

As DEG follows through with the counter strike TW loses possession of his knife forcing it to drop to the floor.

DEG then perceiving an opportunity steps deep into range as he strikes with "palong paakyat" hitting TW square in the chin contacting with the hook of the fire poker.

DEG then pushes through with his strike lifting the head of TW up and forces it backwards.

DEG then grabs the left hand of TW and pulls him forward to imbalance him as he prepares to counter strike.

DEG then strikes TW behind the left ear with the hook of the fire poker as he continues to pull him forward and downwards to keep him imbalanced.

DEG then strikes TW in the temple with the very pointy handle of the fire poker.

DEG then grabs the back of the head of TW and pushes him down making him very vulnerable as he prepares to strike.

DEG then drives the sharp point of the handle of the fire poker deep into the back of the head of TW which drives him closer to the ground.

DEG then strikes with the body of the fire poker once again hitting TW in the back of the head as he collapses to the floor.

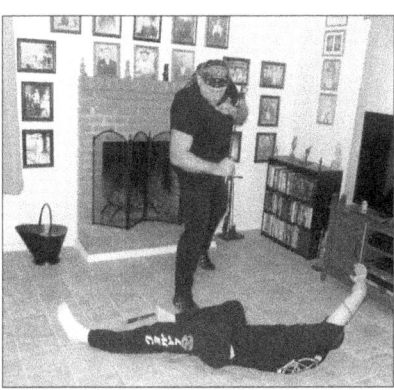

David E. Gould looks on prepared to continue if necessary as he ensures that the situation has been finished as Tad Waltman is laid out on the floor in agony.

The Lameco Eskrima System in Application

Tad Waltman pulls a knife on David E. Gould who has just grabbed a nearby fire poker using it as a weapon of opportunity with which to defend against the knife attack.

TW then initiates with a straight thrust towards the stomach and DEG perceiving the threat simultaneously checks the knife hand of TW with his left hand and simultaneously thrusts into the left eye of TW with the tip of his fire poker.

DEG then pushes his strike through in an effort to gain maximum results with the strike leaving TW a little imbalanced and vulnerable.

TW recovering his position then continues to thrust his knfe forward and DEG intercepts it with a strike to the wrist of the weapon hand of TW hitting with the hook of the fire poker.

DEG perceiving an opportunity closes range as he checks the back of the weapon arm of TW and prepares to thrust to center.

DEG then drives deeper into close range as he pushes the tip of the fire poker up into the throat and under the jaw of TW while he continues to check the back of his weapon arm.

TW counters with a left punch as DEG using the body of the fire poker intercepts the punch as he secures the weapon hand of TW.

DEG then pulls the left hand of TW down using the hook of the fire poker as he continues to secure the weapon hand.

DEG then retracts the fire poker as he prepares and positions himself to disarm the knife of TW.

DEG disarms the knife of TW as he simultaneously delivers a strike into the left temple as TW loses possession of his knife forcing it to drop to the floor.

DEG then follows the strike slightly down and directs it to the outside and up into the right eye of TW.

DEG then follows through with the thrust pushing the head of TW up and back to the outside as he prepares to deliver the final strike of the situation.

David E. Gould then turns his hips and body to the outside using his body weight as he makes hard contact with the right temple of Tad Waltman finishing the situation.

Tad Waltman pulls a knife on David E. Gould who has just grabbed a nearby fire poker and shovel using them as a weapons of opportunity with which to defend against the knife attack.

TW then initiates with a knife thrust towards the chest and DEG perceiving the threat simultaneously checks the knife of TW with the fire shovel as he thrusts the tip of the fire poker into the throat and under the jaw of TW with a technique known as "tusok panipis".

TW then counters with a left punch and DEG perceiving the threat intercepts the punch with the fire poker as he passes the knife hand of TW past center with the fire shovel.

DEG then pulls the left arm of TW down with the hook of the fire poker as he continues to check the knife hand of TW with the fire shovel.

DEG then steps back with "retirada lutang" as he simultaneously passes the knife hand down with the fire shovel as he strikes deep into the head of TW with the fire poker.

DEG then counters with "sumbrada bartikal" hitting TW in the chin with the fire poker after which he perceives TW prepare to counter with another knife thrust.

As TW pushes forward with the knife DEG counters by checking it with the fire shovel as he pulls his strike through with the fire poker.

DEG then shifts his hips and pushes the knife hand of TW down and away from his body with the fire shovel.

DEG then counters right away with "solo kadena" hitting with a high fore hand strike to the temple of TW with the fire poker.

DEG then counters in quick secession with the fire shovel hitting with a high back hand strike to the temple of TW.

David E. Gould completes the "solo kadena" as he hits Tad Waltman behind the ear with a high back hand strike with the fire poker as he finishes the situation.

Tad Waltman pulls a knife on David E. Gould who has just grabbed a nearby fire poker and shovel using them as weapons of opportunity with which to defend against the knife attack.

TW then initiates with a knife thrust towards the stomach and DEG perceiving the threat simultaneously steps back with "retirada lutang" as he intercepts the knife of TW with the fire shovel as he strikes hitting the top of the head of TW the hook of the fire poker.

DEG then closes range as he steps forward and passes the knife hand of TW deep to the inside with the fire shovel and strikes to the head of TW with ta horizontal strike using the fire poker.

DEG perceiving that TW could come back across his body with a knife slash counters with "bagsak" as he hits the forearm of TW with the fire shovel.

DEG then shifts his hips to the outside and counters right away with a hard high fore hand strike using the fire poker striking to the left temple of TW.

David E. Gould pulls his final strike of the fire poker through and past the head of Tad Waltman as he finishes the situation.

Tad Waltman pulls a knife on David E. Gould who has just grabbed a nearby board which was laying on the ground using it as a weapon of opportunity with which to defend against the knife attack.

TW brings the knife into full view and perceiving this DEG brings the board up with which to defend himself.

TW then initiates with a knife thrust towards the stomach as he steps forward and DEG perceiving the threat simultaneously side steps and strikes to the head of TW hitting him with a high fore hand strike using the board, a technique known as "combate heneral".

DEG then pushes the strike through the head as he hits TW in the weapon hand completing the "combate heneral" technique.

TW turns and attacks DEG with a high forehand slash as DEG intercepts the knife hand of TW and delivers a hard counter strike to the ribs of TW with the board.

DEG pulls his strike through the ribs as he secures the weapon hand of TW and positions it where can attempt to disarm TW of his knife.

David E. Gould then shifts his hips to the outside as he simultaneously disarms and strikes Tad Waltman in the head with the board using the same motion to achieve both actions as he finishes the situation.

Tad Waltman picks up a board and threatens to attack David E. Gould who has also just grabbed a nearby board which was laying on the ground using it as a weapon of opportunity with which to defend against the attack.

TW attacks with a high forehand strike as DEG counters with "tala bartikal" (vertical block).

DEG then immediately secures the weapon hand of TW with "bantay kamay" (hand placement) as he simultaneously delivers a horizontal strike to the side of the head of TW.

TW then counters with a punch with his left hand and DEG perceiving the threat shifts his hips as he intercepts the punch with his forearm as DEG prepares to disarm TW of his weapon.

DEG then simultaneously disarms TW of his weapon as he strikes hard into the side of the head of TW.

DEG then pulls the arm of TW and strikes upward with "palong paakyat" (upward strike) to the temple of TW.

David E. Gould in an attempt to finish the situation pulls TW downward as he counters with a heavy strike with the butt of his weapon to the back of the head of Tad Waltman as the impact buckles his knees forcing him to the ground.

David E. Gould and Michael Frazier square off during a training exercise created to test and gauge actual perception, reaction and blocking proficiency regarding "tala bartikal" (a vertical block) in defense of a single stick attack thrown to the head with full intention. The intent is for MF to perceive, react to and try to block the strike of DEG as it is thrown with full power in real time speed. MF is wearing protective headgear so that he will be protected from the strike should he fail in his attempt to block the strike.

DEG initiates a high forehand strike with full speed, power and intention as MF perceives the threat and begins to respond with a vertical block as quickly as he can.

David E. Gould strikes through and collapses the block at full force as the perception, reaction and timing of Michael Frazier regarding the block was a little late enabling DEG to collapse the block on impact and deliver a hard blow to the head.

David E. Gould and Michael Frazier square off during a training exercise created to test and gauge actual perception, reaction and blocking proficiency regarding "sumbrada" (an umbrella block) in defense of a single stick attack thrown to the head with full intention. The intent is for MF to perceive, react to and try to block the strike of DEG as it is thrown with full power in real time speed. MF is wearing protective headgear so that he will be protected from the strike should he fail in his attempt to block the strike.

DEG initiates a high forehand strike with full speed, power and intention as MF perceives the threat and begins to respond with his "sumbrada" (umbrella block) as quickly as he can.

David E. Gould strikes through and collapses the block at full force as the perception, reaction and timing of Michael Frazier regarding the block was a little late enabling DEG to collapse the block on impact and deliver a hard blow to the head.

David E. Gould and Michael Frazier square off during a training exercise created to test and gauge actual perception, reaction and blocking proficiency regarding "pluma" (a pen block) in defense of a single stick attack thrown to the head with full intention. The intent is for MF to perceive, react to and try to block the strike of DEG as it is thrown with full power in real time speed. MF is wearing protective headgear so that he will be protected from the strike should he fail in his attempt to block the strike.

DEG initiates a high backhand strike with full speed, power and intention as MF perceives the threat and begins to respond with his "pluma" (pen block) as quickly as he can.

David E. Gould strikes through and collapses the block at full force as the perception, reaction and timing of Michael Frazier regarding the block was a little late enabling DEG to collapse the block on impact and deliver a hard blow to the head.

David E. Gould and Michael Frazier square off during a training exercise created to test and gauge actual perception, reaction and deflecting proficiency regarding "pasungkit" (an upward outside deflection) in defense of a single stick attack thrown to the head with full intention. The intent is for MF to perceive, react to and try to deflect the strike of DEG as it is thrown with full power in real time speed. MF is wearing protective headgear so that he will be protected from the strike should he fail in his attempt to block the strike.

DEG initiates a high forehand strike with full speed, power and intention as MF perceives the threat and begins to respond with his "pasungkit" (upward deflection) as quickly as he can.

DEG strikes past the deflecting stick with no contact being made at full force as the perception, reaction and timing of MF regarding the deflection was a little late enabling DEG to slip past the deflection attempt and deliver a hard blow to the head.

David E. Gould follows through his trike to the head of Michael Frazier ending in the "pinid" position.

David E. Gould and Michael Frazier square off during a training exercise created to test and gauge actual perception and reaction proficiency regarding a defense regarding leg strikes known as, "retirada lutang" (a defensive step back while 'floating' the foot just off the ground) in defense of a single stick attack thrown to the legs with full intention. The intent is for DEG to perceive, react to and try to move back in defense of the strike of MF as it is thrown with full power in real time speed.

MF initiates with a low forehand strike thrown with full power, speed and intention as DEG perceives the threat he begins to pull his lead leg back to protect it from the ensuing leg attack as he simultaneously initiates his counter strike towards the head of MF.

The leg strike thrown in real time misses the leg of DEG as he pulls it farther back and pushes closer with his counter strike of the head of MF.

David E. Gould now fully protected from the leg strike lands solid with "bagsak" (vertical strike) to the head of Michael Frazier with power.

P.S. In this phase of training all techniques, principles and concepts were tested, evaluated and validated for their true combative value. The training was always done using protective equipment so that the "feeder" could strike with full power, speed and intention in an attempt to assess fair combative value in everything that was trained to determine its over all effect in fighting. Since protective equipment is used during this validation process the person defending the attacks did not have to become overly concerned with being injured during the training but could face strikes thrown with full speed, timing and power in determining over all effect, allowing the student to be held fully accountable to all that he does or hesitates to do.

Example of Random Sparring as it was applied in the Backyard:

In this sequence David E. Gould and Michael Frazier engage in the "sparring" component of the Lameco Eskrima System. This was the most important phase of training as it allowed the student to verify all things previously trained and which are required to fight in forcing the student to negotiate all areas required in mastering a combative situation (a fight) to include, footwork, proper fighting form, speed, timing, power, position, non-telegraphic striking, perception and reaction, location and relocation principles, target acquisition, recovery measures, range, centerline methodology and hand evasions.

Punong Guro Edgar G. Sulite used to tell us that the fight itself was our teacher and that we were in a state of constant learning as students of the combative equation. The more that we fought the better and more efficient that we became at fighting. The fact remains that if you expect to become a great fighter you must frequently spar with intention or fight on a consistent basis to learn its more important lessons and in doing so be able to learn and reform from your mistakes as not to be doomed to repeat them. Simply put, short of actual fighting, sparring yields the highest return on the time that you have invested into your training and will give you much needed experience which serves your need well in preparing you to survive future crisis situations. I have always felt that experience is the best teacher.

Dino Flores Photo Sequence

Dino Flores and Johnathan Balani square off with their "garotes" in the "bukas" (open) position.

JB initiates a high forehand attack and DF prepares to intercept the attack with his "garote".

As JB continues with his attack DF blocks with "tala bartikal" (vertical block).

DF quickly transitions the block into a redirection known as "plumang madulas" as he slips to the negative side of the strike.

DF then continues his counter attack hitting to the neck of JB with the tip of his "garote".

DF then counters with a punch with his weapon hand to the face of JB.

DF then closes range as he slips slightly to the rear of JB setting up a choke attempt on JB using his "garote".

Dino Flores switches hands with his "garote" using "lipat kamay" as he puts the choke on Johnathan Balani as he captures and locks the weapon hand of JB ending with a break of the elbow so that JB can not counter the choke.

Dino Flores and Johnathan Balani square off with their blades in the "bukas" (open) position as JB initiates a high forehand attack as DF prepares to intercept the attack.

DF begins to move forward to breach the gap before JB can complete his attack.

DF intercepts the attack of JB and simultaneously counters with "aldabis" (upper strike) to the right side of JB.

DF continues his counter with his blade as he comes into contact and cuts deep under the right armpit of JB.

DF then capitalizes on an opportunity as he pulls the arm of JB downward to imbalance him as he turns his blade outward cutting into the upper arm of JB using it as leverage to keep him imbalanced.

DF continues to keep JB imbalanced as he straightens and pushes through with his blade towards the throat of JB.

DF brings JB closer to the ground as he cuts into his neck with his blade.

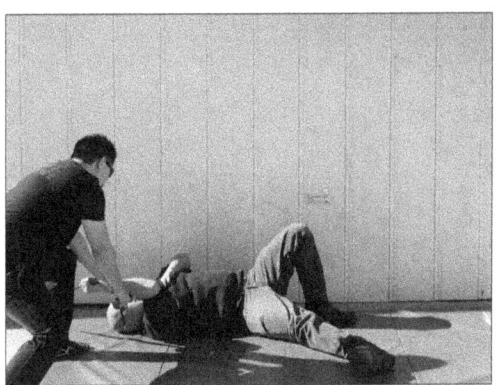

Dino Flores flattens Johnathan Balani out on the ground as he continues to cut into his neck as he ends the situation.

Dino Flores and Johnathan Balani square off with each other in an empty hand altercation.

JB initiates with a punch to the head of DF who repositions to the inside and counters with "pasok sa loob at sunggab" (inside check and eye gouge) hitting JB in the eye with his thumb.

DF then goes from the eye gouge and counters with "tapi-tapi" in preparation to pass the arm.

DF then pushes the arm of JB down with "sakay" (riding on technique) as he repositions to the outside of JB using the "tatsulok babae" (female triangle) foot work.

DF completes his "sakay" successfully passing the arm of JB and positioning to his outside.

DF then pulls the arm of JB forward and down as uses his safety hand to lock the elbow of JB.

DF continues his leverage on the arm of JB as he breaks the elbow while pulling him as he uses his momentum to take JB closer towards the ground.

DF continuing his leverage firmly places JB face first onto the ground and positions to counter.

Dino Flores lets the arm go once Johnathan Balani is firmly placed on the ground then stands and kicks him to the back of the head to end the situation.

Dino Flores and Johnathan Balani square off with each other in an empty hand altercation.

JB initiates with a punch delivered toward DF, who slightly positions to the outside with "tatsulok babae" (female triangle) as he parry's the punch.

DF counters quickly with "dalinas" as he slides his left hand towards the eyes of JB while checking the punch with his right hand.

DF then grabs the right wrist of JB as he sets him up to counter.

DF quickly thrusts his hand downward to the groin of Jb striking him.

DF then brings his right arm upwards to wrap around and trap the arm of JB as he applies a lock and a break of the elbow.

JB in an effort to protect his elbow slips his arm away from the control of DF

DF then reaches and grabs the back of the head of JB in an attempt to regain control of him.

DF pulls the back of the head of JB forward as he punches to his face.

DF then counters with a sharp elbow to the face of JB as he continues to base it with his hand behind the head of JB.

DF continues just past the head of Jb with his elbow strike and positions to get him in a head lock.

DF then drops his body weight in an effort to create momentum as he intends to take JB to the ground.

DF falls straight back using his momentum to further take JB to the ground.

Dino Flores falls on his back as he drives the head of Johnathan Balani into the ground to end the situation.

Gary Quan Photo Sequence

Gary Quan and Johnathan Balani square off with their "garotes" in the "bukas" (open) position.

JB initiates with a high forehand attack and GQ intercepts it with "tala bartikal" (vertical block) as he uses "bantay kamay uno" (hand sector one).

GQ then quickly counters with "waslik" (throwing the hand) to the inside as he positions for a thrust counter.

GQ pushes his thrust forward and positions his hands nearer for a disarm.

GQ continues to push his thrust to the stomach of JB.

GQ then continues his thrust from the stomach of JB and turns it up thrusting towards the face.

GQ continues his thrust past the face of JB as he sets him up for a disarm of his garote.

GQ breaks the "garote" from the hand of JB.

Gary Quan ends the situation as the "garote" of Johnathan Balani falls to the ground.

Gary Quan and Johnathan Balani square off with their "garotes" in the "bukas" (open) position.

JB initiates with a high forehand attack and GQ intercepts it with "tala bartikal" (vertical block).

GQ quickly transitions from the "tala bartikal" to what is known as "plumang madulas" as he slips just to the outside of the strike of JB.

GQ positions farther to the outside of JB using the "tatsulok babae" (female triangle) foot work as he continues to implement his "plumang madulas" to the head of JB.

GQ hits the head of JB while checking his weapon hand at the elbow.

GQ then slides both his safety hand and weapon hand back in an effort to control JB as he sets up a counter to the opposite side of the body.

GQ firmly grabs the wrist of JB as he applies cohesion between the forearm of GQ and the "garote" of JB.

GQ pushes his counter strike forward still keeping good cohesion with the intent to strike the head of JB and disarm him of his "garote".

GQ makes contact with the head of JB as he continues to apply pressure against the garote of JB in an attempt to disarm him.

GQ continues his strike to the head of JB and as he does he tears the "garote" of Jb out of his hand and sends it to the ground.

GQ follows up with the disarm preparing to strike with a high back hand strike to the head of JB.

Gary Quan completes his high back hand strike hitting the head of Johnathan Balani there by ending the situation.

The Lameco Eskrima System in Application

Afterword

What more could one say about the late Edgar Sulite and his Lameco Eskrima system that has not already been well-stated and depicted within the pages of this book? Well, I suppose some perspective on this project might be worth sharing. It began on July 24, 2013 when I received the following message:

> "Mr. Wiley, Hello sir I hope that this message finds you well. I am Guro Dave Gould a certified Instructor in Lameco Eskrima under Punong Guro Edgar G. Sulite and one of his chosen Standard Bearers for the system. I was curious if you would ever consider writing a book about PG Sulite, Lameco Eskrima and his Personal backyard Group "Sulite Orehenal Group" or Lameco SOG for short? There were 25 of us which made up his personal backyard Group in Los Angeles and we have all remained dedicated to him and propagating his legacy to the next generations to come. The Lameco "SOG" have really created a lot of interest in the general Pilipino warrior arts community over the last 16 years since our Founder was sadly taken from us. I think that we would be of great interest to you and a great topic to be written about from you. Please consider this and let me know your thoughts on the matter. Regards, Guro Dave Gould."

I was honored that the Lameco SOG group thought enough of my work to approach me with such a request. I considered the proposal for week, but thought that I was not the right person to write such a book. While I knew Edgar and many of his notable friends in the Philippines, I was not a practitioner of his art. In the past I did write an article or two on Lameco Eskrima and featured chapters on Edgar Sulite and his system within my books *Filipino Martial Culture* and *Filipino Fighting Arts: Theory and Practice*. I did want Tambuli Media to publish this book, but I felt it needed an insider's perspective to be complete and meaningful.

No great book is ever created in a vacuum, and this one is no exception. What makes *Lameco Eskrima: The Legacy of Edgar Sulite* so significant is that from the outset it was meant to be a collaboration. As the late Punong Guro was fond of saying, one can never hope to gain a full understanding of him or his art by seeing it only from one perspective. This book embraces that notion and draws on the support and recollections of his oldest friends, Jun Pueblos and Alex Co, and eight of his backyard students to offer invaluable insights into Lameco Eskrima and the man responsible for developing it.

Fifteen months of collaborating, editing, photo-shooting, designing and proofing have finally led to the book you have just read. A book, I believe, that stands out as being perhaps the most detailed and comprehensive on any single Filipino martial art style published to date. It is part biographical, part historical, part memorial, part instructional, and altogether an invaluable resource providing insight into the life and art of a great man.

Edgar G. Sulite was well respected in the Philippines, where he dedicated his life to learning and mastering the art of Eskrima. He put his reputation on the line, taking challenges for money and honor. He earned the confidence of a collection of legendary masters of the day, including Jose Caballero, Leo Gaje, Jesus Abella, Pablicito Cabahug, Ireneo Olavides, and Antonio Ilustrisimo, among others. He earned the trust and mutual respect of his era's newest masters, including Roland Dantes, Yuli Romo, Tony Diego, Christopher Ricketts and Alex Co. Sulite came to the United States and took the country—and then the world—by storm. He was featured on the cover of countless magazines, starred in numerous instructional videos and had a large seminar following. In short, the poor kid from Tacloban City matured into an international phenomenon, bringing the Filipino arts and his friends up along with him.

I am honored to have known Edgar Sulite and to have helped promote him and introduce his art through my own efforts nearly 20 years ago. I am also honored to have, like Edgar, earned the trust and friendship of Roland Dantes, Yuli Romo, Tony Diego, Christopher Ricketts, Alex Co, Jun Pueblos, Andy Abrian, and our shared teacher, Antonio "Tatang" Ilustrisimo. We traveled similar paths, Edgar and I, but our paths crossed only a few times in person; in his Los Angeles home and at select seminars on the East Coast where he asked me to be a guest judge during promotional exams.

It was also an honor to help Rey Galang assemble *Vortex*, the Lameco Eskrima newsletter, at Galang's home in New Jersey. Rey and I also collaborated closely with Alex Co to assemble Edgar's notes and photographs into the book that was originally titled "Masters of Arnis" but which was retitled for an international audience, *The Masters of Arnis, Kali and Eskrima*. And now at the end of 2014, 17 years after the untimely passing of our friend, I am able once again to bring the world an important work on this unforgettable man and his dynamic fighting art.

In retrospect, it looks as though I have been an unofficial chronicler of a man and his art. But without a doubt, David E. Gould and his fellow SOG contributors are the real, the official, chroniclers and standard bearers of the late Punong Guro Edgar G. Sulite and his Lameco Eskrima system. The late Punong Guro is truly missed by many, but his art lives on in the capable hands of the Lameco SOG group. May Edgar's life and legacy live on in their teachings and within the pages of this book.

Mark V. Wiley
Publisher, Tambuli Media
October 25, 2014

About the Author

David E. Gould began his training in Shotokan Karate in 1977, receiving his black belt in 1982. Since 1983, he has trained in numerous Filipino, Indonesian, and Thai warrior arts in the United States and in their respective countries of origin, but he is best known for his association with the Lameco Eskrima system and its founder, Punong Guro Edgar G. Sulite.

David E. Gould initially joined the Lameco Eskrima International Association on October 20, 1992 in Los Angeles, California and officially began his training as a private student under the direct tutelage of Punong Guro Edgar G. Sulite at the founder's Los Angeles home. Months later, he was invited by Punong Guro Sulite to join his personal and private, invitation-only "backyard" Lameco Eskrima group, which later became known as the "Sulite Orehenal Group." On July 28, 1996, David E. Gould became the last instructor certified by Punong Guro Edgar G. Sulite in Lameco Eskrima. He is recognized by all as one of the standard bearers of the system, appointed directly to that position by Punong Guro Edgar G. Sulite, also in 1996.

From 1992, Gould trained under Punong Guro Sulite several times a week as a private student and as part of the "Sulite Orehenal Group," until Punong Guro was felled by a stroke while training in the Philippines in 1997. Since then, Gould has taught hundreds of Lameco Eskrima seminars, workshops, and training camps in numerous countries around the world. In addition to teaching the Lameco Eskrima system to representatives and students whom he has positioned around the world, he also trains elite military and law enforcement personnel in many countries.

David E. Gould is the featured instructor in six professional training DVDs produced by Budo International in Madrid, Spain, teaching various aspects of Lameco Eskrima. He is also author of the Spanish-language book *Lameco Eskrima: La búsqueda del combate real*. Gould is one of the featured instructors in the 2005 Arjee Enterprises book Masters of the Blade, which was written by renowned author Master Reynaldo S. Galang. Gould has also been featured in several martial arts magazines published in the United States, Mexico, and Europe. Since 1992, he has dedicated himself solely to the task of propagating Lameco Eskrima and perpetuating the legacy of Punong Guro Edgar G. Sulite. In fact, to this day, it is what he has dedicated himself to, in an effort to keep the Lameco Eskrima system well-preserved in its original configuration, exactly as Punong Guro Edgar G. Sulite left it when he passed away on April 10, 1997.

The majority of information contained in this book is based on detailed information and stories told to the author first-hand by Punong Guro Sulite. These were shared during numerous

private training sessions in Los Angeles (1992-1995) and Palmdale, California (1996-1997). These details and stories were written down and included in the author's training notes on a daily basis for the entire time of his training under the late Punong Guro. This book is a reflection of that time.

KaliDave@aol.com
GuroDaveGould@att.net
www.LamecoEskrima.org

Lameco Eskrima Training Gear

Made by the Sulite Family

For those of you who want to maximize your training experience, and do it safely, I cannot recommend more highly the training gear made by the Sulite family. Here you will find whatever training gear you need to train the way you need to become proficient. If you want to excel in the Filipino warrior arts your training equipment has to be able to facilitate that process and last you as it does.

Those who have known me for years know that I do not endorse many things. But with this specific training equipment I speak from many years of experience. I have personally trained with this training equipment for 22 years and it does its job and it does last.

I still have pieces which I purchased from Punong Guro Edgar G. Sulite 22 years ago when I first began my training in the Lameco Eskrima System with him in 1992. I still train with those items to this day as they have lasted me well even though I have a tendency to train hard.

The training gear is made with the best materials available and constructed with the highest quality possible by the Edgar G. Sulite family themselves. Please, if you are in the market for quality training gear at an affordable cost, please visit the Lameco Eskrima International website at www.lamecoeskrima.com.

Thank you in advance for your patronage to the Sulite Family and, as always, train as if your life depends on it... because it does.

Best Regards,

David E. Gould.

TAMBULI MEDIA

Excellence in Mind-Body Health & Martial Arts Publishing

Welcome to Tambuli Media, publisher of quality books on mind-body martial arts and wellness presented in their cultural context.

Our Vision is to see quality books once again playing an integral role in the lives of people who pursue a journey of personal development, through the documentation and transmission of traditional knowledge of mind-body cultures.

Our Mission is to partner with the highest caliber subject-matter experts to bring you the highest quality books on important topics of health and martial arts that are in-depth, well-written, clearly illustrated and comprehensive.

Tambuli is the name of a native instrument in the Philippines fashioned from the horn of a carabao. The tambuli was blown and its sound signaled to villagers that a meeting with village elders was to be in session, or to announce the news of the day. It is hoped that Tambuli Media publications will "bring people together and disseminate the knowledge" to many.

www.TambuliMedia.com

www.ingramcontent.com/pod-product-compliance
Lightning Source LLC
Chambersburg PA
CBHW081345080526
44588CB00016B/2383